THE GUTS OF GRACE

Preparing Ordinary Saints For Extraordinary Ministry

BY GRANT HAWLEY

Bold Grace Ministries
Allen, TX

Copyright © 2013 Bold Grace Ministries

410 N Bonham Dr.
Allen, TX 75013
www.boldgrace.org

Library of Congress Cataloging in Publication Data

Hawley, Grant Cameron (1981-)
The Guts of Grace: Preparing Ordinary Saints for Extraordinary Ministry

1. Hermeneutics. 2. Salvation. 3. Christian Living.
4. Ecclesiology. 5. Eschatology.   I. Title.

ISBN: 978-0-9899665-0-4

Cover Design and Illustrations: 289 Design Ministries
Typesetting: Holly Melton

Unless otherwise noted, all scripture taken from the New
King James Version of the Bible. Copyright © 1979, 1980,
1982, by Thomas Nelson, Inc. All rights reserved.

Printed in the United States of America

Contents

Special Thanks

I want to thank my dear friends and mentors: Bob Wilkin, Jody Dillow, Dale Taliaferro, Ralph Gain, Earl Radmacher, Zane Hodges, Watchman Nee, and Bud Brown. By their obedience to the Lord and tireless work, each of these men contributed to building me up in the Lord and preparing me to write this book.

I want to thank my church family, which has sacrificially supported me in so many ways and joyfully shared me with this project.

Special thanks to my loving wife, Tamara, who has been a constant encouragement to me.

Thank you, Holly Melton, Sky McClure, Jose Serna, Michael DeYoung, Steve Lewis, Titus Penner, the Muysenberg family, the Kirkland family, the Franks family, Pam Esteven, Christie Perkins, Kristen Alewine, and Amy Paige and the 289 Design staff. All of you contributed to this project in important ways.

Thank you, Jeremy Edmondson, for your great encouragement and help in this project.

I want to thank Paul and Lena Miles, for their encouragement and support, but most especially for their help in taking care of many of the day to day tasks of the ministry so that I could focus on writing.

Most of all, I want to thank the Lord Jesus. Everything good in this work originated in Him.

Dedication

This work is dedicated to all of my brothers and sisters in
Christ who desire to serve the Lord Jesus and His Church.

Foreword

There are certain passages of Scripture that immediately stick out when one thinks about the Biblical picture of the church. Some would cite the words of Jesus to "go therefore and make disciples of all nations" (Matt 28:19), while others would speak of the importance to "love one another" for "by this all people will know that you are my disciples, if you have love for one another" (John 13:34-35). Still, others may speak of the crucial task of equipping "the saints for the work of ministry" (Eph 4:12); but regardless of the Biblical picture that is put forward, one thing is evident in all aspects of the Body of Christ: The people of God are to grow!

As a pastor, I am always watching for sound, Biblical materials that will help in aiding the growth of the flock that the Lord has entrusted to me. Many hours are spent in reading various books, Bible study curriculums, workbooks, websites, and even "spiritual growth tests" to discern their integrity in light of the Scriptures, constantly looking for something to help me cover more ground in feeding the sheep so that they will grow biblically. Many times, hours are spent in designing lessons that speak to a Biblical and balanced view of the Scriptures that I have had to write myself due to the lack of sound materials available in the current evangelical landscape. Much of what is being produced for the believer has been drawn from tradition and biased theological systems, and/or poor exegesis and weak application which ends up producing believers of the same nature. By and large, the options are many, but the sound choices are few.

This is why I am thankful for *The Guts of Grace*. Finally, a wonderful tool has come across my path that I can have complete confidence in; whether I am handing it off to my flock for their personal study, or encouraging a small-group situation with confidence and peace that the material being covered constantly points the reader back to the Biblical author's original intentions in their writing. Hawley has successfully laid out many areas that are theologically understandable to the layman, highly practical to how one thinks about God, life, and eternity, and provides opportunities for a contemplative discussion that constantly directs all participants to the truth of the Word of God. Hawley champions the authority of Scripture, the free gift of eternal life through faith alone in Jesus Christ alone, and provides a well-rounded discussion of perspectives that will encourage the reader to return to the text with a desire to understand God's great plan for all of mankind. Where many books are lacking in a balance of "knowing and doing," *The Guts of Grace demonstrates* both while maintaining a focus on grace and truth.

I am most grateful for this work and I look for God's glory to be demonstrated in every flock to which it ministers. Prepare to grow, grow, GROW!

Jeremy Edmondson
Teaching Pastor, Resurgence Church

Introduction

"The harvest truly is great, but the laborers are few; therefore pray the Lord of the harvest to send out laborers into His harvest." Luke 10:2

Jesus' words to His disciples in Luke 10:2 are still true today. The world is full of people ready to hear the good news, but those who are able and willing to do the work are hard to find. There are seminaries that are doing great work, preparing men and women with complete and balanced Biblical and theological education.

But there are problems.

Most seminaries have abandoned God's grace in exchange for works religion, abandoned literal interpretation[1] for allegorizing, and lost their kingdom hope in the process. Freedom has been given up in favor of oppressive legalism. In addition, seminaries typically take years and a fortune to complete, making it impractical for non-professional ministers.

An overdependence on seminaries has greatly slowed the growth of the Church because too few are being prepared, and because it has led to local churches outsourcing ministry preparation. When the local church[2] gives away its vital task of preparing ministers (Eph 4:11-17), the result is the production of consumers of spiritual things rather than ministers.

But we are all called to be ministers, each of us in different ways. We all have the tendency to look at people who have accomplished a great deal for the Lord and think that they must be great men and women. But I love the fact that many of the people in the Bible who did great things were deeply flawed. Moses, David, and Paul all were guilty of murder. Peter denied the Lord repeatedly on the night of His crucifixion. Yet who could deny that God was mighty in their lives?

---

[1] Literal interpretation is a hermeneutical approach that seeks the plain meaning of the original authors.

[2] A local church is an assembly of believers.

David was little more than a boy, a younger brother, a shepherd, when he became God's champion and delivered the Israelites from the threat of Goliath and the Philistines. He did it with simple tools, a sling, five smooth stones, and faith in the almighty God to deliver.

Paul wrote in 2 Cor 12:7-10:

> And lest I should be exalted above measure by the abundance of the revelations, a thorn in the flesh was given to me, a messenger of Satan to buffet me, lest I be exalted above measure. Concerning this thing I pleaded with the Lord three times that it might depart from me. And He said to me, "My grace is sufficient for you, for My strength is made perfect in weakness." Therefore most gladly I will rather boast in my infirmities, that the power of Christ may rest upon me. Therefore I take pleasure in infirmities, in reproaches, in needs, in persecutions, in distresses, for Christ's sake. For when I am weak, then I am strong.

This provides a perspective that should give us great courage. Christ is powerful in weakness. That means you and I and every other believer can accomplish mighty things in Him. An ordinary saint is God's preferred vessel to carry His great treasure to the world.

This book exists to give you a jump start in getting ready to minister to the Body of Christ.

This is not intended to be a complete theological or Biblical education, but simply to get you started off on the right foot. It contains your essential tools: your sling and your five smooth stones. Combined with faith in the Almighty God to deliver, you can begin your journey to become a minister to the people, a man or woman after God's own heart.

If you are working through this by yourself, all of these studies can be done on your own time as you are actively engaged in church ministry. If you are working through it with a group, you have the added benefit of your brothers and sisters in Christ working with you to discern the truth of Scripture.

This book is not infallible. Test everything said here to discern if it is in line with the truth of Scripture. The first section of this book is designed to equip you to do just that with this and any other book you may read in the future. If you are part of a group going through this curriculum, work with your group to compare the teachings here with Scripture.

Lastly, respect your group leader. When your group leader's views differ from those presented in this book, or from your current views, consider his or her views with a humble heart, going to Scripture, ready to learn and be changed.

HELPFUL TOOLS

I have included a glossary of terms in the back of this book that tells in simple language what any word means when it may not be part of every-day language or if it is a word that is often misused. For each word in the glossary, the first time that word appears it has the definition in a foot-note on the same page unless it is immediately defined in the main text.

At BoldGrace.org, you will find our contact info in case you have ques-tions about the book or want to get involved with Bold Grace Ministries. If major additions or corrections are made to future versions of this book, I will try to include those there as well.

Hermeneutics

Hermeneutics: the science and
art of Biblical interpretation.

SECTION GOAL

1. To teach the student how to understand and apply the Bible

WHY STUDY HERMENEUTICS?

Your hermeneutics has an enormous impact on how you view God, yourself, and other people. Having solid hermeneutics will open the Bible up to you and make its content understandable. It equips you to have a well-founded and deep relationship with Christ and prepares you for ministering to others. Having good hermeneutics helps keep you safe from false teachers and spiritual abuse.

Some of the topics in this section in particular will require your diligent effort to take in fully. But when you know and apply the principles here, you will find that a deep understanding of God's Word is within your grasp.

Hermeneutics is the first section of the book, even though it is the most difficult, *because it has to be first.* By our laying the foundation of good hermeneutics, you will be rightly prepared to test the teachings of this book against the Bible. So, if what I have written does not accurately reflect the teaching of Scripture, you will see where I go wrong. But if what I say is true, you can embrace it confidently, having tested it against Scripture. I have done the best I can by God's grace to communicate the truth of God's Word accurately, but I'm not perfect. Test everything you read and hear.

Good hermeneutics is the foundation of an intimate relationship with Christ. The better any two people know each other, the stronger and more intimate their relationship can become. One of the things I do as a pastor is relationship counseling. I have found that if two people in a relationship have trouble communicating, that relationship is bound to have trouble; but fixing that communication goes a long way toward healing and strengthening relationships. Christ already knows you fully—and always has—but we can always know Him more. Having good hermeneutics is learning to understand His communication so that we can know Him more.

My prayer is that you will be greatly blessed through this study of hermeneutics, that you will find the Bible singing with clarity and that you will be prepared to share the truth of Scripture with others confidently.

HELPFUL BOOKS ON HERMENEUTICS AND RELATED TOPICS:

Title	Author	Audience
Living by the Book[3]	Howard Hendricks	All
Basic Bible Interpretation[4]	Roy Zuck	Intermediate
Expository Hermeneutics: An Introduction[5]	Elliot Johnson	Intermediate
Protestant Biblical Interpretation[6]	Bernard Ramm	Intermediate
Validity in Interpretation[7]	E.D. Hirsch	Advanced
Dispensationalism[8]	Charles Ryrie	Intermediate
Law and Grace[9]	Alva J. McClain	All

---

[3] Howard Hendricks, *Living by the Book* (Chicago: Moody Press, 1991).

[4] Roy B. Zuck, *Basic Bible Interpretation: A Practical Guide to Discovering Biblical Truth* (Colorado Springs: Victor, 1991).

[5] Elliot Johnson, *Expository Hermeneutics: An Introduction* (Grand Rapids, MI: Zondervan, 1989).

[6] Bernard Ramm, *Protestant Biblical Interpretation* (Grand Rapids, MI: Baker Academic, 1980).

[7] E. D. Hirsch, Jr. *Validity in Interpretation* (New Haven and London: Yale University Press, 1967).

[8] Charles Ryrie, *Dispensationalism Revised and Expanded* (Chicago: Moody Press, 2007).

[9] McClain, Alva J., *Law and Grace* (United States: BMH Books, 1991).

Introduction to Hermeneutics

"But know this first of all, that no prophecy of Scripture is a matter of one's own interpretation, for no prophecy was ever made by an act of human will, but men moved by the Holy Spirit spoke from God." 2 Peter 1:20-21 NASB

LESSON OBJECTIVES

1. To define hermeneutics
2. To introduce the principle of literal interpretation
3. To introduce some common hermeneutical errors
4. To define the Holy Spirit's role in interpretation

DEFINITION

Hermeneutics: The science and art of Biblical interpretation.

Interpretation is a science because there are laws that guide it. It is an art because the laws must be applied skillfully.

LITERAL INTERPRETATION

Correct hermeneutics is the foundation for a correct understanding of Scripture. And because the Scripture is God-breathed (2 Tim 3:16) and intended to lead us into freedom (John 8:32), so much rides on being able to understand what the Bible means by what it says.

For those who love God, who believe that the Bible is God's revealed truth and that it is "...profitable for doctrine,[10] for reproof, for correction, for instruction in righteousness, that the man of God may be complete, thoroughly equipped for every good work" (2 Tim 3:16-17), it is essential that a correct interpretation of the Bible be the cornerstone of our ministry. We must not only practice good interpretation, we must also teach others to do the same. This provides a check against destructive doctrines, as any step away from solid interpretation will be noticed by those being taught.

As we discuss hermeneutics, there are a lot of complex things to consider. But even the complex can be simple when we keep one thing in mind—the one correct interpretation is what the author intended by what he wrote. Anything else simply darkens the pure light of Scripture with man-made presuppositions.

This is what I mean by *literal interpretation*. Literal interpretation does not mean that we do not recognize figures of speech, but that we are seeking the original intention of the author. If I say, "I slept like a log," I don't mean that I lay down in the forest and slept under the stars. I mean, "I slept well." "I slept well" is the literal interpretation of the statement, "I slept like a log," because that is what I mean. The intention of the author determines the literal interpretation.

SPOTTING NON-LITERAL INTERPRETATION

There are a few different kinds of non-literal interpretation, all of which should be rejected.

ALLEGORIZING

When allegorizing, the interpreter[11] casts aside the literal meaning entirely and turns plain-literal statements into metaphors.[12]

For example: Many interpreters treat all of the promises to Israel[13] as having allegorical fulfillment in the Church. The promise that Christ

---

[10] A doctrine is a theological teaching on a subject.

[11] An interpreter is a person who derives a meaning from a text.

[12] A metaphor is a figure of speech that describes something by comparing it to an unrelated object.

[13] Israel is the nation consisting of descendants of Jacob, the son of Isaac, the son of Abraham.

will rule from David's throne (2 Sam 7:11-16) is treated as if it means that Christ will rule in the hearts of Christians.

THEOLOGICAL INTERPRETATION

Theological interpretation, also called eisegesis,[14] involves reading a theological concept into a text that has nothing to do with that concept.

For example: Some scholars have argued that because Lazarus could not have heard Jesus' call to come out of the grave until he had been resurrected (John 11:38-43), people must be born again before they can believe in Jesus. This passage clearly has nothing to do with that concept.

IGNORING HISTORICAL CONTEXT

This is incorrectly applying a primary application[15] of passages across dispensations[16] (see Lessons 3 and 8), ignoring (or changing) the intended audience, or failing to understand the historical situation the book of the Bible is addressing.

For example: Seventh-Day Adventists mistakenly apply the command to keep the Sabbath to Christians today. The command to keep the Sabbath was given to Israel and is not intended to be binding for the Church (Rom 14:5-6).

SOME KEY PRINCIPLES THAT ARE OFTEN MISUNDERSTOOD OR MISUSED

ANALOGY OF SCRIPTURE—ITS USE AND ITS DANGERS

Analogy of Scripture (and the related principle, the Analogy of Faith) is the principle that "Scripture interprets Scripture." This is a valuable tool because unclear passages can become clear when compared with clear ones. Many times, we can rule out certain interpretations of a passage because it would conflict with other clearer passages.

---

[14] Eisegesis is a poor approach to Bible study that seeks to impose the interpreter's meaning into the text rather than taking the authors' intended meaning out of the text.

[15] Primary application is the way the originally intended audience of a command or moral teaching should respond.

[16] A dispensation is a distinct economy through which God relates to man.

For example, some interpreters look at Luke 17:21b, "the kingdom of God is within you," on its own and interpret[17] it as suggesting that the coming kingdom is not a literal kingdom but a metaphorical one in the hearts of believers. This interpretation can be ruled out by a host of other passages that clearly describe the kingdom as literal (compare Gen 15:18-21; 2 Sam 7:8-16; Psalm 122; Ezek 37:14-25; Rev 20:4-6. See also Lesson 30: The Kingdom Described).[18]

Sadly, however, Analogy of Scripture has been badly abused by theologians.

Instead of looking to see what the clear intention of a passage is, some theologians often read away the clear intention by going to other passages for refuge. The passages they use as a refuge are often less clear and mis-interpreted, but fit better with the interpreter's preconceptions.

The Analogy of Scripture says that we can interpret unclear passages in light of clear ones. This is not the same as interpreting hard passages in light of easy ones. If we run to passages that are easy for us in order to explain away passages that, though clear, are hard to fit into our belief system, we will never be able to progress in our understanding of God's Word. In this way, a theology can become a set of shackles that keep us chained in spiritual infancy.

Many times, conversations I have about simple and crystal-clear passages like John 6:47, "Most assuredly I say to you, he who believes in Me has everlasting life," go something like:

> Me: Isn't this simple? All that someone needs to do is believe in Jesus to receive eternal life.[19]
>
> My friend: But what about, "If anyone loves me, he will keep My word..." John 14:23?
>
> Me: That is also true, but that passage was for the faithful disciples, and we aren't talking about love, we are talking about faith.

---

[17] To interpret is to ascribe a meaning to a text, either correctly or incorrectly.

[18] Another clear reason that Luke 17:21b cannot be saying that the kingdom of God is in the hearts of believers is that Jesus wasn't talking to believers when He said, "the kingdom of God is within you." He was talking to the antagonistic Pharisees. The kingdom is in no sense in the hearts of unbelievers. Jesus, as the promised King, was referring to Himself as representative of the kingdom, and the word *within* should be translated *among*. Jesus' point is that they will not see the kingdom by looking here or there, because they don't even recognize the King when He is among them.

[19] Eternal life is the spiritual life that begins for Christians in the moment they put their faith in Christ. Eternal life cannot be lost and never ends.

My friend: But what about James 2?

Me: I then explain that James 2 is not about justification before God, but about justification before men.

My friend: Sure, but what about Matthew 7:20-21?

The cycle continues. Rather than reserving the Analogy of Scripture for the explanation of unclear passages, my friend has read away the clear intention of one of the most straightforward verses in the Bible. In this circumstance, Analogy of Scripture becomes a way to run away from what God is saying, rather than a tool to help us understand what He is saying.

The Bible conveys God's thoughts, and God's thoughts are not the same as ours (Isa 55:8-9). This means that what the Bible says can be challenging. When we come across a passage that is difficult for us, we have to deal with it honestly and reassess ideas that we are comfortable with but which may contradict what a passage says.

ILLOCUTIONARY FORCE

Illocutionary force is the intention behind a word or phrase. Some examples of illocutionary force are: command, exhortation, warning, and statement—though there are many more variations and the differences can be somewhat subtle at times. Is the author expressing an expectation of something that *should* happen or something that is inevitable? Is he asking a rhetorical question to guide a reader gently toward a conclusion, or is he delivering a stinging rebuke?

Often, the same exact phrase with the same grammar can be used to express different things, because there is a difference in illocutionary force. Grammatically, the phrase "eat your vegetables" is an imperative. This imperative could be a command or an exhortation, or simply advice. The context helps us determine the illocutionary force of any given phrase. If I'm talking to my son, it's probably a command. If I'm talking to a friend who is asking me about how to have more energy, it's most likely advice. If I'm talking to myself, I probably mean it as an exhortation.

By ignoring or misinterpreting illocutionary force, many interpreters have essentially reversed the meaning of many key passages in Scripture.

For example, translators and interpreters often incorrectly turn 1 Cor 12:31a into a command or exhortation. The NKJV reflects this incorrect understanding by translating the passage, "But earnestly desire the best gifts."

In the Greek, the grammar can be taken as either an imperative (a command) or an indicative (a statement of fact). In the context, Paul has already said that the Holy Spirit gives gifts to individuals as He chooses (1 Cor 12:11), and that this comes when we are (spiritually) baptized into the body of Christ (1 Cor 12:13), i.e., when we first believe. Paul has also just labored to communicate that all of the spiritual gifts should be considered as necessary and of great value, especially those gifts that aren't automatically honored (1 Cor 12:14-25). Finally, the phrase "and yet I show you a more excellent way" (1 Cor 12:31b), as an introduction to the need to love with a humble love (1 Cor 13:1-8a), should indicate to us that the Corinthians were lacking in that area.

So what Paul intended as a rebuke, "But you are jealously desiring the best gifts, and yet I show you a more excellent way," has been turned into an exhortation to do the very thing Paul is rebuking. As you can see, properly discerning illocutionary force can mean a great deal when interpreting Scripture.

Keep in mind the different options of illocutionary force when reading the Bible. Often, looking at a phrase with a different illocutionary force in mind can help the pieces all fall into place.

While context helps a great deal, determining illocutionary force can often be more art than science (hermeneutics involves both). Perhaps more than anything, it takes familiarity with the Lord, and with the human author of a particular book and his purpose in writing. Best friends often communicate with subtle references and changes in tone that others may not pick up. While the Biblical authors were not necessarily writing to their best friends (except perhaps Paul's letters to Timothy), knowing their personalities goes a long way in understanding what they mean by what they say.

Some New Testament books and passages that give us intimate pictures of many of the personalities involved in crafting Scripture are: Matthew 6; Mark 14; Luke 15; John 13–17; Acts 9–10; 15; 2 Corinthians 1–5; 11–12; Galatians; Second Timothy; Hebrews 2; 13; 1 John 1; 4.

ILLEGITIMATE TOTALITY TRANSFER

The *illegitimate totality transfer* is an interpretive error in which the entire context of a particular usage of a word or phrase is transferred into that word or phrase's meaning elsewhere.

For example, in Exod 3:7-8, God promises to deliver (save) Israel by freeing them from Egyptian bondage and taking them into a land of their own, a land flowing with milk and honey. But it would be committing the *illegitimate totality transfer* to read deliverance from physical slavery and land ownership into the word *deliver* or *save* in another context that has nothing to do with those concepts.

ILLEGITIMATE IDENTITY TRANSFER

A related concept is the *illegitimate identity transfer*. In this interpretive error, a definition of a word in one context is incorrectly read into another context. For example, the Hebrew word *barak*, which often means *to bless* is correctly translated as *curse* in Job 1:5. Both definitions are part of the possible semantic value of that word. But it would be inappropriate to use the definition *curse* for that word in Job 42:12, where clearly the word should be translated *blessed*.

WHERE DOES THE HOLY SPIRIT COME IN?

Second Corinthians 2:9-16 teaches that apart from the Holy Spirit, man cannot receive *or* know (intimately) "the things of the Spirit of God" (v 14). Many people think this means that diligent study of the Bible is needless. However, the Holy Spirit was not given to make Bible study needless, but to make it effective.[20] Bible study is hard work, and we are called to study God's Word with care and perseverance (2 Tim 2:15).

The Holy Spirit was not given to lead the interpreter (you) into an understanding of the text that goes beyond or is not contained in the normal sense of the text. "For the word of God is living and powerful, and sharper than any two-edged sword, piercing even to the division of soul and spirit, and of joints and marrow, and is a discerner of the thoughts and intents of the heart" (Heb 4:12). But as soon as we seek a meaning that is not in the words written, we no longer have the word of God; we have the word of man masquerading as the word of God.

---

[20] Thanks to Dr. Earl Radmacher for teaching me this important truth.

As we approach the Bible, it is absolutely vital that we depend upon the Holy Spirit to lead us every step of the way, not because the Bible itself is unclear, but because as human beings we have a tendency to let our pride and biases blind us to what is clearly in the text. Even our human loyalties can influence our interpretation. We can be concerned about how people we love will react to our views. Or we might be inclined to give the benefit of the doubt to people we respect. We *should* hold those who have given themselves to ministry in high esteem (Phil 2:29), and we *should* humbly consider their views in comparison to Scripture. But if the Bible is saying something different than what they say, we need to accept the Bible's teaching. Only God's Word is infallible.

By depending upon the Holy Spirit, we are able to let go of these biases and let the Bible sound its clear voice.

This leads us to understanding the attitude we should have when we approach Scripture. We must be committed to believing everything the Bible says, even if it means we must fundamentally change our theology, our world view, and/or our behavior, even if it results in persecution or other difficulties. The Bible was given to mold us, and it is only as we are willing to accept God's truth, whatever it is, that His truth will make us free (John 8:32). We must be willing to let go of values, traditions, desires, and anything else that conflicts with the word of God. This is only possible by the power of the indwelling Holy Spirit.

TREASURE THE TOUGH PASSAGES

Coming across a tough passage in Scripture is a cause for rejoicing. I know this sounds counter-intuitive, but if we are approaching Scripture with the goal of being transformed by the renewing of our minds (Rom 12:2), doesn't it make sense that the passages that don't seem to (or don't in actuality) match our current thinking are great opportunities? But if we want to be transformed, we can't run from these passages or try to change what they say.

Sometimes it can be really easy to be frightened by a passage and what implications it may have. But I have found that Jesus' promise in John 8:32, that if we abide in His Word we will "know the truth, and the truth shall make [us] free," has always proven true. When I've let down my guard and really sought to understand difficult passages, I have always found that the truth being expressed leads to a greater understanding of

God's goodness, His love for His creation, and His desire for us to experience the freedom His Son has purchased for us with His blood.

The tough texts are treasures to be uncovered. It may take some digging, but the wealth they contain is far more than worth the effort.

PRACTICE

1) It is common for people to use the phrase "You will know them by their fruits" (Matt 7:16, 19) to mean that you can tell who is and is not a believer by their works. However, in verse 15 Jesus says who it is we are to know by their fruits. Whom are we to know by their fruits?

2) In Matt 12:33-35, Jesus uses the same illustration. In that context, what are the fruits?

3) Is the definition of fruits from Matt 12:33-35 an appropriate way to understand the fruits in 7:16 and 19? How can you tell?

4) Given what you have learned above, is it appropriate to use the phrase "You will know them by their fruits" to mean that you can tell by their works who is and is not a believer?

5) What does the phrase "You will know them by their fruits" mean?

6) How does this change your perspective?

DISCUSS

1) How do figures of speech relate to literal interpretation?

2) In what ways have you noticed non-literal interpretation outside of Bible teaching (i.e. in relationships, in media, etc.)?

3) How can Analogy of Scripture be helpful?

4) How can Analogy of Scripture be a hindrance?

5) Have you ever had problems with people misinterpreting your email or text messages? How can this illustrate the need for care in determining illocutionary force?

6) Discuss how the Holy Spirit interacts with us when we are interpreting Scripture.

Context

> "Hermeneutics is needed...because of the historical, cultural, linguistic, and philosophical gaps that block a spontaneous, accurate understanding of God's Word" *Henry A. Virkler*[21]

LESSON OBJECTIVES

1. To introduce the importance of considering context
2. To describe different aspects of context to consider

INTRODUCTION

The Bible is not a collection of unconnected spiritual sayings.[22] Every verse has a larger context that helps to determine its meaning. As with any work of literature, to take one phrase or sentence out of context is to divorce it from many things that help determine its meaning.

If I said, "this is my home," I could mean, *this is where I live*, or, *this is where I spent my childhood*. In a particular context, it could even mean something like, *you need to leave*. But if you read that phrase in a context that said, "As we ended our trip to India, my wife said to me, 'Let's go home,' and I told her, 'As long as you are here with me, this is my home,'" you would understand that I was telling my wife that I love her. Context clearly plays a huge role in the meaning of this and any other word, phrase, paragraph, or even a whole book.

---

[21] Henry A. Virkler, *Hermeneutics: Principles and Processes of Biblical Interpretation* (Grand Rapids, MI: Baker, 1981), p. 20.

[22] The Book of Proverbs is somewhat of an exception. While the individual proverbs are grouped together by theme, and cultural idioms must be understood, each proverb is a complete statement in itself and can be understood without literary context.

Every single word has a range of possible meanings, and the context determines which meaning is intended. For example, the Greek word for repentance, *metanoia*, originally meant *a change of mind*. But language changes over time, and in some contexts it is clear that the author intends the word to mean *a turning from sin*. There is much scholarly debate about whether *metanoia* means *a change of mind* or *a turn from sin*. What is the reality? It does not mean *a change of mind* or *a turn from sin*, but it can mean either one. It can mean *a turn from sin* (as in Matt 9:13 and Luke 15:7), but it can just as easily mean *a change of mind* (as in 2 Tim 2:25 or Heb 12:17; see also the LXX[23] in Jonah 3:9-10). The meaning is determined by its use. When we approach a passage that uses the word *repent*, or the word *repentance*, or any other word for that matter, we need to keep the range of meanings in mind and see which fits the context best.

HISTORICAL CONTEXT

Historical context plays a significant role in the interpretation of every book of the Bible. The Bible is a collection of sixty-six books written over the course of up to 2000 years, and each book has at least one set of historical circumstances that helped to shape its purpose.

When studying the historical context, there are many questions that we must ask ourselves. Here are a few examples: Are any historical figures mentioned? How is God working with Israel? Is Israel in the Promised Land?[24] At peace? Are they experiencing God's judgment? Do they even exist as a nation, in the political sense, at the time of the book? Is it before or after the death and resurrection of Christ? Is it before or after the gospel was taken to the Gentiles?[25] These and many other questions can help us get a better feel of what the book's author means by what he says.

For example, when God said to Ezekiel: "Then they [Israel] shall dwell in the land that I have given to Jacob My servant, where your fathers dwelt; and they shall dwell there, they, their children, and their children's children, forever; and My servant David shall be their prince forever" (Ezek 37:25), David had long since been dead. Therefore, either David

---

[23] The LXX, also known as the Septuagint, is an ancient translation of the Old Testament from Hebrew and Aramaic to Greek. It was commonly used in the time of Jesus' earthly ministry.

[24] The Promised Land is the land which God promised to Abraham in Gen 15:7-21.

[25] A Gentile is any non-Israelite person.

must represent His Son Jesus, or this must be talking about David after the resurrection of the saints.

DISPENSATIONAL CONTEXT

Dispensationalism and the dispensations will be discussed at length in Lesson 3. Dispensationalism is fundamentally a system of hermeneutics, because it is the application of consistent literal-historical-grammatical interpretation.[26]

One result of this application is that we recognize that God works with different people in different ways at different times. These different systems are called dispensations. The interpreter needs to be careful not to give primary application across all dispensations to principles that are unique to one dispensation. See more on this topic in Lesson 3: Dispensationalism.

GEOGRAPHICAL CONTEXT

The geographical context can often be significant. Under the law, when Israel was disobedient, they were chastised by being taken from the Land (Deut 28:63-65). When reading an Old Testament book, see if Israel is in the Promised Land or not. If not, why not?

In the Book of Acts, every geographical context (there are many) is significant. In Acts 1:8, Jesus uses geographical references to express to the apostles their mission to be His witnesses to Jerusalem, then to all of Judea, then to Samaria, and eventually to the whole world. This foreshadows the whole book, and each time the Apostles move to the next step, important things happen.

Another illustration of the importance of geographical context in the Bible is First and Second Corinthians. Corinth was a large port city that housed the temple of Aphrodite, the Greek goddess of love, beauty, and sexuality. The temple had many prostitutes, and Corinth was widely known as a city of vice. How might this help you to understand the Corinthians' struggles and Paul's letters to them?

---

[26] Literal-historical-grammatical interpretation is a hermeneutic approach that seeks the plain meaning of the original authors.

CULTURAL CONTEXT

The cultures to which the Bible was written are all very different from our own. We are removed by close to 2000 years or more. We do not share the same cultural norms, governments, expectations, or taboos. We need to learn the cultural norms of the various societies that are addressed in the Bible so that we can fully understand God's Word. This takes diligent study.

Some helpful resources on this topic are:

Title	Author	Audience
The Life and Times of Jesus the Messiah[27]	Alfred Edersheim	Advanced
New Testament Introduction[28]	Donald Guthrie	Intermediate
New Testament History[29]	F.F. Bruce	Intermediate
The Words and Works of Jesus Christ: A Study of the Life of Christ[30]	J. Dwight Pentecost	All

AUDIENCE

One aspect of context that is often ignored or not taken into account is the audience. Is the audience made up of Jews,[31] Christians, non-believers? Is it written to a church? To an individual? Often this is explicitly stated (see Isa 1:1; Jer 2:1-4; Acts 1:1; Rom 1:7-8; 1 Cor 1:2; 1 John 2:12-14, 21, 27).

At other times, one can clearly identify the audience, even though it is not explicitly stated. For example, Jas 1:2, 18, 19; 2:1, 5, 12, and many other verses confirm that his audience is an audience of believers. By contrast, the purpose statement in John 20:31, "but these are written that you may believe that Jesus is the Christ, the Son of God, and that believing you may have life in His name," demonstrates that his audience is an audience of those who had not yet believed in Jesus—"that *you* may

---

[27] Alfred Edersheim, *The Life and Times of Jesus the Messiah* (McLean, VA: n. d.).

[28] Donald Guthrie, *New Testament Introduction, Revised Edition* (Downers Grove, IL: Intervarsity Press, 1990).

[29] F. F. Bruce, *New Testament History* (New York: Doubleday, 1969).

[30] J. Dwight Pentecost, *The Words and Works of Jesus Christ: A Study of the Life of Christ* (Grand Rapids, MI: 1981).

[31] A Jew is a member of the nation of Israel, or more specifically, the tribe of Judah.

believe" (emphasis added). In fact, The Gospel of John is the only book in the New Testament that was written to an unbelieving audience, and it is thus the only book of the Bible with an evangelistic[32] purpose.

Within the audience of the book, there is often a second audience, the audience of a speaker within the book. For example, while the Gospel of John was written to non-believers, it is crucial to recognize when reading the Upper Room Discourse (chapters 13–17), that only the eleven faithful disciples are present from 13:30 through the end of chapter 17. This lets us know that Jesus' purpose in what He says in this portion of the book could not be evangelistic, because only believers were present.[33]

PURPOSE OR THEME OF A BOOK

Each book in the Bible was written for a purpose. Misunderstanding the purpose of any book is one way to fall into serious error, but a correct understanding of a book's purpose is a big step in the right direction. Understanding that First John was written to believers to tell them how to have fellowship with God and the joy that comes with it (see 1 John 1:3-4) helps us to avoid the serious error of looking to our works, rather than the promises of God, for our assurance of salvation.[34] The same can be said for knowing that Matthew was not written to tell people how to receive eternal life, but to answer the question, "If Messiah has come, why do we still wait for His kingdom?"

DEVELOPMENT OF THE BOOK'S ARGUMENT OR NARRATIVE

Nearly every book in the Bible has a progression of argument or narrative. When studying each book of the Bible, look for clues that the author is concluding a point or section and moving on to another point. A few good examples are: Matthew 12–13; Rom 5:1; 9:1-4; 12:1; Gal 3:1-3; and Eph 4:1.

---

[32] Evangelistic is an adjective pertaining to the work of teaching the gospel to non-believers (evangelism).

[33] While Jesus' purpose in the Upper Room Discourse was not evangelistic, the passage can still help support John's evangelistic purpose. In this passage, the reader is able to peek into a very personal expression of Jesus' love for His disciples, better understand who Jesus is, and therefore be helped along in the path toward believing in Him.

[34] Assurance of salvation is a regenerate person's confidence in his own salvation.

IMMEDIATE CONTEXT

The immediate context of any verse in the Bible has a great impact on its meaning and uses. For example, many times Rom 14:21, "It is good neither to eat meat nor drink wine nor do anything by which your brother stumbles or is offended or is made weak" is used to say that a Christian should not express his or her Christian liberty because it may cause someone to stumble. But the immediate context in vv 1-14 shows us that the brother who is strong in faith does express his Christian liberty and is free to do so. On the other hand, vv 15-21 demonstrate that a brother must express his Christian liberty with love and sensitivity. Therefore the freedom that is confirmed in the first half of the chapter must be tempered by love. Noting the immediate context helps to keep us from two extremes: complete restriction of Christian liberty on one hand, and callous and uncaring expression of Christian liberty on the other. For more information on the topic of Christian Liberty, see Lessons 17 and 27.

PRACTICE

1) Historical Context: Read Gen 15:18-21; 2 Sam 7:8-17; Psalm 89:20-37; Jer 33:19-22; Ezek 37:21-28. What would the people of Israel have understood the word *kingdom* to mean when Jesus said, "Repent, for the kingdom of heaven is at hand." (Matt 4:17)?

2) Dispensational Context: Read Rom 6:14; 7:1-6; Second Corinthians 3; Gal 2:19–3:5; 5:16-18; Eph 2:14-15; and Col 2:16-23. How does this affect your understanding and application of Lev 19:27-28?

3) Audience: The phrase "Therefore, brethren, be even more diligent to make your call and election sure," (2 Pet 1:10a) is often quoted to say that we need to persevere in good works to the end of life to ensure our final salvation. But are there any clues in the context (see 1:1-9) that tell us whether or not the audience is made up of true believers (who are eternally secure, see Section 2: Free Grace)? What are those clues? In light of this, is it possible that Peter was warning false professors (those who are not really Christians) in v 10? Why or why not?

4) Context of the Book: In Rom 5:1 Paul says, "Therefore, having been justified [that is, declared righteous] by faith, we have peace with God through our Lord Jesus Christ," giving us a clue that he is considering the issue of justification as settled, and is moving on to a new topic. How does this impact the interpretation of verses like 6:23 and 8:1? The first command given in the book is found in 6:11. Why do you suppose there are no commands prior to Paul's leaving the justification discussion?

5) Cultural Context: Luke 1:24-25 says, "Now after those days his [Zacharias] wife Elizabeth conceived; (…) saying, 'Thus the Lord has dealt with me, in the days when He looked on me, to take away my reproach among people.'" Prior to this, Elizabeth had grown to be "well advanced in years" (v 7), yet had no offspring. Given the promise in Deut 28:11 (see also 28:1), why do you think being childless would have been a reproach to her?

DISCUSS

1) What are some different ideas that can be expressed by the word "friend" in different contexts?

2) What are some examples of historical context that I did not mention in the lesson?

3) What things are accepted in your culture that would not have been thought normal in Israel at the time of Jesus' earthly ministry?

4) What things were normal for first century Israel that are not normal for your culture?

5) What problems could arise from incorrectly identifying the audience of a book?

6) When you read an editorial in a newspaper or on a news website, how does knowing the reason the writer is writing help you to understand the piece? What could happen if you don't know why he or she is writing?

Dispensationalism

> "Be diligent to present yourself approved
> to God, a worker who does not need
> to be ashamed, rightly dividing the
> word of truth." *Second Timothy 2:15*

LESSON OBJECTIVES

1. To define Dispensationalism
2. To show that the dispensational method is the correct method for interpreting the Bible
3. To teach the student how to apply the distinctions among the dispensations, when interpreting the Bible
4. To warn the student of the dangers of non-dispensational methods

WHAT IS DISPENSATIONALISM?

Dispensationalism is a system for understanding God's program for the ages that arises out of consistent literal hermeneutics. If you approach every portion of the Bible with the intention to seek only the original intention of the author, then you are a Dispensationalist. As soon as non-literal interpretation is brought in, the interpreter is allowed to twist the Bible to say whatever he or she wants. Only consistent literal interpretation leaves God's Word pure and unmixed with human ideas, and only Dispensationalism applies consistent literal interpretation to the entire Bible. This is the primary reason that Dispensationalism is preferable to other systems.

WHAT IS A DISPENSATION?

The word *dispensation* is from the Greek word *oikonomia*, meaning "house rule." Our English word, *economy*, is related to the Greek word for dispensation. Essentially, a dispensation is a system of rule whereby God sets the standard for His people to live by. There are seven dispensations mentioned in the Bible, each for a distinct time period, and each with a different set of standards by which God's people of that time are meant to live.

The dispensations have a cyclical nature because they all start with a set of instructions from God, move to showing man's failure to heed those instructions, and end with a decisive judgment that starts a new dispensation.

But it is more appropriate to understand the dispensations together as forming an upward spiral, because each dispensation reveals a greater step toward the revealing of God's glory[35] through His program for the ages.

Non-dispensationalists also recognize that there is more than one dispensation spoken of in the Bible, but the distinctions are minimalized.

THE FIVE ESSENTIAL ASPECTS OF DISPENSATIONALISM

1. LITERAL-HISTORICAL-GRAMMATICAL INTERPRETATION SHOULD BE APPLIED TO ALL PORTIONS OF SCRIPTURE (WHAT IS THE AUTHOR'S INTENTION?).

This point has been explained elsewhere, but it should be noted here that all other aspects of Dispensationalism flow from this singular point.

In addition, it should be noted that not all non-literal methods of interpretation involve allegorizing. If a passage is taken out of context, or applied in a way that the author did not intend, a non-literal method is being used. This is because literal interpretation involves recognizing the historical situation, the intended audience, and the circumstance it was written to address. For example, it may not be allegorizing to apply the Sermon on the Mount to an evangelistic context, but neither is it literal

---

[35] Glory is high honor and magnificence.

interpretation because 1) that is clearly not the Lord's intention, 2) the disciples to whom it is addressed were already believers, as is affirmed throughout the sermon, and 3) Matthew was not writing to an unbelieving audience.

2. THE CHURCH AND ISRAEL ARE DISTINCT PEOPLES IN GOD'S PROGRAM FOR THE AGES.

The Church is not Israel, and Israel is not the Church. Israel is the chosen nation. It is a race of individuals in which God has founded and advanced His kingdom program throughout its history. The Church, on the other hand, is a Body of all those who are spiritually baptized into Christ. The Church began during this current age, and no more people will be added to it after the Rapture. In Christ, all distinctions based on race and other natural factors are eliminated (Gal 3:28; Col 3:11).

Non-dispensationalists do not make a clear distinction between Israel and the Church. They might call Israel the Old Testament Church, or they might call the Church New Testament Israel or spiritual Israel.

3. THE LORD JESUS CHRIST WILL RETURN BODILY TO EARTH AND REIGN ON DAVID'S THRONE IN JERUSALEM FOR ONE THOUSAND YEARS.

This aspect of Dispensationalism is called *premillennialism*. Because Dispensationalists take kingdom prophecies literally, we understand that Christ will reign on David's throne in Jerusalem for 1000 years (see 2 Sam 7:8-17; Psalms 89:20-37; 122; Ezekiel 37; Luke 1:32-33; and Rev 20:1-6). Christ's reign will continue forever in the New Earth after the 1000 years is completed. This will be discussed at length in Section 5: The Kingdom.

4. THE UNDERLYING PURPOSE OF GOD'S DEALINGS WITH THE WORLD IS HIS GLORY, NOT MERELY THE SALVATION OF MAN; THUS THE SCRIPTURE GOES FAR BEYOND EVANGELISM.

One major error of non-dispensational approaches to interpretation is to see everything through a lens of soteriology (the doctrine of salvation). This is a serious error because the vast majority of the Bible was written to those who were already justified. Because Dispensationalists recognize that the glory of God (especially as revealed in His kingdom program), and not the salvation of man, is the overarching theme of the Bible, the Dispensationalist is less likely to read soteriological[36] concerns into passages that have nothing to do with soteriology.

5. THE CHRISTIAN IS FREE FROM THE LAW IN ITS ENTIRETY FOR BOTH JUSTIFICATION AND SANCTIFICATION.

The death of Christ (including our death with Him, see Rom 6:1-6; Gal 2:19-21) resulted in the fulfilling of and abolition of the law in its entirety. This is *explicitly* stated many times by the Apostle Paul (Rom 6:14; 7; Second Corinthians 3; Galatians [entire book]; Eph 2:14-16; Phil 3:1-8; Col 2:16-23 and elsewhere).

Serious harm has been done to the Church by limiting the application of this truth to the ceremonial aspects of the law while keeping the believer under the "moral law." But the law is one unit and cannot be broken apart (Gal 5:3; Jas 2:10). Furthermore, Romans 7, for instance, deals with the believer's freedom from law related to coveting, a moral issue. Those who would seek to limit the believer's freedom from the law to ceremonial issues are guilty of the error of Judaizing,[37] not recognizing that the law has no power over sin, and that it even arouses and revives sin (Rom 7:5-11). Instead of using legalism to attempt to control the sin problem, the believer is to reckon himself dead to sin and alive to God in Christ (Rom 6:11). This empowers the believer to have true victory over indwelling sin. This is discussed at length in Section 3: Life and Liberty.

Teachers who place the Christian under the law are guilty of bringing those believers into the bondage described in Rom 7:14-25. Paul says that anyone who does this should be considered accursed by the brethren (Gal 1:6-9, see also 5:12). Passages like these are intended to be a solemn warning to all who would become teachers, and we should take them as such. Jesus was always gentle toward sinners, but toward teachers who would bring His people into bondage, the gentleness was not to be found.

---

[36] Soteriological means in relation to soteriology (the doctrine of salvation).

[37] Judaizing is the forcing of Jewish culture and Jewish religious laws onto Gentiles.

WHAT ARE THE DISPENSATIONS?[38]

The Bible shows a pattern among the dispensations, namely that each dispensation begins with a set of instructions for men,[39] moves to demonstrate man's failure to obey, and ends in judgment. A dispensation's ending does not necessarily wipe away its instructions for future dispensations, but where a conflict occurs, new commands supersede those of previous dispensations.

INNOCENCE—FROM THE CREATION OF MAN TO THE FALL

Man was to refrain from eating from the Tree of Knowledge of Good and Evil, to fill the earth and subdue it, and to have dominion (Gen 1:28). This is the first discussion in Scripture of God's mission, His kingdom program. Man failed the test during this dispensation when Adam and Eve ate of the Tree of the Knowledge of Good and Evil (Gen 3:1-13). God blocked off access to the Tree of Life and the Garden of Eden. Instead of man having dominion over the world and spreading the blessings of Eden throughout the whole world, fallen angels (temporarily) took over rulership of the world (see 2 Cor 4:4; Eph 6:12; compare Hebrews 1–2), death became an oppressive reality for all men (Rom 5:12-14; Heb 2:15), and the advancement of God's kingdom program was delayed.

CONSCIENCE—FROM THE FALL OF MAN TO THE FLOOD

Man was to live according to his own understanding of right and wrong. No specific commands were given during this dispensation, though neither did God abolish His command to fill the earth and subdue it. Man failed in this dispensation when God "saw that the wickedness of man was great in the earth, and that every intent of the thoughts of his heart was only evil continually" (Gen 6:5). God then flooded the earth, saving only Noah's family.

---

[38] If you are familiar with various dispensational systems, you may notice that the description of the various dispensations are slightly different from what you have seen in the past. I call this system Missional Dispensationalism. It is a refinement of Classical and Revised Dispensationalism, and I believe it relieves the tension between the two systems. I am indebted to my dear friend Bud Brown for his insights here.

[39] The dispensation of Conscience is an exception. See below.

HUMAN GOVERNMENT—FROM THE FLOOD
TO THE CALLING OF ABRAHAM

God instituted capital punishment, bringing in the responsibility for men to govern each other. God also repeated the call for man to "be fruitful and multiply and fill the earth" (Gen 9:1). Man failed the test during this dispensation when instead of filling the earth, mankind remained together in one location, all working together to build the Tower of Babel as they reached to heaven in pride. In judgment for this failure, God confused the languages of the people and spread man throughout the earth (Gen 11:1-9), correcting this disobedience.

PROMISE—FROM THE CALLING OF
ABRAHAM TO THE GIVING OF THE LAW

This dispensation was a bit unique. It began with the promise to Abraham in Gen 12:1-3. During this time, God was working to call out a nation (Israel) to be His people. His people were commanded also to "be a blessing" (Gen 12:2, literal translation). This explicitly reintroduces the mission of God, i.e., God's plan to restore His blessing to the entire world through His human representatives.

This working with a small group of people, however, is not a dispensation in itself. The responsibility to all mankind was to bless Abraham and His children. God promised to bless those who bless Abraham and curse those who curse him (Gen 12:3). Man failed this test when Egypt brought the Children of Israel into slavery. God judged Egypt and brought His people out of slavery (Exodus 1–15).

LAW—FROM THE GIVING OF THE LAW
TO THE DEATH OF CHRIST

Under the law, seemingly every minute detail of life was codified with a system of dos and don'ts. While many transgressions could be forgiven through a system of sacrifices, others carried severe penalties, including death. Material and physical blessings were promised to those who kept the law. Material and physical curses, including removal from the Promised Land and oppression from wicked Gentiles, were assured for the disobedient (Deuteronomy 27–28).

In addition, Israel was to participate in God's mission by calling the world's attention to God's goodness and righteousness through their obedience (Deut 4:1-8).

Israel as a nation never had a significant time period of complete or near-complete obedience to the law, though David's reign is seen as the golden age to which all other reigns are compared. Hezekiah was said to approach David's goodness as a king. Other than a short exception under Solomon, Israel never took their call to be a missionary nation to heart (see especially Jonah). But the final disobedience was the crucifixion of Christ, who came to offer fulfillment of Israel's purpose as originally given to Abraham. As a result, Jerusalem was destroyed by the Romans (AD 70), the people were scattered, and they have undergone terrible oppression at the hands of wicked Gentiles.

THE CHURCH—FROM THE DEATH OF CHRIST TO THE RAPTURE

During the dispensation of the Church, men are to live by faith in Christ in freedom from sin and law, and to be transformed into His image (Second Corinthians 3). In the Church, we are tasked with using our special spiritual gifts (all believers have them) toward edifying the Body in love (Eph 4:11-16). This includes taking on the mission of Abraham to share God with the world (Acts 1:8). All of this is to be done from a position of security and assurance, and with a view toward anticipating the return of Christ, when He will reward the saints for the works they have done to build up the Body (1 Cor 3:9-15; Phil 3:10-21; Rev 3:21; 22:12).

One important distinction needs to be made. While this dispensation is characterized by the existence of the Church, the Church itself is not a dispensation. The dispensation is related to our participation in God's mission, bringing His blessing to the world. In one sense the Church will succeed, in that when all is said and done, many believers will live forever with God as a result of the spread of the Church's witness, and a Bride of overcomers will be prepared to rule with Christ in His kingdom. However, the Church will not be successful in filling the earth with God's righteousness, and the world will continue to spiral into wickedness until the Lord's return to set up the kingdom.

This dispensation will end when the Church is removed from the earth to meet the Lord in the air. This event is known as the Rapture (1 Thess 4:13-5:6). After the Rapture, God will resume His work with Israel.

KINGDOM—FROM THE RETURN OF
CHRIST TO THE FINAL BATTLE

During the Dispensation of the Kingdom, Jesus Christ will rule in person from David's throne in Jerusalem. Jerusalem will be the world's capital with Israel as the lead nation to which all others serve as vassals. This will be the only truly righteous government the world has ever seen (Isaiah 11). There will be no injustice or oppression. In addition, the creation will be freed from futility (Rom 8:19-22), and the fruit of the ground will be abundant. Even the mountaintops will produce fruitful grain (Psalm 72:16). During this time, man will not be in danger from animals (Isa 11:6-8), and Satan will be bound and unable to tempt the people (Rev 20:2-3). Those who overcome in life now will rule with Christ then. The kingdom is the fulfillment of God's mission.

This dispensation will end when Satan is released after one thousand years to recruit (through deception) and lead a rebellion against Christ (Rev 20:7-8). Christ will call down fire from heaven to consume the rebellion (Rev 20:7-9), and this world will be consumed by fire (2 Pet 3:10-12). After this, a New Heaven and a New Earth will be created, sinless and perfect, and all believers from every age will live there with God for all eternity. The Eternal State is not considered a dispensation because it happens outside of this world's history.

COMMON MISCONCEPTIONS

MISCONCEPTION #1—DISPENSATIONALISTS
TEACH VARIOUS MEANS OF SALVATION
DURING THE DIFFERENT DISPENSATIONS.

The truth is that Dispensationalists do not teach various means of justification salvation. That has always been by grace alone, through faith alone. The Dispensationalist does recognize, however, that the Bible speaks of many kinds of salvation. Salvation from the penalty of sins has only one condition, but salvation from sickness or physical death has other conditions (see Jas 5:19-20). In addition, the word salvation can refer to kingdom blessing or can refer back to receiving the promises of blessing in Deuteronomy 27, and these are clearly conditioned upon works. The word *salvation*, as it occurs in the Old Testament, never looks toward new birth or eternal destiny; thus the salvation discussed in the

Old Testament often has requirements in addition to faith (cf. Ezek 33:5). This is often the case in the New Testament as well (cf. Jas 1:21). But throughout both the Old and New Testaments, a person's eternal destiny is based upon faith alone (see Rom 4:1-5).

MISCONCEPTION #2—DISPENSATIONALISM WAS NEVER FOUND IN CHURCH HISTORY UNTIL RECENTLY.

The truth is that while Dispensationalism was first systematized in the early 1800s, many dispensational concepts can be found (and even had near universal acceptance) in the early church fathers. Dispensationalists do admit that Dispensationalism was lost at the beginning of the Dark Ages, and that it was not recovered at the beginning of the Reformation.

MISCONCEPTION #3—DISPENSATIONALISTS DO NOT BELIEVE THE WHOLE BIBLE IS FOR THE CHRISTIAN.

The truth is that Dispensationalists do believe that the whole Bible is *for* the Christian, but we recognize that many portions of the Bible are not *to* the Christian. Even the Law, which is non-binding to the Christian, reveals God's justice, mercy, and concern for the whole world and points to the reality that we have in Christ (See Col 2:16-17).

DISPENSATIONALISM AND FREE GRACE: INTIMATELY LINKED

Dispensationalism and Free Grace[40] go hand-in-hand for many reasons. Those interested in further study, please see, "Dispensationalism and Free Grace: Intimately Linked," originally published in the *Journal of the Grace Evangelical Society* (Spring 2011 though Spring 2012), available online at:

www.boldgrace.org/pdfs/DAFG-part1.pdf

www.boldgrace.org/pdfs/DAFG-part2.pdf

www.boldgrace.org/pdfs/DAFG-part3.pdf

---

[40] Free Grace is a soteriology that teaches that salvation is granted through faith alone regardless of works.

PRACTICE

1) Read Gal 3:22-25 and 4:1-9. What is Paul comparing living under law to in 4:8-9? How does this impact your understanding of law living? What does this mean regarding the application of principles from one dispensation to another?

2) What is the primary reason that Dispensationalism is preferable to other systems?

3) Read Matt 5:17-18 and Eph 2:14-15. Did Jesus abolish the Law, or did He not? As you read, keep in mind the audience, at what point in time Jesus is talking, etc.

4) Read Gen 15:18-21. What is significant about specifying all the land area Abraham's descendants will inherit? (Hint: What does it tell us about the nature of the inheritance promised to Abraham's descendants?)

5) Try to name the seven dispensations in order without looking back on the lesson. If you miss any, memorize the ones you missed.

DISCUSS

1) Does Dispensationalism mean that God changes? Why or why not?

2) Read Rom 7:4-13. Are the Ten Commandments a good thing?

3) Should Christians place themselves under the Ten Commandments at all?

4) Read Jer 29:10-14. Does Jer 29:11 apply directly to the Church? Can it be applied to the Church at all?

5) Read Exod 34:27-28 and John 16:5-15. Do you have trouble believing that what we have now is better than what Moses had, meeting with God face to face? Why or why not?

Figures of Speech

The voice said, "Cry out!"
And he said, "What shall I cry?"

"All flesh is grass,
And all its loveliness is like the flower of the field.
The grass withers, the flower fades,
Because the breath of the Lord blows upon it;
Surely the people are grass.
The grass withers, the flower fades,
But the word of our God stands forever."
Isaiah 40:6-8

LESSON OBJECTIVES

1. To introduce the concept of figures of speech
2. To define the various common figures of speech
3. To help the student recognize figures of speech in the Bible
4. To help the student understand how to interpret figures of speech in the Bible

INTRODUCTION

The simple phrase "The LORD is my shepherd" (Psalm 23:1), conjures up a wealth of feelings and thoughts. David, himself a shepherd, knew all about what a shepherd means to his flock. Sheep need the feeling of security, or they will not lie down and sleep; so a shepherd protects his sheep from predators, self-inflicted harm, and thieves. A sheep cannot provide for its own needs, so a shepherd provides his sheep's food and drink. Each sheep is unique in its needs, so a shepherd knows every little detail about every one of his sheep. A sheep's condition openly displays the quality of its shepherd, so in taking up the care of sheep, a shepherd stakes his own reputation. A sheep has no offensive or defensive weapons and is unable to fend off predators, so a shepherd puts himself between his flock and predators, and lays down his life in its protection if necessary. This tells us a great deal about the Lord and His relationship with David. All of this barely scratches the surface of the depth of meaning that is communicated in five words—"The LORD is my shepherd."

By using figures of speech, an author can: express complex ideas with few words, emphasize a certain important point, make complex ideas understandable, and create artful expression. Even while maintaining the principle of consistent literal interpretation, we must take figures of speech into account. To fail to do this is to lose the author's intention.

METAPHOR

A metaphor is substituting one object or idea with another to express a similarity. Metaphor is often used to draw a comparison for the purpose of illustration.

Examples: The phrase "The LORD is my shepherd" (above), is an example of metaphor. Also, "You are the salt of the earth" (Matt 5:13), and "You are the light of the world" (Matt 5:14) are metaphors.

SIMILE

A simile is a comparison using *like* or *as*.

Examples: "...*he who doubts is like a wave* of the sea driven and tossed by the wind" (Jas 1:6); "For *you were like sheep going astray*, but have now returned to the Shepherd and Overseer of your souls" (1 Pet 2:25); "...*your adversary the devil walks about like a roaring lion*, seeking whom he may devour" (1 Pet 5:8). Emphasis added.

ALLEGORY

An allegory is an extended metaphor. The Lord as the Good Shepherd in John 10, and the Lord as the True Vine in John 15 are good examples of allegory. The use of allegory and what is called *allegorizing* are not the same thing. Allegorizing is the process of treating something as an allegory when that was not intended by the original author. For example, treating the promise God made to David, that his Son would rule on his throne forever, as an allegory about Christ ruling in the hearts of those in the Church is allegorizing. The use of allegory in the Scripture should not be seen as license to allegorize Scripture.

TYPE AND ANTITYPE[41]

Types are real persons, events, or things in the Old Testament that have a substantial relationship with corresponding New Testament persons, events, or things. The New Testament fulfilling is called an *antitype*. For a type and antitype to be genuine, they must have five characteristics: 1) Similarity: the antitype must be similar to the type. 2) Historical Reality: both the type and the antitype are actual persons, events, or things. 3) Predictive Element: A type must point towards its antitype. 4) Fulfilling or Heightening: The antitype must be greater than its corresponding type. 5) Divine Design: types are a beautiful illustration of the providence and activity of God. Real people, events, or things exist or happen in anticipation of a greater reality. This can only happen by divine working.

Example:

Paul wrote in Col 2:16-17:

> So let no one judge you in food or in drink, or regarding a festival or a new moon or sabbaths, which are a shadow of things to come, but the substance is of Christ.

Likewise, the author of Hebrews wrote:

> For if the blood of bulls and goats and the ashes of a heifer, sprinkling the unclean, sanctifies for the purifying of the flesh, how much more shall the blood of Christ, who through the eternal Spirit offered Himself without spot to God, cleanse your conscience from dead works to serve the living God? (Heb 9:14-15)

These passages show us that the Law of Moses is a type of Christ and His work. Christ is the antitype which the Law of Moses prefigures.

---

[41] This definition of type and antitype is adapted from the definition given by Roy Zuck in *Basic Bible Interpretation* (Colorado Springs: Victor, 1991), pp. 169-74.

METONYMY

Metonymy is referring to something by naming a related thing or concept.

Example: "I will arise and go to my father, and will say to him, "Father, I have sinned against heaven..." (Luke 15:18). In this example, the prodigal son employs metonymy by using the term "heaven" to refer to God.

SYNECDOCHE

Synecdoche is referring to something by naming one of its parts, or the reverse.

Example: "Your throne shall be established forever" in 2 Sam 7:16, means that David's kingdom will be established forever.

DRAMATIC IRONY

Dramatic irony occurs when the audience understands an unusual circumstance that the people within the situation do not understand. John 11:45-52 is a classic example of dramatic irony. In this passage, the reader is to understand that when Caiaphas said, "one man should die for the people," it was a prophecy about the substitutionary death of Christ, though Caiaphas did not understand this when he spoke.

Passages that exhibit dramatic irony (like John 11:45-52) have been used by allegorizing interpreters as proof that there is a dual meaning to many texts in the Bible, one that the author intended and a spiritual meaning that is beyond or different from what the author intended. But there is a key difference between dramatic irony and having a dual meaning to any text. The *author's* intention determines the literal meaning, not the *speakers* within the text. Usually the author's meaning and the speaker's meaning are the same, but during moments of dramatic irony, this may not be the case. The existence of dramatic irony does not validate allegorizing.

ANTHROPOMORPHISM

Anthropomorphism is ascribing human characteristics to God.

Example: Psalm 44:3 says, "For they did not gain possession of the land by their own sword, nor did their own arm save them; but *it was Your right hand, Your arm, and the light of Your countenance*, because You favored them" (emphasis added).

ZOOMORPHISM

Zoomorphism is ascribing animal characteristics to God, to angels, or to people.

Example: Psalm 63:7 says, "Because You have been my help, therefore in the shadow of Your wings I will rejoice." This phrase brings to mind an image of a mother bird protecting her chicks.

PERSONIFICATION

Personification is ascribing characteristics or actions of a person to inanimate objects.

Example: Genesis 4:10 says, "And [God] said [to Cain], "What have you done? The voice of your brother's blood cries out to Me from the ground." Abel's blood does not have a literal voice. God means that He knows about the spilling of Abel's blood. Additionally, God asking the question, "What have you done?" is an example of anthropomorphism because God is omniscient (He knows everything).

HYPERBOLE

Hyperbole is an exaggeration intended to emphasize.

Example: Psalm 6:6 says, "I am weary with my groaning; all night I make my bed swim; I drench my couch with my tears." David's bed did not actually swim because of a flood of tears, but by using this hyperbole, David was able to help us relate to his experience more than if he had said, "I cried a lot."

LITOTES

Litotes is a deliberate understatement. Like hyperbole, litotes can be used to show emphasis.

Example: Acts 15:2 says, "Therefore, when Paul and Barnabas had no small dissension and dispute with them..." means that Paul and Barnabas had an enormous dispute with the Judaizers in verse 1.

Litotes can also be used in antithetic parallel phrases by downplaying what is stated in the second line (opposing line), in order to emphasize what was stated in the first line. For example, in Rev 2:10-11, "... Be faithful until death, and I will give you the crown of life. He who has an ear, let him hear what the Spirit says to the churches. He who overcomes shall not be hurt by the second death," litotes is used in v 11 to stress the truth expressed in the previous verse, "...Be faithful until death, and I will give you the crown of life." Far from being hurt by the second death, the one who overcomes will be given "the crown of life," a reward given for perseverance in faithful obedience. The text does not say that failure to overcome would cause the believer to be hurt by the second death. Recognizing that this is an example of litotes given to emphasize the reward of the crown of life helps the interpreter to avoid the incorrect assumption that these believers are being threatened with loss of salvation.

PARABLES

"Jesus' stories [parables] are like wrapped gifts. The packaging of the story can either distract or captivate. But unless the package is opened, the gift itself remains unseen. Likewise unless one seeks the core of the parable—its truth and application—the lessons will remain hidden. Yet when discovered, these lessons prove extremely valuable."[42]

Parables are simple stories, using familiar topics, told to illustrate spiritual or moral truths. While parables exist in the Old Testament as well, in this lesson, I focus primarily on the kingdom parables in the Gospels.

---

[42] *Nelson Study Bible*, Earl D. Radmacher, Editor (Nashville: Nelson, 1997) p. 1613.

WHY WERE THE PARABLES GIVEN?

Parables are intended for the purpose of illustration, but the kingdom parables (most of the parables in the Gospels) have an added purpose as well. In Matt 13:10-12, Jesus reveals His reason for speaking the kingdom parables:

> And the disciples came and said to Him, "Why do You speak to them in parables?" He answered and said to them, "Because it has been given to you to know the mysteries of the kingdom of heaven, but to them it has not been given. For whoever has, to him more will be given, and he will have abundance; but whoever does not have, even what he has will be taken away from him."

This reveals a double purpose. Jesus spoke in parables 1) to increase the disciples' understanding of the mysteries related to the kingdom, and 2) to hide these truths from the unresponsive (and even hostile) religious leaders ("them") and to even take away what little understanding they had.

In other words, to those who are responsive to the truth about the kingdom, the parables will help them gain a fuller understanding of kingdom truths. To those who are unresponsive to kingdom truth, the parables will serve only to further confuse them. This was true when Jesus spoke the parables about the kingdom, and it has remained true throughout the Church's history.

When interpreting parables, ask the following questions:

What is the subject of the parable (is it the kingdom)?

What is the main point being communicated?

How do the details of the parable support the main point?

RECOGNIZING KINGDOM PARABLES

Kingdom parables are easy to recognize because they usually begin with statements such as, "The kingdom of heaven is like..." Other times, the context makes it clear that the kingdom is the subject. The most important thing to remember when interpreting kingdom parables is that they are about the future kingdom of Messiah[43] (See Section 5: The

---

[43] Messiah is an Anglicized spelling of the Hebrew word, meshiach (מָשִׁיחַ), which means "anointed one."

Kingdom). This should be obvious, but due to centuries of non-literal interpretation of things related to the kingdom, this point is often missed. Unfortunately, kingdom parables are commonly interpreted as if they are about the free gift of eternal life (confusing the gift and the prize, and making eternal life far from free) or about the Church.

For an excellent work on the parables of Matthew 13, see Stanley Toussaint's, *Behold the King*.[44]

INTERPRETING PARABLES

Like any portion of the Bible, the correct interpretation of any parable is what the original author intended. Anything else is simply reading our own biases and opinions into the text.

A word of caution when interpreting parables: Parables are generally given to illustrate a single point. Theological conclusions should not be made based solely on the details of parables. In fact, the details should only be considered theologically relevant as they are related to the main point being made. For example, it is appropriate to consider the differences in rewards received by the servants in the Parable of the Minas in Luke 19:11-27, because they relate to the parable's main point. However, it is not appropriate to go to the Parable of the Lost Coin in Luke 15:8-10 and build a theology based on the fact that the Holy Spirit is there typified by a woman. That is clearly not related to the main point of the parable.

It is also essential that we do not, based on our theological bias, make assumptions or conclusions that are not explicitly stated in the text. This is true in all portions of the Bible, but the figurative language in parables provides a strong temptation for dishonest and/or careless interpreters to read theological bias into the text. A small point of possible comparison can be manipulated to bring in ideas that are totally foreign to the parable. This further illustrates the second purpose Jesus stated for His use of parables—to confuse those who are hardened to kingdom truth.

CONCLUSION

Figures of speech are powerful tools. Figures of speech allow a great deal to be communicated in a few words, whereas it would be difficult or

---

[44] Stanley Toussaint, *Behold the King: A Study of Matthew* (Grand Rapids, MI: Kregel, 1980).

impossible to communicate the same ideas and feelings without them, no matter how many words are used. Correctly interpreting figures of speech in the Bible helps us to grasp the richness of God's Word and to avoid being carried away by error.

PRACTICE

1) What prompted Jesus' telling of the Parable of the Rich Fool (Luke 12:13-21)? How does it relate to the meaning of the parable?

2) What is the main point of the Parable of the Pharisee and Tax Collector (Luke 18:9-14)? Would it be appropriate to use this parable to say that we should always be looking down, beating our chests while worshiping God? Why or why not?

3) What primary figure of speech is being employed in Psalm 23?

4) What is the significance of the allegory of Christ as the Good Shepherd in John 10:1-16 and 26-30?

5) What figures of speech are used in Isaiah 40:28-31? What do these figures of speech mean?

DISCUSS

1) The Gospel of John contains no kingdom parables. Why (see John 20:31)?

2) In Matt 13:18-23, Jesus explains the Parable of the Soils, given in vv 3-9. How does this help you to understand how parables should be interpreted? Does Jesus mention anything about eternal life? Why do many interpreters read eternal life into the text?

3) Read Gen 2:18-24 and Eph 5:22-32. Are Adam and Eve a type of Christ and the Church? Why or why not?

4) In John 15:1-5, Jesus gives a very expressive metaphor to explain to his disciples the type of relationship that they can have with Him. What does this metaphor reveal about the nature of our relationship with Jesus and the Father?

5) What are the dangers of seeing a figure of speech where there isn't one being employed?

6) Zoomorphism, anthropomorphism, and personification are used throughout the Bible. What are some dangers of not recognizing these figures of speech?

Interpreting Prophecy

"If it were possible to straighten out the confusion existing about us in the professing church, the proper starting point would be, no doubt, to teach God's purposes concerning Israel." *A. C. Gaebelein*[45]

LESSON OBJECTIVES

1. To demonstrate that prophecy that has already been fulfilled has been fulfilled literally

2. To show the reasonable expectation for literal fulfillment of prophecy that has not yet been fulfilled

3. To demonstrate the danger of non-literal interpretation of prophecy, as illustrated in Church history

4. To introduce the great value of interpreting prophecy correctly

LITERAL FULFILLMENT OF ALREADY FULFILLED PROPHECY

All conservative scholars agree that prophecies regarding things that have now taken place have all been fulfilled literally. Several examples are below.

THE VIRGIN BIRTH

PROPHECY:

Isaiah 7:14, "Therefore the Lord Himself will give you a sign: behold, the virgin shall conceive and bear a Son, and shall call His name Immanuel [Hebrew for, 'God with us']."

LITERAL FULFILLMENT:

Luke 1:26-35 reads:

> Now in the sixth month the angel Gabriel was sent by God to a city of Galilee named Nazareth, to a virgin betrothed to a man whose name was Joseph, of the house of David. The virgin's name was Mary. And having come in, the angel said to her, "Rejoice, highly favored one, the Lord is with you; blessed are you among women!"

> But when she saw him, she was troubled at his saying, and considered what manner of greeting this was. Then the angel said to her, "Do not be afraid, Mary, for you have found favor with God. And behold, you will conceive in your womb and bring forth a Son, and shall call His name Jesus. He will be great, and will be called the Son of the Highest; and the Lord God will give Him the throne of His father David. And He will reign over the house of Jacob forever, and of His kingdom there will be no end."

> Then Mary said to the angel, "How can this be, since I do not know a man?"

> And the angel answered and said to her, "The Holy Spirit will come upon you, and the power of the Highest will overshadow you; therefore, also, that Holy One who is to be born will be called the Son of God.

DESTRUCTION OF THE TEMPLE

PROPHECY:

Matthew 24:1-2, "Then Jesus went out and departed from the temple, and His disciples came up to show Him the buildings of the temple. And Jesus said to them, 'Do you not see all these things? Assuredly, I say to you, not one stone shall be left here upon another, that shall not be thrown down.'"

Literal fulfillment: In AD 70, the Romans destroyed Jerusalem. During this destruction, the temple was taken apart stone by stone so that the gold between the stones could be plundered. Not one stone was left upon another.

THE CRUCIFIXION OF CHRIST

PROPHECY:

In Psalm 22:6-8, 14-18, David wrote:

> But I am a worm, and no man;
> A reproach of men, and despised by the people.
> All those who see Me ridicule Me;
> They shoot out the lip, they shake the head, saying,
> "He trusted in the Lord, let Him rescue Him;
> Let Him deliver Him, since He delights in Him!" (…)
> I am poured out like water,
> And all My bones are out of joint;
> My heart is like wax;
> It has melted within Me.
> My strength is dried up like a potsherd,
> And My tongue clings to My jaws;
> You have brought Me to the dust of death.
> For dogs have surrounded Me;
> The congregation of the wicked has enclosed Me.
> They pierced My hands and My feet;
> I can count all My bones.
> They look and stare at Me.
> They divide My garments among them,
> And for My clothing they cast lots.

Likewise, Isaiah wrote in Isa 53:4-12:

> Surely He has borne our griefs
> And carried our sorrows;
> Yet we esteemed Him stricken,
> Smitten by God, and afflicted.
> But He was wounded for our transgressions,
> He was bruised for our iniquities;
> The chastisement for our peace was upon Him,

And by His stripes we are healed.
All we like sheep have gone astray;
We have turned, every one, to his own way;
And the Lord has laid on Him the iniquity of us all.
He was oppressed and He was afflicted,
Yet He opened not His mouth;
He was led as a lamb to the slaughter,
And as a sheep before its shearers is silent,
So He opened not His mouth.
He was taken from prison and from judgment,
And who will declare His generation?
For He was cut off from the land of the living;
For the transgressions of My people He was stricken.
And they made His grave with the wicked—
But with the rich at His death,
Because He had done no violence,
Nor was any deceit in His mouth.
Yet it pleased the Lord to bruise Him;
He has put Him to grief.
When You make His soul an offering for sin,
He shall see His seed, He shall prolong His days,
And the pleasure of the Lord shall prosper in His hand.
He shall see the labor of His soul, and be satisfied.
By His knowledge My righteous Servant shall justify many,
For He shall bear their iniquities.
Therefore I will divide Him a portion with the great,
And He shall divide the spoil with the strong,
Because He poured out His soul unto death,
And He was numbered with the transgressors,
And He bore the sin of many,
And made intercession for the transgressors.

These prophecies lay out many of the details of Jesus' crucifixion, which took place several hundred years later.

LITERAL FULFILLMENT:

Mark 15:16-37 reads:

> Then the soldiers led Him away into the hall called Praetorium, and they called together the whole garrison. And they clothed Him with purple; and they twisted a crown of thorns, put it on His head, and began to salute Him, "Hail, King of the Jews!" Then they struck Him on the head with a reed and spat on

Him; and bowing the knee, they worshiped Him. And when they had mocked Him, they took the purple off Him, put His own clothes on Him, and led Him out to crucify Him.

Then they compelled a certain man, Simon a Cyrenian, the father of Alexander and Rufus, as he was coming out of the country and passing by, to bear His cross. And they brought Him to the place Golgotha, which is translated, Place of a Skull. Then they gave Him wine mingled with myrrh to drink, but He did not take it. And when they crucified Him, they divided His garments, casting lots for them to determine what every man should take.

Now it was the third hour, and they crucified Him. And the inscription of His accusation was written above:

THE KING OF THE JEWS.

With Him they also crucified two robbers, one on His right and the other on His left. So the Scripture was fulfilled which says, "And He was numbered with the transgressors."

And those who passed by blasphemed Him, wagging their heads and saying, "Aha! You who destroy the temple and build it in three days, save Yourself, and come down from the cross!"

Likewise the chief priests also, mocking among themselves with the scribes, said, "He saved others; Himself He cannot save. Let the Christ, the King of Israel, descend now from the cross, that we may see and believe."

Even those who were crucified with Him reviled Him.

Now when the sixth hour had come, there was darkness over the whole land until the ninth hour. And at the ninth hour Jesus cried out with a loud voice, saying, "Eloi, Eloi, lama sabachthani?" which is translated, "My God, My God, why have You forsaken Me?"

Some of those who stood by, when they heard that, said, "Look, He is calling for Elijah!" Then someone ran and filled a sponge full of sour wine, put it on a reed, and offered it to Him to drink, saying, "Let Him alone; let us see if Elijah will come to take Him down."

And Jesus cried out with a loud voice, and breathed His last.

See also Matt 27:32-61; Luke 23:26-56; John 19:17-37

CYRUS

PROPHECY:

In Isa 44:26–45:3, Isaiah prophesies that a man named Cyrus will be used by God to declare that Jerusalem and the other cities of Judah will once again be inhabited by Israel.

> Who confirms the word of His servant,
> And performs the counsel of His messengers;
> Who says to Jerusalem, 'You shall be inhabited,'
> To the cities of Judah, 'You shall be built,'
> And I will raise up her waste places; Who says to the deep,
> 'Be dry!
> And I will dry up your rivers';
> Who says of Cyrus, 'He is My shepherd,
> And he shall perform all My pleasure,
> Saying to Jerusalem, "You shall be built,"
> And to the temple, "Your foundation shall be laid."'
> "Thus says the Lord to His anointed,
> To Cyrus, whose right hand I have held—
> To subdue nations before him
> And loose the armor of kings,
> To open before him the double doors,
> So that the gates will not be shut:
> 'I will go before you
> And make the crooked places straight;
> I will break in pieces the gates of bronze
> And cut the bars of iron.
> I will give you the treasures of darkness
> And hidden riches of secret places,
> That you may know that I, the Lord,
> Who call you by your name,
> Am the God of Israel.
> For Jacob My servant's sake,
> And Israel My elect,
> I have even called you by your name;
> I have named you, though you have not known Me.

This prophecy occurred 150 years before Cyrus (who would later become king of the Medo-Persian Empire) was born. Jeremiah added to this prophecy by declaring that Judah[46] would be carried away into captivity by Nebuchadnezzar (King of Babylon) and that the captivity would last for 70 years (Jer 25:1-14).

FULFILLMENT:

Exactly seventy years after Judah was carried away into captivity, Cyrus made a declaration to allow the Jews to return to the Promised Land, facilitating their homecoming. Second Chronicles 36:22-23 records this fulfillment:

> Now in the first year of Cyrus king of Persia, that the word of the Lord by the mouth of Jeremiah might be fulfilled, the Lord stirred up the spirit of Cyrus king of Persia, so that he made a proclamation throughout all his kingdom, and also put it in writing, saying,
>
> Thus says Cyrus king of Persia:
>
>> All the kingdoms of the earth the Lord God of heaven has given me. And He has commanded me to build Him a house at Jerusalem which is in Judah. Who is among you of all His people? May the Lord his God be with him, and let him go up!

See also Ezra 1:1-4, 7, 8; 3:7; and 4:3.

THE 69 WEEKS OF DANIEL

PROPHECY:

Daniel wrote in Dan 9:25:

> Know therefore and understand,
> That from the going forth of the command
> To restore and build Jerusalem
> Until Messiah the Prince,
> There shall be seven weeks [literally, sevens, i.e. seven groups
> of seven years] and sixty-two weeks [sevens]..."

This prophecy tells us that after the command to rebuild Jerusalem, 69 groups of seven years (483 years) would pass before Messiah is revealed

---

[46] 1. The tribe of Judah, one of the twelve tribes of Israel 2. The Southern Kingdom of Israel after the kingdom was split into two. Here I refer to the second definition.

as the coming Prince. This baffled interpreters for some time, because they were using the wrong calendar year. Using the Jewish[47] 360-day year (which Daniel would have been using), gives a total of 173,880 days.

LITERAL FULFILLMENT:

The decree given by Artaxerxes to rebuild Jerusalem (Neh 2:1-8) was given on March 14, 445 BC. Jesus' triumphal entry, riding on the foal of the donkey (see Zech 9:9 and Matt 21:4-10), occurred on April 6, AD 32, exactly 173,880 days later.[48]

EXPECTATION OF LITERAL FULFILLMENT OF FUTURE PROPHECY

In Gen 15:18-21; 2 Sam 7:8-17; and many other passages, God promises a literal and eternal kingdom to His chosen nation, Israel.

One theological group argues that due to the disobedience of Israel, all prophecies regarding the kingdom of Messiah will not be fulfilled literally in Israel, but allegorically through the Church. This not only breaks with the Bible's long history of literal fulfillment of prophecy, it also goes against plain statements in which God says that His promises regarding the kingdom are not conditioned upon Israel's obedience (Psalm 89:20-37; Jer 33:17-22). In fact, in Psalm 89:20-37, God explicitly says that He will not break His covenant with David even if Israel is disobedient. See Lesson 30: The Kingdom Promised and Confirmed for a detailed look at this issue.

In addition, to deny that the kingdom will have literal fulfillment is an explicit denial of the original intention of the authors.

TELESCOPING

At times, prophets describe events as occurring together, when in fact there can be long intervals in between. One clear example of this is the events of the first and second comings of Christ. In the Old Testament, Christ's coming as the Suffering Servant and His coming as Triumphant King seem to occur together, when, in fact, there are at least 1988 years

---

[47] Jewish is an adjective meaning, "of the nation of Israel."

[48] Sir Robert Anderson, *The Coming Prince* (Grand Rapids, MI: Kregel, 2008).

in between (as of 2013 + 7 years of Tribulation[49]). *Telescoping* is a descriptive name of this principle. If one were to look at a mountain range through a telescope, the peaks would appear together, even if large valleys are in between.

Telescoping is vital. Telescoping allowed God to make a legitimate offer of the kingdom to Israel, while still allowing for the Church and the inclusion of Gentiles in His kingdom program.

THE DANGER OF NON-LITERAL INTERPRETATION OF PROPHECY

When interpreters deny a literal fulfillment of prophecies regarding the kingdom, many theological and practical problems are created. For starters, throughout the New Testament, kingdom inheritance (that is, gaining a share in ownership of this kingdom) is clearly conditioned upon good works and faithful endurance of trials (see Matt 4:17; 5:1-10; 25:34-36; Rom 8:17; 1 Cor 6:9-10; Gal 5:19-21; Eph 5:5; 2 Thess 1:4-5; 2 Pet 1:5-11; Rev 3:21; and elsewhere). When the kingdom is confused with the free gift of justification and eternal life, works are inappropriately added as a condition of what is often called *final salvation*.[50]

St. Augustine and A.W. Pink are classic examples of scholars who, when they held to a literal fulfillment of kingdom prophecies, also held firmly to justification by faith alone and assurance of salvation based upon the promises of God alone. Yet when they adopted a non-literal approach to kingdom prophecies, both men abandoned grace and taught that assurance was impossible without a lifetime of good works. There are very few

---

[49] Generally, a tribulation is a difficulty. Specifically, the Tribulation is a seven year period that precedes a literal millennial reign of Christ.

[50] The term *final salvation* is used by people who hold to the view described here. They view salvation from the penalty of sins as essentially probationary, and believe it is not really finalized until the Great White Throne judgment. By contrast, the Biblical picture of salvation related to eternal destiny is that it is final at the first moment of faith, and that there is no future judgment for the believer to determine eternal destiny (John 5:24).

scholars who allegorize kingdom passages and also hold firmly to salvation by grace alone, through faith alone, in Christ alone.[51]

In addition, the Dark Ages idea of the church's ruling over the world's governments, rather than a separation of church and state, comes from allegorizing Scripture related to the kingdom. An untold number of tragedies and oppressions has been justified due to this unbiblical concept.

THE VALUE OF INTERPRETING PROPHECY CORRECTLY

Literal interpretation of prophecy results in a greater understanding of God's faithfulness. If God has broken his promise to Israel because of their disobedience, how do we know His promise stands firm with us? But if God is faithful, even through Israel's disobedience, we know He will remain faithful with us. "If we are faithless, He remains faithful; He cannot deny Himself" (2 Tim 2:13). A right picture of God depends upon literal interpretation of prophecy.

Throughout the New Testament, believers are exhorted to live in light of the coming kingdom of Messiah. Having a real and literal picture of His coming kingdom helps us keep a right perspective, letting go of the things of this world and waiting eagerly for His return.

FIGURATIVE LANGUAGE IN PROPHECY

Prophecy is full of figurative language, and each of these figures must be handled with care. Prophecy that has already been fulfilled gives us a good template of how to interpret prophecy that is yet to be fulfilled. But God has given us an even greater tool to help us interpret prophecy. In Daniel 2; 4; 7; and 8, we have detailed examples of visions full of figurative language that are interpreted under divine inspiration. There are other examples of this in Scripture, but these are a great starting point.

A full treatment of these examples is beyond the scope of this lesson. I encourage you to take some time and read carefully through these

---

[51] For further discussion of this principle, see Grant Hawley, "Dispensationalism and Free Grace: Intimately Linked, Parts 1, 2, and 3" *Journal of the Grace Evangelical Society* (Spring and Autumn 2011 and Spring 2012). Also available online at www.boldgrace.org/pdfs/DAFG-part1.pdf, www.boldgrace.org/pdfs/DAFG-part2.pdf, and www.boldgrace.org/pdfs/DAFG-part3.pdf. Last accessed, July, 29th, 2013.

passages to get a good idea of how to interpret figurative language in prophecy.

SIMPLE CHART OF END TIME EVENTS

Below is a simplified chart of some of the most significant end time events as pictured in the Bible:

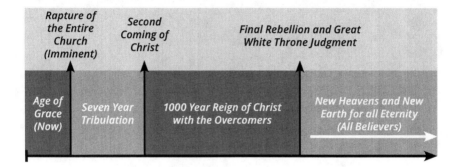

PRACTICE

1) Read Hos 3:4-5. What does this mean for Israel's future?

2) Read Rom 11:25-29. How does 11:29 relate to prophecy concerning Israel's future?

3) Read Matt 24:1-14. Verse 13 states "But he who endures to the end shall be saved." Does the context say what the one who endures will be saved from?

4) Read Ezek 37:1-14. What do the dry bones represent?

5) Read Isa 61:1-2 and Luke 4:16-21. What does Jesus leave off from Isa 61:1-2 when He quotes it? How does the principle of telescoping help us to understand these passages?

DISCUSS

1) How should we understand Isa 11:1-10? Has this already happened?

2) What does the detail and accuracy of prophecy and its fulfillment tell us about God?

3) In Jonah, God said that in forty days, Nineveh would be overthrown. But the people of Nineveh repented, and God relented of His judgment. What does this tell us about prophecy of judgment?

4) Suppose we did not know that Jesus will bring justice and peace to the world when He returns. How would this change the way we view current affairs and our role in them?

5) Read 2 Tim 2:14-18 together. Discuss how this illustrates the importance of having a right understanding of prophecy.

Languages, Translations, & Language Tools

"...it was Greek to me." Casca in Shakespeare's Julius Caesar

LESSON OBJECTIVES

1. To introduce the languages of the Bible
2. To discuss some English translations and their philosophies of translation[52]
3. To introduce helpful tools for English-only readers
4. To teach the reader how to do word studies

THE LANGUAGES OF THE BIBLE

The Bible was not originally written in English, but in Hebrew (Old Testament), Koine Greek[53] (New Testament), and some small sections of Aramaic (much more in the Old Testament than in the New). Koine Greek in particular is wildly different from English grammatically. In English, the part of speech for each word is determined largely by word order. In Greek, the words take on different forms to express their grammatical relationship to each other. Word order means much

---

[52] Translation is converting a text from one language/culture to another.

[53] Koine Greek is the language of the Greek world from 300 B.C.-300 A.D. The New Testament and Septuagint were written in Koine Greek.

less in Greek than it does in English, though it is a primary tool for adding emphasis.

The language differences present the Bible interpreter with an additional challenge. Because it is impossible to translate exactly from one language to another, Bible translators must choose how best to express what the original language means by what it says. The result has been a wide variety of translations, some with translation philosophies very different from others.

TRANSLATIONS

Translations vary from literal[54] (NASB, NKJV) to complete paraphrase[55] (The Message), and everything in between. One popular method is Dynamic Equivalence,[56] which is a blend between literal and paraphrase. When the translators feel that the purpose of a phrase is easily expressed with a literal translation, they will translate it literally. When they feel that the theological meaning of the text is lost or unclear when translated literally, they will paraphrase. Even within a sentence, the product may be part literal and part paraphrase, with no indicator of a change between the two. To many, this philosophy makes good sense. But this is a particularly dangerous philosophy of translation because the reader often does not know that what he is reading is the editor's theological opinion rather than the literal meaning of the words. The NIV, NET Bible, Good News Bible, and the New Living Translation are some examples of Dynamic Equivalence Bibles.[57] The NET Bible is the most literal of these Dynamic Equivalence translations, but a literal translation is preferable.

When using a translation, the serious Bible student (and we all should be) should always choose a literal translation. In the chart below, I

---

[54] Literal translation is an approach of translating to a new language that seeks to maintain the voice of the original language as much as is reasonable.

[55] A paraphrase is a translation philosophy that expresses the translators' understanding of the text with little regard to maintaining the structure of the text itself.

[56] A dynamic equivalence is a translation philosophy in which the translators' understanding of the text prioritizes the reader's comfort over a strict adherence to the original words and grammar.

[57] The NIV is particularly dangerous because not only is it very popular, but all of the editors of the NIV held to one extreme theological perspective, and the philosophy of translation allowed for a great deal of manipulation of the text for theological purposes. See *The NIV Reconsidered: A Fresh Look at a Popular Translation*, by Earl Radmacher and Zane Hodges, for a fuller discussion.

attempt to list some literal Bible translations in order starting at the top with the most literal. This list is unavoidably subjective:

Translation	Philosophy
Recovery Version	This translation is literal to the point of being almost wooden. In addition, the notes are quite helpful on the Christian life at times, though they sometimes venture into allegorizing and theological error, and should be read with discernment. *The Recovery Version New Testament* is available free of charge from its publisher, Living Stream Ministries.
Darby Version	John Nelson Darby rediscovered the importance of literal interpretation, was a world-class linguist, and took great care in making a fresh literal translation. It is about 150 years old, however, and can be a bit archaic. This translation is available online for free, and is a free option for the e-Sword Bible Study Software.
New King James Version	The NKJV is, in my opinion, the finest English translation available. It is literal, insightful, and quite readable (even out loud). Perhaps best of all, it notes textual differences at the bottom of the page. Some people mistakenly believe that the NKJV is simply a reworking of the KJV (taking out the *Thees* and *Thous*). But this is not the case. The NKJV is a completely new translation. The NKJV is still far from perfect, but it is very good.
New American Standard Version	The NASB has a reputation for being the most literal popular translation. This is true in many places. However, in certain key passages, the translators have made some very unfortunate, theologically driven translations. Some examples are John 3:36; 15:2; 1 Cor 5:11; Jas 2:14. The translations chosen for these verses are not novel, and overall the NASB is quite literal. But it does fall a bit short of its reputation.
King James Version	The KJV is beautifully written, but it is a bit archaic which can hinder people from correctly understanding.
English Standard Version	The ESV is a literal translation, but where there are questions about how a passage could be translated, it tends to side with the Calvinistic view.
New English Translation	The NET Bible is a Dynamic Equivalence, though it does tend to be more literal than others.

Below are a few non-literal English Bibles (literal translations are preferable):

- New International Version
- The Message
- Today's New International Version
- New Living Translation
- Contemporary English Version
- The Living Bible

LANGUAGE TOOLS

While every teacher of the Bible should learn the original languages if able, this is no easy task. However, many helpful tools are available to assist the English-only Bible student in getting closer to the original meaning of the Bible.

LEXICONS

Lexicons[58] are essentially dictionaries of ancient languages, though they often contain more information than a typical dictionary. Many lexicons are available, but some especially helpful lexicons are *Thayer's Greek Lexicon, Bauer's Greek Lexicon,*[59] and *Brown-Driver-Briggs Hebrew and English Lexicon.*

STRONG'S CONCORDANCE

Strong's Concordance[60] is an especially useful tool, because it not only contains a simple lexicon of Greek and Hebrew, but it has also assigned a number to each Greek and Hebrew word and listed each occurrence of those words in the Bible. This is extremely valuable for doing word studies.

---

[58] A lexicon is a word list that includes words and their meaning as they are used throughout literature.

[59] Because the newest edition, BDAG, has an added theological bias, BAG and BAGD, the first and second editions, are preferable for personal study. See Michael Makidon, "Soteriological Concerns with Bauer's Greek Lexicon," *Journal of the Grace Evangelical Society* (Autumn, 2004).

[60] A concordance is a book that includes a list of English words as they appear in the Bible.

PARSING GUIDES

For students who know some Greek, parsing guides can be a tremendous help. Parsing guides parse (tell the grammatical function of) each word as it occurs in the text.

But caution should be exercised. Sometimes, words in a certain form can have more than one possible grammatical function, and which function we choose can radically change our understanding of a passage.

DEEPER STUDY

For example, the Greek word *tetagmenoi*, found in Acts 13:48, can be either middle voice[61] or passive voice.[62] If it is middle voice, the verse would mean, "Now when the Gentiles heard this, they were glad and glorified the word of the Lord. And as many as had *appointed themselves* toward eternal life believed." If it is passive, it would mean, "Now when the Gentiles heard this, they were glad and glorified the word of the Lord. And as many as *had been appointed* to eternal life believed," as in the NKJV. The difference between the two is clearly significant, as the first supports the idea of human freedom, while the latter supports the Calvinistic view of unconditional election.[63]

Contextually, verse 46, "Then Paul and Barnabas grew bold and said, 'It was necessary that the word of God should be spoken to you first; but since you reject it, and *judge yourselves unworthy* of everlasting life, behold, we turn to the Gentiles,'" supports the middle voice rendering in v 48. Those who rejected Paul and Barnabas' appeal *judged themselves unworthy*. Those who did not reject Paul and Barnabas' appeal had appointed themselves toward eternal life. Against the context, Han's *Parsing Guide*, along with the NKJV, has the passive.[64] For this reason, parsing guides should be used only as a help, and should not be seen as authoritative, even though Han's *Parsing Guide* is jokingly nicknamed "The Pope," because people often refer to it as if it is authoritative.

---

[61] Middle voice is a grammatical structure in which the subject performs the action for its own result (not found in English grammar).

[62] Passive voice is a grammatical structure in which the subject receives the action.

[63] Biblically, election is God's choosing of people, places, and things to carry out His work, but in Calvinism, it is the idea that God has chosen in advance whom He will save and whom He will condemn.

[64] Nathan Han, *A Parsing Guide to the Greek New Testament* (Scottsdale, PA: Herald Press, 1971), p. 260.

<u>Warning for Greek Students</u>: *Heavily using parsing guides can make it difficult to retain what you have learned about Greek grammar.*

COMMENTARIES

Commentaries (and Study Bibles) can be very helpful but should not be seen as authoritative, nor should they be used as a substitute for diligent study of the Bible itself. It is best to read commentaries from more than one theological perspective and to observe whether or not the authors are following sound hermeneutics.

Some helpful commentaries are listed below:

Title	Description	Audience
The Grace New Testament Commentary[65]	A Free Grace commentary on the New Testament	All
The Bible Knowledge Commentary[66]	From Dallas Theological Seminary faculty. This commentary contains various theological perspectives but is often worth checking. The notes on Psalms, Hebrews, and Second Peter are especially helpful.	All
Robert Govett's Commentaries[67]	Archaic, but extremely helpful in studying Dispensational and soteriological (salvation) issues. Govett held to a partial rapture[68] and should be read with discernment in these passages.	Advanced
RCH Lenski's *Commentary on the New Testament*[69]	Lenski is a Lutheran and this does affect his comments. However, his insights into the Greek grammar are invaluable.	Advanced—some Greek knowledge required

---

[65] Various Authors, *The Grace New Testament Commentary* (Denton, TX: Grace Evangelical Society, 2010).

[66] John F. Walvoord and Roy B. Zuck, ed., *The Bible Knowledge Commentary: An Exposition of the Scriptures by Dallas Seminary Faculty* (Place Unknown: Victor Books, 1983).

[67] See Schoettle Publishing Company for more information.

[68] A partial rapture is the theory that faithful believers will be raptured, but unfaithful believers will not.

[69] R. C. H. Lenski, *Commentary on the New Testament*, 13 vols. (Place Unknown: Hendrickson Publishers, 1943, 1963).

Title	Description	Audience
Zane Hodges's commentaries on James and The Epistles of John[70]	These commentaries are unparalleled. They should be read by every serious Bible student.	All/ Intermediate

WORD STUDIES

Words have a range of possible meanings. For example, the word *run* has 430 possible definitions listed in the Oxford English Dictionary and can mean anything from a tear in a stocking to melted or liquefied. Greek and Hebrew words are no different.

Word studies are the best way to find the range of possible meanings for each particular word. If you are unsure about the definition of a word, use a *Strong's Concordance* to find every occurrence of that word in the Bible, and see how it is used in each context. Does that word appear in any similar contexts? What does that word mean in those contexts? Does that same meaning make sense in the current context?

For example, the Greek word *sunechō*, which appears in 2 Cor 5:14, is often translated there as *compels* or *controls*, as in, "the love of Christ compels us" (NKJV), or "the love of Christ controls us" (ESV). But a simple word study reveals another meaning that makes more sense in the context. The word only appears twelve times in the New Testament (only one other time by Paul, Phil 1:23), and never in a similar context. None of the other uses seem to mean "controls." But in the LXX[71] (a Greek translation of the Old Testament which was often quoted by the writers of the New Testament) the idea of *joining* or *putting together* emerges as a common meaning, especially when the ideas of creating, making garments, and building are concerned (a few very clear examples of this are Gen 1:9; Exod 28:7; 1 Kgs 6:10, 15). This is significant because all of those concepts are apparent in Second Corinthians 5.

---

[70] Zane Hodges, *The Epistle of James: Proven Character through Testing* (Denton, TX: Grace Evangelical Society, 2009), and *The Epistles of John: Walking in the Light of God's Love* (Denton, TX: Grace Evangelical Society, 2009).

[71] The LXX is an abbreviation for the Septuagint, a Koine Greek translation of the Old Testament, so called because of the committee of 72 scribes who translated it.

How does understanding that Paul likely means "the love of Christ joins us together" in 2 Cor 5:14 open up the meaning of the passage?[72]

USING THE E-SWORD BIBLE SOFTWARE

The e-Sword is a wonderful free tool available online at www.e-sword. net. You can download the program, many translations, commentaries, and language tools for free. Some translations and other materials cost extra. However, the free material includes the Greek and Hebrew texts, several literal translations (Young's Literal Translation, the Darby Bible, the King James Version, and the Modern King James Version), *Thayer's Greek Lexicon*, and *Strong's Concordance* and a Parsing Guide in line with the text of the KJV and Greek, respectively.

The e-Sword makes word studies very simple. When using the KJV+ translation, simply right click the Strong's number next to the word (example: believeth[G4100]) and select "Quick Search > New Testament" to see every time that Greek word appears in the New Testament. If you do not like using the KJV, you can open up your printed Bible and look up each reference in context in your favorite translation.

When doing a word study, however, do not depend upon what the translation says. Instead, within the range of possible meanings from each word, use contextual clues to determine what the right understanding of each word is in its context.

---

[72] For further discussion on this passage, see Grant Hawley, "Joined Together at the Bema" *Grace in Focus Magazine*, March-April 2012. Available online at http://faithalone.org/magazine/y2012/12B4.html, and also at http://www.boldgrace.org/biblestudy/2cor5-14.html.

HOW TO USE THE E-SWORD TO DO A WORD STUDY:

Below are pictures from the main screen of the e-Sword Bible Study Software. In the first picture, the user has right clicked on the Strong's number for "believeth, G4100." He then selected "Quick search on: G4100" and "New Testament" in the pop-up menus.

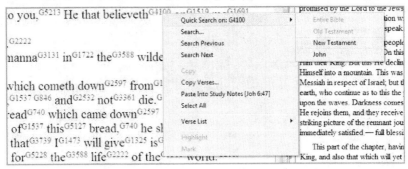

Once the user selected "New Testament," a list of every verse where that word appears in the New Testament comes up in a pop-up screen.

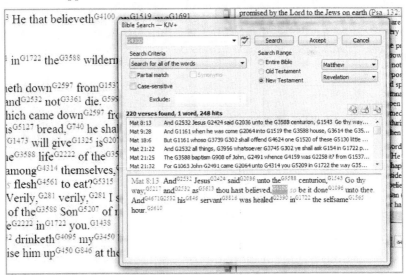

When you click on the number G4100 in the main Bible text, the dictionary window will select that word and show the definition according to the dictionaries or lexicons you have installed.

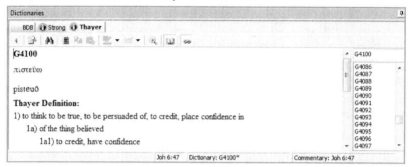

By looking at the selected definitions and the word's use in context, the Bible student can get a good idea of the range of meanings of each word he studies.

PRACTICE

Download the e-Sword Bible Software. Using the KJV+, do a word study (look up each time the word is used in context to determine how the word is used) on the Hebrew word translated "salvation" in Exod 14:13. If you do not have a way to get the e-Sword software, a bound copy of Strong's Exhaustive Concordance will also work. It can be found inexpensively at used bookstores or online. To use it, you can look up the word "salvation" and follow the Hebrew word listed. What are some ways the word is used?

DISCUSS

1) Suppose a paraphrase of the Bible does not accurately reflect the meaning of the passage it is paraphrasing. Do you still have the Bible? Discuss.

2) Now, suppose a paraphrase does accurately reflect the meaning of the passage it is paraphrasing. Do you still have the Bible? Discuss.

3) Mormons and Catholics both claim divine inspiration in Bible translation and interpretation. In this system, does the Bible or the Mormon or Catholic church truly claim higher authority?

4) Translations of the Bible are only God's Word to the extent that they reflect the original writings. True or false? Why?

5) Many seminaries teach that any particular interpretation must have support in commentaries in order to be valid. What are the implications of this thinking? Is it right?

6) How might word studies be more useful than lexicons?

Literary Structure

"The more you know of the patterns, styles, and forms of the various units in a book of the Bible the more you will know of that book's purpose and unique character, and the better you will understand it." *Roy B. Zuck*[73]

LESSON OBJECTIVES

1. To introduce the concept of literary structure[74]
2. To define various forms of literary structure in the Bible
3. To help the student be able to recognize literary structure in the Bible
4. To help the student be able to apply the significance of literary structure to interpretation

INTRODUCTION

Literary structure can play an important role in Bible interpretation. Not only does it help us to appreciate the extreme care that went into crafting each book of the Bible, but it also helps us to gain a better understanding of the author's intention—which is one major goal of Bible interpretation (the ultimate goal being Christlikeness).

---

[73] Zuck, *Basic Bible Interpretation*, p. 124.

[74] Literary structure is the framework of a piece of literature.

PARALLELISM

One of the ways Hebrew poetry is distinct from many other forms of literature is in the extensive use of parallelism. Parallelism compares and contrasts two or more lines in order to express a single idea.

SYNONYMOUS PARALLELISM

In synonymous parallelism, the corresponding lines express the same idea.

Example:

> "You are all fair, my love,
> And there is no spot in you." Song 4:7

ANTITHETIC PARALLELISM

In antithetic parallelism, the corresponding lines express a contrasting but related idea.

Example:

> "There is one who makes himself rich, yet has nothing;
> And one who makes himself poor, yet has great riches." Prov 13:7

SYNTHETIC PARALLELISM

In synthetic parallelism, the second of two corresponding lines completes the thought of the first.

Example:

> "He who goes about as a talebearer reveals secrets;
> Therefore do not associate with one who flatters with his lips"
> Provs 20:19

CHIASM

Another type of parallelism that is a bit more complex is called chiasm. A *chiasm* (or chiasmus, plural = chiasmi) is a literary tool in which lines or phrases are arranged in an ascending and then descending structure.

A chiasm is very different from the linear structure that is common in western literature in which a concept builds throughout until a climax near the end of the literary work. Rather than a linear structure (example: I., A, B, II., A, III., IV., A, B, C, etc.) the structure is cyclical (example: A, B, C, C', B', A').

In a chiasm, parallel lines are related, and the middle point (or related middle points) is emphasized. Chiasmi can be more complex, containing multiple cycles and taking on structures like: A, B, C, D, D', C', B', C, D, C', B', A'.

Keeping an eye out for chiasmi (which are common throughout both the Old Testament and the New Testament) can help us to see important points being made by the Biblical authors.

For example, Eph 4:3-6 forms a chiasm:

> A. ...endeavoring to <u>keep the unity</u> of the Spirit in the bond of peace.
> > B. There is <u>one body</u>
> > > C. and <u>one Spirit</u>,
> > > > D. just as you were called in <u>one hope</u> of your calling;
> > > > > E. <u>one Lord</u>,
> > > > D'. <u>one faith</u>,
> > > C'. <u>one baptism</u>;
> > B'. <u>one God</u> and Father of all,
> A'. who is above all, and through all, and <u>in you all</u>.

Recognizing this chiasm in Ephesians 4:3-6 is especially helpful to show us how Paul is relating similar concepts. Relating lines C ("and one Spirit") and C' ("one baptism") demonstrates that Paul is basing this aspect of our unity upon spiritual baptism, not water baptism. This shows us that it is the fact that God has baptized us all into the Body of Christ by His Spirit that is the source of our unity, not the expression or (God forbid) method of expressing obedience in water baptism. Thus, all believers in Christ share this unity.

The phrases "keep the unity" and "[the Father is] in you all" in lines A and A' respectively, show us that our unity that we have is not something that we need to create upon some false pretense. We are to keep the unity that God has already accomplished by putting Himself "in [us] all."

Note also that the line "one Lord" (line E) is in the middle position. This gives us a clue that it carries the greatest emphasis in this chiasm. The structure of this chiasm shows that our unity with our brothers and sisters in Christ is primarily based upon our having one Lord, the Lord

Jesus Christ. This should help us to see the importance of unity with *all* brothers and sisters in Christ, not just the ones we most naturally get along with. The chiasm here helps us to see all of these points.

INCLUSIO

An inclusio is a phrase that occurs twice within a book, which indicates the start and end of a section. It may be helpful to understand an *inclusio* as a set of bookends within a text, inserted to let the reader know that the content between is related.

For example, Jesus uses the phrase "Let not your heart be troubled" in both John 14:1 and 14:27, letting the reader know that He was addressing the emotional turmoil of the disciples.[75]

BOOK STRUCTURE

Keeping a close eye on book structure[76] can help the interpreter to avoid choosing an incorrect purpose statement for a Bible book. As mentioned in Lesson 2, correctly diagnosing a book's purpose is a major key to interpretation.

Many interpreters incorrectly choose 1 John 5:13a, "These things I have written to you who believe in the name of the Son of God, that you may know that you have eternal life..." as the purpose statement for the book. This has an enormous impact on the interpreter's understanding of the doctrine of assurance. First John contains many tests which are intended to help us determine if we are walking in fellowship with God and with the brethren. When interpreters misdiagnose the purpose statement of the book, they turn all of these tests of fellowship into tests of whether or not we have eternal life at all. As a result, interpreters have to read away clear statements that John's audience is made up of believers only (see 1 John 2:12-14, 21; 3:1-2; 4:4). Thus, the supposed purpose statement becomes self-defeating. If we must persevere in holiness and love for the brethren until the end of life to know that we have eternal life, we cannot know we have eternal life until we have already persevered until the end

---

[75] It should also be noted that His closing statement in 16:33—and the repeated use of the words peace, joy, and love—are intended to let the reader know that Jesus has been continuing this theme throughout the discourse.

[76] Book structure is the framework of a book of the Bible.

of life. We can only *know* we have eternal life if we are looking to Jesus alone and not to our works for our assurance.

We can avoid this error by noting that the phrase "These things I have written to you" and other very similar phrases are used four times in the book,[77] each referring to the immediately preceding context. In the immediately preceding context to 5:13a, namely 5:9-12, John assures the reader concerning the promise of eternal life to all who believe in Jesus:

> If we receive the witness of men, the witness of God is greater; for this is the witness of God which He has testified of His Son. He who believes in the Son of God has the witness in himself; he who does not believe God has made Him a liar, because he has not believed the testimony that God has given of His Son. And this is the testimony: that God has given us eternal life, and this life is in His Son. He who has the Son has life; he who does not have the Son of God does not have life. These things I have written to you who believe in the name of the Son of God, that you may know that you have eternal life... (1 John 5:9-13a)

We can know we have eternal life by taking God at His word.

The purpose statement for First John is found in the prologue. This purpose is much broader than simply to know we have everlasting life:[78] "that which we have seen and heard we declare to you, that you also may have fellowship with us; and truly our fellowship is with the Father and with His Son Jesus Christ" (1:3). John is writing so that his readers might have fellowship with the apostles and with God.

In addition to the points above, recognizing the parallels between 1 John and the Upper Room Discourse in John 13–17, marvelously brings out the emphasis on fellowship and abiding in Christ.

Similarly, interpreters often read the concept of justification into Romans 6–11, but in Rom 5:1, Paul says, "Therefore, having been justified by faith, we have peace with God through our Lord Jesus Christ." This verse lets us know that Paul considers the discussion of justification to be settled, and he is moving on to a new topic.

Recognizing a book's structure is a key factor in interpretation. As you read individual books of the Bible, look for verses like Rom 5:1 or 11:32

---

[77] "[T]hese things we write to you" 1:4; "these things I write to you" 2:1; "These things I have written to you" 2:26.

[78] Everlasting life is spiritual life that begins for Christians in the moment they put their faith in Christ. Everlasting life cannot be lost and never ends.

that wrap up topics, and verses like Rom 9:1-4 and 12:1 that introduce new topics.

Look for repeated phrases, such as "the children of Israel did evil in the sight of the LORD" found seven times in Judges. These kinds of phrases can help us to understand themes in books.

When repeated phrase changes, this can often emphasize the change. For example: "And God saw (…) it was good" in Genesis 1:4, 10, 12, 18, 21, 25, and "And God saw (…) it was very good" in 1:31, after man had been created. Noting these repeated phrases and the changes can help us better to see the literary structure of a book or of one of its sections.

Sometimes books can be structured in absolutely amazing and illustrative ways. For example, the Gospel of John is structured to mirror the physical structure of the Temple. Every aspect of the Temple has a great deal of symbolic significance. By learning of this significance, we can see the symbolic richness intended by John in each section. Next time you read through the Gospel of John, see if you can recognize the correlation.

CONCLUSION

Recognizing literary structure takes practice, but when you are able to see it, the meaning of the text becomes clearer. You can then identify emphasis, avoid reading ideas into the text that aren't intended, and add depth to your understanding of the book.

PRACTICE

In the following passages, outline the chiasmi and state what is emphasized:

1) John 1:1

2) John 6:47-51

3) Heb 1:1-4

4) Eph 2:14-15

5) Find an example of synonymous, antithetic, and synthetic parallelism: one from Psalms, one from Proverbs, one from Ecclesiastes.

DISCUSS

1) Psalm 119 is arranged so that each line in each section starts with the same Hebrew letter and these sections are arranged according to the Hebrew alphabet. What does this tell you about the care that was put into its crafting? How does this contrast with some teachers who do no preparation because of Matt 10:19-20? What is the right perspective to have on preparing lessons?

2) In the Book of Daniel, chapters 1 and 8-12 were written in Hebrew (the language of Israel), and chapters 2-7 were written in Aramaic (the language of Babylon, the world's dominant superpower at the time). Why do you suppose Daniel structured the book that way?

3) What does the chiasm in John 6:47-51 (from Practice, above) tell us?

4) In Matthew 12, the religious leaders credit the demons with the power behind Jesus' miracles. Jesus never again in Matthew tells the people that the kingdom of heaven is at hand. What does this element of the book structure tell us?

5) Watchman Nee noted that Ephesians breaks up into three sections: sit (1:1–3:21), walk (4:1–6:9), and stand (6:10-24). Discuss how this might illustrate Paul's purpose in writing.

Bible Study Method and Application

"He who has my commandments and keeps them, it is he who loves Me. And he who loves Me will be loved by My Father, and I will love him and manifest Myself to him." *John 14:21*

LESSON OBJECTIVES

1. To teach various effective methods for studying the Bible
2. To help the student know how to apply the Bible correctly

INTRODUCTION

Everyone has a different method for studying the Bible. Some of the principles listed below are principles that everyone should apply. Many of these tools, however, will prove helpful for some, but not all, students of the Bible. Take these tools and use them in whatever way works best for you.

PRAYER

Before studying (and while studying), pray that the Holy Spirit will illuminate the Word of God, help you to lay aside your biases, and open your heart to what the Bible says.

READING

Ironically, simply reading the Bible is one step that is often missed. All of the letters of the New Testament were meant to be read aloud in a single setting. Reading a book cover to cover, even aloud, is a great way to catch the flow of the book and see the big picture that the author is drawing. When we see the big picture, the details make more sense. The Bible is literature, prose and poetry from the very mouth of God. Don't miss its voice and its beauty by never looking at a book in its entirety.

In Howard Hendricks's wonderful book, *Living By the Book*, he lays out "Ten Strategies to First-Rate Reading." They are listed below:[79]

Read Thoughtfully

Read Repeatedly

Read Patiently

Read Selectively (rightly dividing dispensations and situations)

Read Prayerfully

Read Imaginatively (Try to place yourself in the shoes of those being spoken to or about.)

Read Meditatively

Read Purposefully

Read Acquisitively (reading to possess the truths inside)

Read Telescopically (viewing each part in light of the whole)

Howard Hendricks devotes an entire chapter to each of these ten strategies in Living By the Book.

THE INDUCTIVE METHOD

One helpful method for Bible study is the Inductive Study Method. It is detailed in the beginning of the *Inductive Study Bible*.[80] Each step with a brief description (where needed) is included below:

Step 1: Pray (see discussion above)

Step 2: Ask the "5 W's and an H"

Ask who (and to whom)

Ask what

---

[79] Howard Hendricks, *Living By the Book* (Chicago: Moody, 1991), p. 75.

[80] Kay Arthur, *International Inductive Study Bible*, NASB Version (Eugene: Harvest House, 1992), p. IISB-17-IISB-25

Ask when

Ask where

Ask why

Ask how

Step 3: Mark key words and phrases

Does the passage repeat any words or phrases?

Does the author use a word or phrase in a way that you would not have expected?

Key words and phrases can be marked with symbols or highlighted in different colors.

Step 4: Look for lists

The Bible contains many lists. Noting them can help us to understand how the Biblical author is structuring his argument.

Step 5: Watch for contrasts and comparisons

Step 6: Note expressions of time

Step 7: Identify terms of conclusion

Such as: *wherefore, therefore, for this reason,* and *finally.*

Step 8: Develop chapter themes

The Inductive Study Bible leaves chapter titles blank for you to fill in your own. In your own Bible, it is OK to cross out chapter or section titles and write in your own.

Step 9: Discover lessons for life

Apply it.

Step 10: Complete the At A Glance Chart

An *At A Glance Chart* is a chart included for each book in the *Inductive Study Bible*. In addition, you can create your own charts for organizing books and customize them to your tastes using a word processor. An example chart, empty and completed is included in the next pages.

SAMPLE BOOK STUDY CHART—ROMANS

Theme of Romans:

Segment Divisions

Author:

Date:

Purpose:

Key Words:

				Chapter Themes
			1	
			2	
			3	
			4	
			5	
			6	
			7	
			8	
			9	
			10	
			11	
			12	
			13	
			14	
			15	
			16	

Theme of Romans: Christian Liberty

Segment Divisions

Author: Paul

Date: Fall of 57

Purpose:
Ending Strife
by
Showing Christian
Liberty

Key Words:

Faith
Justified
Righteousness
Law
Glorified
Death
Life
Love

Structure of Book	Purpose	Subject		Chapter Themes
Justification	To know we have been justified	Gentiles/Jews	Every Believer	1 "It's all by faith / Disobedience of the Gentiles
				2 Disobedience of the Jews
				3 Everyone Guilty / Justification by faith alone
				4 Justification by faith alone
				5 In Adam to In Christ
Sanctification / Glorification	Walk by faith not by law			6 Dead to sin Alive to God
				7 Free from Law
				8 Free from sin / Kingdom Hope
Dispensation	God is faithful to keep his promises	Israel		9 Israel's Fall
				10 Means of Restoring Israel
				11 Israel's Restoration
Liberation	Don't judge one another. Live in love.	Every Believer		12 Live in Love by Using Your Gifts
				13 Live in Love by Obeying Authority
				14 Live in Love by Accepting Differences
				15 Live in Love by Being One Minded
				16 Live in Love by Greeting One Another

THE COMPREHENSIVE METHOD

PREPARATION

When I use this method, I prefer to print out copies of the Biblical text with lots of space between the lines and put it, along with some notebook paper, in a three-ring binder. Be prepared to spend at least one month of diligent study on each book.

READING

After praying, read through the book you wish to study in one sitting, using the "Ten Strategies for First Rate Reading" noted above. With some of the longer books, this can take a significant time commitment. If you are very familiar with the book you have chosen, try reading it in a new translation the first time you read through. If it is a shorter book, read through it a few times. If it is a longer book, spend several days reading through the book a few times.

As you are reading, note any indicators about the book's audience. Note phrases and passages that call to mind other phrases and passages, especially if the authors are the same. For example, when you read Eph 2:8-9, Rom 4:1-5 might stand out as a parallel. Note this connection. Also, note any difficult or unclear verses or passages. Write all of these things on a separate sheet of paper.

OBSERVING – THE BIG PICTURE

After you have read through the book a few times, read through it again, looking for literary structure. Note any repeated phrases and see if they form an inclusio or if they are just setting a theme. Look to see if chiasm is being employed. Note any other interesting or unusual literary structure.

LITERARY STRUCTURE IN EPHESIANS 1:3-14

In the great doxology[81] found in Eph 1:3-14, Paul blesses God because of what He has done in Christ. The doxology breaks up into three sections, each punctuated with "to the praise of His glory." The three sections also each focus on one Person in the Godhead, first the Father, second, the Son, and third, the Holy Spirit, yet in each of the three sections, the phrase "in Christ" and its equivalent is repeated, showing that all three Persons in the Godhead are glorified in God's placing us in Christ. Below is the NKJV translation of the doxology, with added emphasis and typesetting to show the literary structure.

---

[81] A doxology is an expression of praise to God.

Blessed be the God and Father of our Lord Jesus Christ, who has blessed us with every spiritual blessing in the heavenly places in Christ, just as He chose us in Him before the foundation of the world, that we should be holy and without blame before Him in love, having predestined us to adoption as sons by Jesus Christ to Himself, according to the good pleasure of His will, <u>to the praise of the glory of His</u> grace [literally, to the praise of His glory-grace], by which He made us accepted in the Beloved.	*The Father is blessed.*
In Him we have redemption through His blood, the forgiveness of sins, according to the riches of His grace which He made to abound toward us in all wisdom and prudence, having made known to us the mystery of His will, according to His good pleasure which He purposed in Himself, that in the dispensation of the fullness of the times He might gather together in one all things in Christ, both which are in heaven and which are on earth—in Him. In Him also we have obtained an inheritance, being predestined according to the purpose of Him who works all things according to the counsel of His will, that we who first trusted in Christ should be <u>to the praise of His glory</u>.	*The Son is blessed.*
In Him you also trusted, after you heard the word of truth, the gospel of your salvation; in whom also, having believed, you were sealed with the Holy Spirit of promise, who is the guarantee of our inheritance until the redemption of the purchased possession, <u>to the praise of His glory</u>.	*The Holy Spirit is blessed.*

Finally, look to see if there are any indicators that a book's argument or narrative is moving to a new section. After doing this, see if you can sum up the theme of each section for the book.

DETAILS

Now, take out your list of verses that you found difficult or unclear and compare to your notes on the literary structure of the book. Does the meaning of any of these verses now become clear? If the meaning is clear and you are sure that you understand it correctly, yet it contradicts a view you currently hold, revisit that view and the passages you use to support it to see if you are misunderstanding them.

For those verses that are still not clear, it is time to do word studies. Find all of the key words to the passage and use the e-Sword or a concordance to look up the usage of those words as they appear in their own contexts. Does the word appear elsewhere in the same book? Are any of the contexts parallel to the one you are studying? How is the word used in those contexts?

If a passage is still not clear after doing word studies, discuss these verses with a trusted mentor or look up the reference in some helpful commentaries. Be careful to see if what you learn from these sources really does match what the passage is saying. Be wary of easy outs that read away the passage.

If all of these things do not help, put it on the back burner and come back to it later. It may be that you are still waiting to learn something important that will help you understand the verse or passage. This happened to me when studying Romans 6 in college. After a great deal of study, certain verses still did not make sense to me. I spoke about it with my mentor for hours on more than one occasion and was still confused. A few months later, I heard a sermon from my mentor that taught some basic principles to the Christian life that I had not understood and immediately Romans 6 made sense. It was all in God's timing.

WRITE A SUMMARY

When finished studying the whole book thoroughly, write a summary paragraph for each chapter of the book. After doing this, write down your thoughts about the book, its significance, and its application. Store these notes where you can easily find them later.

THE IMPORTANCE OF APPLICATION

James 1:22-25 says:

> But be doers of the word, and not hearers only, deceiving yourselves. For if anyone is a hearer of the word and not a doer, he is like a man observing his natural face in a mirror; for he observes himself, goes away, and immediately forgets what kind of man he was. But he who looks into the perfect law of

liberty and continues in it, and is not a forgetful hearer but a doer of the work, this one will be blessed in what he does.

This passage tells us that failure to apply the word of God is self-deception, but that *doing* the word, continuing in the law of liberty, will result in blessing.

God gave us the Bible to provide us with an understanding of life, of God's faithfulness in the past, and of His promises regarding the future. But He also gave us the Bible to set us free from sin (John 8:32), and to equip us offensively for battle with Satan (Eph 6:17). The Bible is not only "God-breathed" (2 Tim 3:16, literal translation), it is also "profitable for doctrine, for reproof, for correction, for instruction in righteousness, that the man of God may be complete, thoroughly equipped for every good work" (3:16-17).

It has been said that the Bible is the handbook for perfect human happiness, but this will be our experience only if we apply the Bible to our lives. Those who are called to lead and teach are to help others apply the Bible to their lives, too.

CORRECT APPLICATION OF SCRIPTURE

If all of the Bible is *for* us, but not all of the Bible is written *to* us, this clearly has an impact on application. Determining the intended audience of each portion of the Bible is an essential step in the interpretation process that must be taken before application is made. Without this essential step, some Christians might be killing animals in order to atone for sins.

The principle of primary and secondary application[82] helps us to avoid this error. Below is an extended quote from Dr. Lewis Sperry Chafer regarding this principle:

> Each dispensation, therefore, begins with man divinely placed in a new position of privilege and responsibility, and closes with the failure of man resulting in righteous judgments from God. While there are certain abiding facts such as the holy character of God which are of necessity the same in every age,

---

[82] Secondary application is the way someone who is not part of the originally intended audience should respond to a command or moral teaching.

there are varying instructions and responsibilities which are, as to their application, limited to a given period.

In this connection, the Bible student must recognize the difference between a primary and a secondary application of the Word of God. Only those portions of the Scriptures which are directly addressed to the child of God under grace are to be given a personal or primary application. All such instructions he is expected to perform in detail. In the matter of a secondary application it should be observed that, while there are spiritual lessons to be drawn from every portion of the Bible, it does not follow that the Christian is appointed by God to conform to those governing principles which were the will of God for people of other dispensations. The child of God under grace is not situated as was Adam, or Abraham, or the Israelites when under the law; nor is he called upon to follow that peculiar manner of life which according to the Scriptures will be required of men when the King shall have returned and set up His kingdom on the earth.[83]

After determining the audience and the meaning of a passage, you are ready for the application step of Bible interpretation. Begin by asking yourself:

1. Does this have primary application to me?

2. If not, what is the secondary application?

3. What is the application to me?

BEING OR KNOWING VERSUS DOING

Many times what the Bible is teaching us relates to our being or knowing rather than our doing. For example, Eph 3:14-19 teaches us that we are to know (in experience) the love of Christ and that by doing so we may "be filled with all the fullness of God." It would be a mistake to turn this passage into a "do" passage rather than a "know" passage. In fact, large sections of Scripture (like Ephesians 1–3 and Romans 1:1–6:10) contain no commands. Instead, the author focuses the believer on things that God has done and on who we are in Christ. When studying these passages, let the application be what it is, a change of mind and a resting in what God has done. Do not try to force a "do" into passages like these.

---

[83] Lewis Sperry Chafer, *Major Bible Themes: 52 Vital Doctrines of the Scripture Simplified and Explained* (Grand Rapids, MI: Zondervan, 1926, 1954), p. 127.

The Church must learn to rest in what God has already done, and become what it is supposed to be before moving on to doing what it is supposed to do. Much harm has been done by teachers thinking they are always needing a "do."

AVOIDING LEGALISM

It is easy to turn the New Testament into nothing more than a list of dos and don'ts, simply replacing one set of ordinances (the Mosaic Law) with another. For example, out of context, "Do not lie to one another..." (Col 3:9a) has a great deal of similarity to the 9th Commandment, "You shall not bear false witness against your neighbor." But there is a vital difference. Colossians 3:9-10 says: "Do not lie to one another, since you have put off the old man with his deeds, and have put on the new man who is renewed in knowledge according to the image of Him who created him." In the New Testament, our holy living is to flow out from our unity with Christ and with His Church. It is always the case in Paul's letters that the foundation for obedience is our unity with Christ. As we will see in Section 3, law living (whether it is the Mosaic Law, man-made religious laws, or even commands in the New Testament taken out of context) produces failure and disobedience. When teaching the Bible, focus—as Paul does—on our union with Christ, and let the dos and don'ts flow out of that union. A Bible teacher's failure to keep this focus will lead people into an endless cycle of defeat.

PRACTICE

1) What is the primary application of Lev 4:1-12? What is the secondary application? Which applies to the Church?

2) Read Ephesians 1–3. On a separate piece of paper, write out a list of everything Paul says that God has done. How should this section be applied? Note: save this list for later.

3) Apply the Inductive Study Method to Romans 6. What did you learn?

DISCUSS

1) What are some common ways that people misapply Scripture, even when they understand the passage correctly?

2) Why are word studies important?

3) What are some issues that arise from forcing a "do" into a "be" passage? When we make this mistake, what do we miss?

4) How does the big picture of Ephesians 1–3 help us understand why Paul calls us a glorious inheritance for Christ in 1:18?

5) Read Romans 7. In the experience he relates here, how was Paul incorrectly applying the command "You shall not covet"? (Hint: See Rom 6:14).

Free Grace

SECTION GOALS

1. To help the student to be absolutely sure that eternal life is a free gift given to all who believe, and that the gift of everlasting life, once given, can never be lost.

2. To equip the student to be able to share this truth confidently with others.

3. To equip the student to be able to answer common questions and objections about the freeness of the gift of eternal life.

4. To show how and why Free Grace provides the right setting for growth in holiness.

WHAT IS FREE GRACE?

The doctrine of Free Grace is essentially the belief that justification before God and the gift of eternal life is given freely to all who believe in Jesus. Moreover, once we have received this gift, we cannot lose it under any circumstances.

INTRODUCTION

Free Grace is dear to me for many reasons. I came out of a legalistic mindset, from a church family that called us to test ourselves by looking to our works to see if we were truly saved. For me, this meant that I struggled with assurance. I saw the high standard we are called to live by in the Bible. Because I understood that high standard to be the definition of a true Christian, I was never sure of my salvation unless I blinded myself to my own sin. When I blinded myself in this way, I judged others.

But I thank God that He made me uncomfortable with the doctrine I was taught. It no longer made sense to me that I should have to look to my works to determine what I believed. Nevertheless, I didn't have a better answer for reconciling passages like Eph 2:8-9 and Gal 5:19-21. I thought Arminianism (a belief system that teaches you can lose your salvation) was the only option other than what I had been taught, and I knew that was wrong (Rom 8:31-39; 11:29). So, I waited.

In His perfect timing, God put me in exactly the right place at exactly the right moment to learn about Free Grace. The apparent contradictions melted away, and the Bible finally made sense.

This new understanding brought me into a season of persecution. As my friend Marty Cauley says, "When I learn that someone is Free Grace, I want to see his scars." So many Free Grace people I talk to have been through trials just like mine. But through those trials and my new confidence in the sureness of God's love for me, God brought me into a much deeper relationship with Him. He was always there with me, even when everything else seemed to fall apart. In the end, I can trace a lot of the sweetest blessings in my life to that time of trial—and I thank God for it. I can now joyfully say with Paul, "But what things were gain to me, these I have counted loss for Christ" (Phil 3:7).

Once God's Free Grace sank into my heart enough to heal old wounds and insecurities, my relationship with God was transformed. His perfect love had cast out fear (1 John 4:18), and instead of wanting to prove *myself*, I wanted to please *Him*.

Lastly, Free Grace, when put in right perspective, erases the judgmentalism that plagues the Church, and that plagued my own heart for years. We all need Him for everything, and when we can accept our helplessness to save ourselves or to prove our own salvation, we are truly free to love without hypocrisy (Rom 12:9).

Free Grace is so precious to me. I hope that it is or soon will be to you, too.

HELPFUL WORKS ON FREE GRACE

Title	Author	Audience
Absolutely Free![84]	Zane Hodges	All
The Gospel Under Siege[85]	Zane Hodges	Intermediate
Confident in Christ[86]	Bob Wilkin	All
Final Destiny[87]	Jody Dillow	Advanced
Lordship Salvation: A Biblical Evaluation and Response[88]	Charles Bing	Advanced
Free Grace Soteriology[89]	David R. Anderson	Intermediate
The Five Points of Calvinism: Weighed and Found Wanting[90]	George Bryson	All
Journal of the Grace Evangelical Society	Various Authors. Back issues available online at www.faithalone.org/journal.html	Intermediate/ Advanced

---

[84] Zane Hodges, *Absolutely Free! A Biblical Response to Lordship Salvation* (Grand Rapids, MI: Zondervan, 1989).

[85] Hodges, *The Gospel Under Siege: Faith and Works in Tension* (Dallas, TX: Redención Viva, 1981).

[86] Robert Wilkin, *Confident in Christ: Living by Faith Really Works* (Irving, TX: Grace Evangelical Society, 1999).

[87] Joseph Dillow, *Final Destiny: The Future Reign of the Servant Kings* (Monument, CO: Paniym Group Inc., 2012).

[88] Charles C. Bing, *Lordship Salvation: A Biblical Evaluation and Response* GraceLife Edition (Burleson, TX: GraceLife Ministries, 1992).

[89] David R. Anderson, *Free Grace Soteriology* (Place Unknown: Xulon Press, 2010).

[90] George Bryson, *The Five Points of Calvinism: Weighed and Found Wanting* (Costa Mesa, CA: The Word For Today, 1996, 2002, 2006).

The Free Gift

"...there is but one condition of eternal salvation, believing in Christ. The moment one believes, he has eternal life. Nothing can reverse that, since eternal life is eternal." *Bob Wilkin*[91]

LESSON OBJECTIVES

1. To help the student understand what Free Grace is and why it is important

2. To help the student see how the Bible presents the free offer of justification before God and eternal life in Christ Jesus

WHY STUDY FREE GRACE?

Confusion abounds concerning what a person must do to receive and keep eternal life. In fact, it is very difficult to find a Bible teacher, evangelist, or gospel tract that is clear about it (though one large gospel tract publisher, *Evantell*, is consistently clear). Most of the confusion about the gospel arises out of a failure to understand what the Bible says about the kingdom, and all of it can be traced to poor hermeneutics.

Furthermore, when people are looking to their performance of good works to gain assurance of salvation, God is robbed of His glory regarding their salvation.

Finally, a full understanding of the security and assurance of the believer is the foundation of a spiritual walk. Without this foundation, it

---

[91] *Confident in Christ*, p. 133.

becomes impossible to take our eyes entirely off ourselves and focus on the Lord Jesus.

AN EXTENDED DEFINITION OF FREE GRACE

The price—Jesus Christ, the Son of the Living God (John 6:69), died on the cross for the sins of the world, was buried, and rose from the dead on the third day (1 Cor 15:1-4).

The message—All who believe in Jesus have been justified before God (Rom 3:21-4:5), have been given everlasting life (John 3:16; 5:24; 6:47; 11:25-26; Eph 2:8-9), and are guaranteed bodily resurrection (John 6:39-40) to eternal happiness with God in Paradise (Luke 23:43; 2 Cor 5:1-8; Rev 2:7, compare Rev 22:2).

What is faith?—Faith is belief. It is persuasion that something is true (Acts 17:4; 18:4; 28:24; Rom 4:21), and does not include works or obedience as part of its definition.

Faith does not save—Faith does not save; Christ saves through faith in Him. This is because faith is not meritorious. It is not the cause of eternal life, nor is it something we trade for eternal life. Faith is merely the channel to the giver of eternal life, Jesus Christ.

Salvation is through faith alone—Turning from sin, obedience, commitment, baptism, and perseverance are not conditions for everlasting life (John 4:10-14; Rom 4:1-5; 11:6; Eph 2:8-9), nor are they the inevitable outcome of faith (Luke 8:13; 2 Pet 1:4-9).

Eternal security—Once granted, eternal life cannot, under any circumstances, be lost or given up. As those who have believed, we are the gift of the Father to the Son, and no one is able to snatch us from His hand (John 6:39; 10:27-29; Rom 8:38-39; 11:29).

Assurance—Every believer can and should have full assurance of his/her salvation. Nothing other than a failure to believe the gospel should be invoked to make anyone doubt the security of his eternal destiny (John 6:47; 11:25-27; 1 John 2:25; 5:13).

WORKS-BASED SYSTEMS

The most prevalent Protestant form of the opposing view to Free Grace is called *Lordship Salvation*.[92] Lordship Salvation can take many forms, but the most basic element that defines Lordship Salvation is the belief that in addition to simple belief in Jesus, a person must commit his life in obedience to Him and follow that belief with good works to obtain final salvation from the penalty of sins.

Lordship Salvation is a very popular view among Christians. In fact, it and other works-oriented views have dominated Christian thinking since before the founding of the Roman Catholic Church. Even in the earliest days of the Church, works salvation mindsets similar to Lordship Salvation had already begun to spread. See Acts 15:1-11 and Galatians.

HOW DOES THE BIBLE PRESENT THE OFFER OF ETERNAL LIFE?

As noted in previous lessons, only one book of the Bible was written to an unbelieving audience, and it is the only book that was written with the expressed purpose of telling people how to receive eternal life. That book is the Gospel of John. John 20:30-31 says: "And truly Jesus did many other signs in the presence of His disciples, which are not written in this book; but these are written that you may believe that Jesus is the Christ, the Son of God, and that believing you may have life in His name."

There are many statements in John that state clearly that every single person who believes in Jesus Christ has everlasting life. A few of them are below.

John 1:12

> But as many as received Him, to them He gave the right to become children of God, to those who believe in His name.

John 3:14-15

> And as Moses lifted up the serpent in the wilderness, even so must the Son of Man be lifted up, that whoever believes in Him should not perish but have eternal life.

---

[92] Lordship Salvation is a theological error that redefines faith to include works, so that one must believe and work in order to be saved.

John 3:16

For God so loved the world that He gave His only begotten Son, that whoever believes in Him should not perish but have everlasting life.

John 3:36

He who believes in the Son has everlasting life; and he who does not believe the Son shall not see life, but the wrath of God abides on him.

John 4:10

Jesus answered and said to her, "If you knew the gift of God, and who it is who says to you, 'Give Me a drink,' you would have asked Him, and He would have given you living water."

John 5:24

"Most assuredly, I say to you, he who hears My word and believes in Him who sent Me has everlasting life, and shall not come into judgment, but has passed from death into life.

John 6:40

And this is the will of Him who sent Me, that everyone who sees the Son and believes in Him may have everlasting life; and I will raise him up at the last day."

John 6:47

Most assuredly, I say to you, he who believes in Me has everlasting life.

John 6:51

I am the living bread which came down from heaven. If anyone eats of this bread, he will live forever; and the bread that I shall give is My flesh, which I shall give for the life of the world."

John 11:25-26

Jesus said to her, "I am the resurrection and the life. He who believes in Me, though he may die, he shall live. And whoever lives and believes in Me shall never die. Do you believe this?"

John 20:30-31

And truly Jesus did many other signs in the presence of His disciples, which are not written in this book; but these are written that you may believe that Jesus is the Christ, the Son of God, and that believing you may have life in His name.

One of the most straightforward of these verses is John 6:47, "Most assuredly, I say to you, he who believes in Me has everlasting life." This is so clear, in fact, that if anyone believes in Jesus and does not have everlasting life, the statement would be untrue.

In John, the Greek word for "believe," *pisteuō*, appears one hundred times (Majority Text). The words *repent, repentance, obey, obedience, submit,* and *submission* do not occur even once. The word confess only appears once and it is not related to the offer of eternal life. Nowhere is anyone asked to pray a prayer to receive Jesus into his heart. The *only* condition that is ever communicated is to believe in Jesus.

Other books of the Bible that talk about receiving justification before God and eternal life are focused on helping believers look back at what Christ has done for them, rather than telling them how to receive eternal life. These passages are intended to help believers avoid being deceived into thinking that their works, commitment, or obedience contributed to their obtaining justification before God.

NO STRINGS ATTACHED

In the Bible, the offer of eternal life is presented without any strings attached, and without casting doubt upon expressed faith in Christ.

In John 4:1-26, Jesus speaks with a Samaritan woman. Even though she had been married five times and was involved in a sexual relationship with someone who was not her husband, Jesus says simply, "If you knew the gift of God, and who it is who says to you, 'Give Me a drink,' you would have asked Him, and He would have given you living water" (4:10). Jesus did not demand that she change her life before she could receive the living water (a metaphor for eternal life, see v 14).

It is popular for people to say that you cannot really know if you are a believer until you have had a life full of good works to prove it. Once I heard a pastor say in a sermon (and this kind of teaching is surprisingly common), "How do you know if you are truly a believer? Why don't you come back here in fifty years and we'll check ya." Fruit checking of this sort is far from what we see in the Gospel of John. In John 11:25-27, Jesus had a conversation about Himself with Martha, a woman whose brother, Lazarus, had recently died. The conversation went like this:

> Jesus said to her, "I am the resurrection and the life. He who believes in Me, though he may die, he shall live. And whoever lives and believes in Me shall never die. Do you believe this?" She said to Him, "Yes, Lord, I believe that You are the Christ, the Son of God, who is to come into the world."

If it were impossible for someone to know whether he or she believes in Jesus until after a life of perseverance and good works, Jesus' question, "Do you believe this?" would be an absurdity. Also, the very next verse says, "And when she had said these things, she went her way..." (John 11:28). If a person cannot know whether he or she believes in Jesus without a life of good works, Jesus would have said something to cast doubt on Martha's statement "Yes, Lord, I believe..." But immediately after finishing her statement, she left without a comment from the Lord.

We know what we believe, and we don't need action to convince us. As prideful human beings (and in our flesh, all of us are prideful), we have a difficult time letting it be so simple. We want to be able to point to something in ourselves that validates our expectation of heaven. But we must remember that faith is not the cause of our justification salvation; it is merely the channel to the cause, Jesus Christ. God made it perfectly simple, so that no room was left for boasting.

JESUS PAID THE WHOLE COST

Real grace, Free Grace, is often called "cheap grace" by well-meaning people who simply do not understand that because Christ paid the entire cost for our salvation, nothing is left for us to pay. The phrase "the high cost of salvation," should only be applied to what Christ did on the cross and never to what a person must do to receive the free gift. Christ paid it all. There is nothing left for me to pay. Our eternal salvation[93] is free to us, and it cost Christ His life. It isn't cheap to anyone.

---

[93] Eternal salvation is Christian slang, usually used in reference to the reception of eternal life (regeneration). As a term, eternal salvation only occurs once in the Bible, in Heb 5:9, where it is in reference to an eschatological promise that believers who persevere in obedience will rule with Christ forever. I am using the slang term here.

IT IS TRULY GOOD NEWS

Nothing this world can offer compares to the gospel. The gospel is matchless in simplicity and magnitude. In the world, everything, no matter how insignificant, has a cost. In the gospel, nothing less than a righteous standing before God, the unending, empowering life of God, unity and brotherhood with the Eternal Son of God, and an eternity of happiness and purpose with God are absolutely free, given without cost to the one who simply believes in Jesus Christ. The word *gospel* means "good news." The gospel sounds too good to be true, but the things of God often are.

PRACTICE

1) Read Rom 11:6. If justification salvation is by grace, can our works play any role?

2) Read John 3:14-15 and Num 21:5-9. How does Christ's comparison illustrate the simplicity of the gospel?

3) Read Rom 3:28; 4:1-6; 11:6; Gal 2:16; Eph 2:8-9; Titus 3:5. What do all of these passages explicitly deny as a condition for receiving eternal salvation?

4) Phrases such as, "Give your heart to Jesus," "give your life to Jesus," "accept Jesus as Lord" and, "commit your life to Christ" are often used in gospel presentations. Given the following passages: John 3:15-16; 5:24; 6:47; 11:25-26; 20:31; Acts 16:31; Rom 3:21-22, 24-26, 28; 5:1; 1 John 5:1, are any of the above phrases appropriate as conditions for receiving eternal life? Why or why not? What condition or conditions are appropriate?

5) Is there someone you would like to share this good news with? If so, share it with him, even if he already believes. We all need encouragement, and you can be that encouragement for someone.

DISCUSS

1) In what ways is God robbed of His glory if we look to our works for assurance of salvation?

2) Why do you suppose so many people flock to Lordship Salvation teaching?

3) Why is assurance of salvation important for the Christian life?

4) Can something truly be a free gift if it has strings attached?

5) What are some common beliefs people hold that they do not always prove with action? Do they still believe those things?

The Nature of Faith

"The Greek word for believe
means believe." *Bob Wilkin*[94]

LESSON OBJECTIVES

1. To demonstrate that faith is nothing more than simple belief or persuasion that something is true
2. To equip the student to answer common objections about the nature of faith

INTRODUCTION

The Bible teaches clearly that justification before God is by faith alone, apart from works. Romans 4:1-5 says:

> What then shall we say that Abraham our father has found according to the flesh? For if Abraham was justified by works, he has something to boast about, but not before God. For what does the Scripture say? "Abraham believed God, and it was accounted to him for righteousness." Now to him who works, the wages are not counted as grace but as debt. But to him who does not work but believes on Him who justifies the ungodly, his faith is accounted for righteousness.

Despite this clear Biblical truth, many scholars have added works to the definition of faith, making works a condition for what they call *final salvation*. Over time, the idea that the words *faith* and *believe* include works as part of their definition has taken hold. Many people just assume it is true without critically thinking about it. This confusion comes out of

---

[94] Told to me in a personal conversation.

the attempt to reconcile two irreconcilable views: 1) that justification is by faith alone apart from works, and 2) that justification requires works.

At the face of it, phrases like, "For by grace you have been saved through faith...not of works..." (Eph 2:8-9), and, "to him who does not work but believes" (Rom 4:5), are complete nonsense, if works are part of the definition of the words faith and believe. If a woman at a wedding reception said, "The one who does not move, but dances, enjoys the reception," you would wonder if she had had too much to drink because moving is part of the definition of the word *dances*. For some reason, when we talk about the Bible, drunk logic can seem to make sense.

The Greek words translated *faith* and *believe* are not complicated words loaded up with secret meaning. They are as simple as can be.

SYNONYMS FOR *PISTIS* (FAITH) AND *PISTEUŌ* (BELIEVE) IN THE BIBLE

By looking at synonyms for faith in the Bible, we can get a clearer picture of what it means to believe.

In the following passages, Luke uses the passive form of the word *persuaded* (Greek: *epeisthēsan* and *epeithonto* from *peithō*) as synonyms for *pisteuō* (believe):

Acts 17:2-4

> Then Paul, as his custom was, went in to them, and for three Sabbaths reasoned with them from the Scriptures, explaining and demonstrating that the Christ had to suffer and rise again from the dead, and saying, "This Jesus whom I preach to you is the Christ." And some of them were persuaded; and a great multitude of the devout Greeks, and not a few of the leading women, joined Paul and Silas.

Acts 28:24

> And some were persuaded by the things which were spoken, and some disbelieved.

Likewise, Luke said that Paul "persuaded" people concerning the gospel:

Acts 18:4

> And he [Paul] reasoned in the synagogue every Sabbath, and persuaded both Jews and Greeks.

Acts 19:8-9a

> And he went into the synagogue and spoke boldly for three
> months, reasoning and persuading concerning the things of
> the kingdom of God. But when some were hardened and did
> not believe...

Paul, discussing Abraham's faith in Rom 4:20-21, uses "being fully
convinced" as a synonym for *believing*: "He did not waver at the promise
of God through unbelief, but was strengthened in faith, giving glory to
God, and *being fully convinced* that what He had promised He was also
able to perform." In this context, Abraham's faith is described as his being
"fully convinced" concerning God's promise to make a great nation from
his descendants.

Looking at these synonyms, we can see that to have faith is to be persuaded that something is true. It is to be fully convinced that what God
says is true.

METAPHORS FOR FAITH USED IN THE BIBLE

In Gal 3:5-6, Paul uses "hearing" as a metaphor for faith:

> Therefore He who supplies the Spirit to you and works mira-
> cles among you, does He do it by the works of the law, or by
> the hearing of faith?—just as Abraham "believed God, and it
> was accounted to him for righteousness."

Jesus uses "drink" and "eat" as metaphors for believing:

John 4:13-14

> Jesus answered and said to her, "Whoever drinks of this water
> will thirst again, but whoever drinks of the water that I shall
> give him will never thirst. But the water that I shall give him
> will become in him a fountain of water springing up into ever-
> lasting life."

John 6:47-51

> Most assuredly, I say to you, he who believes in Me has ever-
> lasting life. I am the bread of life. Your fathers ate the manna
> in the wilderness, and are dead. This is the bread which comes
> down from heaven, that one may eat of it and not die. I am the
> living bread which came down from heaven. If anyone eats of

this bread, he will live forever; and the bread that I shall give is My flesh, which I shall give for the life of the world."

In John 6:47-51, the word for "eats" (*phagō*) is in the aorist tense, and is a simple action. By itself, the aorist does not necessitate simple action, but in this context it is differentiated from another Greek word, *trōgō*, which means to chew on (as a cow chews cud). Jesus uses *trōgō* in the present tense when focusing on discipleship. By using *phagō* here in the aorist, Jesus is stressing the simplicity of the action.

Perhaps the most powerful metaphor for the simplicity of faith that is used in the Bible is found in comparing John 3:14-15 with Num 21:4-9.

John 3:14-15 reads:

> And as Moses lifted up the serpent in the wilderness, even so must the Son of Man be lifted up, that whoever believes in Him should not perish but have eternal life.

Jesus is referring to Num 21:4-9:

> Then they journeyed from Mount Hor by the Way of the Red Sea, to go around the land of Edom; and the soul of the people became very discouraged on the way. And the people spoke against God and against Moses: "Why have you brought us up out of Egypt to die in the wilderness? For there is no food and no water, and our soul loathes this worthless bread." So the Lord sent fiery serpents among the people, and they bit the people; and many of the people of Israel died.
>
> Therefore the people came to Moses, and said, "We have sinned, for we have spoken against the Lord and against you; pray to the Lord that He take away the serpents from us." So Moses prayed for the people.
>
> Then the Lord said to Moses, "Make a fiery serpent, and set it on a pole; and it shall be that everyone who is bitten, when he looks at it, shall live." So Moses made a bronze serpent, and put it on a pole; and so it was, if a serpent had bitten anyone, when he looked at the bronze serpent, he lived.

These passages are a great treasure for many reasons, but for the purposes of this lesson, I only want to point out the simplicity of the illustration. The Israelites needed only to look at the bronze serpent and they lived. We must only believe in Jesus to live forever.

All of these metaphors represent simple and passive concepts. Hearing, eating, drinking, and looking are active verbs, grammatically, but they all have to do with receiving something. When we hear, we receive sound. When we eat, we receive food. When we drink, we receive water. And when we look, we receive an image of what we look at.

This illustrates that to believe is passive as well. When we believe, we receive truth.

FAITH IS NOT BLIND

The world thinks of faith as believing something with no valid reason to do so. Unfortunately, Christians often fall into this way of thinking as well. Biblically, the phrase "faith to believe" is nonsensical, because faith is belief. It is the noun form of the Greek verb, *pisteuō*, which means *believe*.

Scripturally, there is nothing about faith that is blind. In fact, it is exactly the opposite. Paul wrote:

> But even if our gospel is veiled, it is veiled to those who are perishing, whose minds the god of this age has blinded, who do not believe, lest the light of the gospel of the glory of Christ, who is the image of God, should shine on them. (2 Cor 4:3-4)

Believing is seeing the light—the truth—for what it is. Faith isn't blind; a lack of faith is blindness.

A LITTLE GREEK:[95]

Many scholars argue that the Greek word for believe (*pisteuō*) and its noun form, faith (*pistis*) carry the meaning of obedience because they share a root (*pith*) with *peithō*, which can mean "obey."

The argument goes something like this:

> Major Premise: *pistis, pisteuō,* and *peithō* share a Classical Greek root (*pith*).
>
> Minor Premise: *peithō* means "obey."
>
> Conclusion: *pistis* and *pisteuō* carry obedience as part of their meaning.

---

[95] For a fuller discussion, see Fred Chay and John Correia, *The Faith That Saves: The Nature of Faith in the New Testament* (USA: Grace Line Inc. 2008), and Charles Bing, *Lordship Salvation.* Available for free online at www.gracelife.org.

There are many reasons this argument is not valid, linguistically or logically. These fallacies are explained below.

1. This commits the root fallacy, which is, "[t]he presupposition that every word actually has a meaning bound up with its shape or its components."[96] Word meanings change as those words are used. The more a word is used, the more likely it is to change meaning. For example, the word "goodbye" comes from the phrase "God be with ye," but it would be a mistake to assume that most people have God in mind when they say, "goodbye." Some other common words that as they are normally used have nothing to do with their root are: hotdog, tweet, and pedigree (which is from the French words for crane's foot). See Lesson 1 for more discussion on this topic.

2. This commits the illegitimate totality transfer, which occurs when an interpreter reads all of the possible definitions of related words into the definition of one word in a given context. This is like saying that because "running" can have to do with mucus coming out of a nose, therefore the word "running" always has to do with mucus.

3. *Peithō* can mean "to obey," but out of the fifty times it occurs in the New Testament, it is only translated "to obey" four times (NKJV). The other forty-six times it is translated (correctly) with "to persuade," "to convince," "to trust," or simply, "to believe." "Obey" is the least common meaning. The lexical evidence suggests that by far the most common usage of *peithō* is "to persuade."

4. Though *peithō* can mean either "persuade" or "obey" it cannot mean both at the same time, as Lordship Salvation proponents would suggest. Additionally, it can only mean "obey" under certain grammatical conditions (either the passive voice or the middle voice + dative[97]), and even under these circumstances, it only sometimes means "obey."

5. If the writers of the New Testament want to use *peithō* they use *peithō*, not some other word. More to the point, if they want to say "obedience" (Greek: *hupakoē*), why would they use an entirely

---

[96] D. A. Carson, *Exegetical Fallacies*, Second Edition (Grand Rapids, MI: Baker Academic, 1996, 2006), p. 28.

[97] See entry *"peithō"* in Liddell and Scott, *An Intermediate Greek-English Lexicon*. (Oxford: Clarendon Press. 1889).

different (and seemingly incompatible) word (*pistis* or *pisteuō*) to express it? Interestingly enough, *peithō* does not occur in the Gospel of John at all.[98]

6. Every occurrence of *pisteuō* in the LXX except one (Jer 25:8) is translated from the Hebrew word *aman* which means to believe or trust.

It is inappropriate to point to the shared root with *peithō* and read the idea of obedience into the Greek words for believe and faith. Obedience is not part of the meaning of *pisteuō*.

FAITH WITH MODIFIERS

It is common for teachers of Lordship Salvation to talk about certain kinds of faith in Christ that are saving versus faith in Christ that is not saving. One way to have this focus is to use many adjectives with faith. These are all commonly used by Lordship Salvation teachers.

Faith with positive adjectives: saving faith, repentant faith, true faith, heart faith.

Faith with negative adjectives: spurious faith, unsaving faith, demon faith, false faith, temporary faith, head faith, defective faith, insufficient faith, cheap faith, meaningless faith.

The Bible does not share this focus. Out of 245 uses of the word "faith" in the Bible, only five times are adjectives of quality used with it. Two hundred forty times, no qualitative adjectives are used. And out of the five times when qualitative adjectives are used, only two are referring to activity produced by faith (both in James 2). Both of these are in a non-soteriological (not having to do with eternal salvation) context (see Lesson 14).

All other instances in which adjectives are used with faith are listed below.

First Timothy 1:5 uses the adjective "sincere" or "unfeigned" to modify faith. The word in Greek means "not pretend." The context is non-soteriological.

The second qualitative adjective is "like precious" (one word in Greek) from 2 Pet 1:1. Peter is affirming that the faith of his

---

[98] In John 3:36 the related word *apeitheō* does appear. *Apeitheō* in John 3:36 means, "not persuaded." See Acts 19:8-9 for a similar use.

readers is the same in content as the faith of the apostles. This one does have to do with eternal salvation.

The third qualitative adjective is "holy" in Jude 20, and it also refers to the content of the faith. This is a non-soteriological context.

In the Bible, faith is faith. The question is, "what is the object of your faith" not, "how good is your faith."

CONCLUSION

"Faith" and its verbal counterpart, "believe," consist of nothing more than passively accepting certain propositions as true. We should not twist faith into something meritorious or give the impression that it has to impress God to result in salvation. Jesus saves, not faith. Even the feeblest faith that is persuaded of the truth in Christ is sufficient for Jesus to save the lowest of sinners.

PRACTICE

1) It is becoming increasingly popular for scholars to say that the distinction we should be making is between grace and merit, rather than grace and works. This is supposed to give them room to make final salvation dependent upon works without abandoning grace. How do Rom 4:1-5; 11:6; and Eph 2:8-9 address this theological sleight of hand?

2) Using the e-Sword or a *Strong's Concordance*, do a word study on *believe* (Greek *pisteuō*). What did you learn?

DISCUSS

1) Lordship Salvation teachers use the term "head faith" to describe faith that is not sufficient, and "heart faith" to describe faith that is sufficient. Does this add to the postmodern notion that feelings are superior to thoughts? Why or why not?

2) Is faith an act of the will?

3) What are some common wrong ideas about faith?

4) If faith is simply being convinced that something is true, how does this impact your understanding of walking by faith?

5) Why do you suppose people can be comfortable with the idea that salvation is by faith alone apart from works, but that works are necessary for salvation?

Security and Assurance

"There could never be such a thing as a justification before God which is based upon human worthiness. On the other hand, a justification which is not subject to human merit could hardly be subject to human demerit." *Lewis Sperry Chafer*[99]

LESSON OBJECTIVES

1. To demonstrate that the one who believes in Christ can never lose eternal salvation

2. To demonstrate the believer's right to assurance of salvation

3. To demonstrate the importance of the believer's assurance for the Christian life

4. To establish the connection between the freeness of eternal life and the glory of God

JESUS ON ETERNAL SECURITY

The Bible teaches that without a doubt all believers in Jesus are eternally secure. John 6:37 makes this abundantly clear: "All that the Father gives Me will come to Me, and the one who comes to Me I will by no means cast out." Christ will never, under any circumstances, cast out anyone who has come to Him. This should be sufficient to settle the

---

[99] Lewis Sperry Chafer, *Systematic Theology, Vol. 3* (Dallas, TX: Dallas Seminary Press, 1948), p. 325.

issue, but there are some who would raise the objection: "He may not cast them out, but He doesn't say that they cannot leave."

While it is clear to me that Jesus includes our own will when He says "by no means," Jesus understood this may not be sufficient for some. This is why He adds, "This is the will of the Father who sent Me, that of all He has given Me I should lose nothing, but should raise it up at the last day. And this is the will of Him who sent Me, that everyone who sees the Son and believes in Him may have everlasting life; and I will raise him up at the last day" (John 6:39-40). Not only will He never throw us out, but He will also never lose us, and He guarantees that He will raise each and every one of those whom the Father gives Him on the last day. If you have believed in Jesus, you will be raised on the last day. None are excluded.

But Jesus doesn't stop there. He goes on to say, "Your fathers ate the manna in the wilderness, and are dead. This is the bread which comes down from heaven, that one may eat of it and not die. I am the living bread which came down from heaven. If anyone eats of this bread, he will live forever" (John 6:49-51a). As discussed in the previous lesson, the term "eats" here is in the aorist tense. The aorist is often said to describe an action that takes place in a single moment in time, and is set in contrast to other Greek tenses which imply duration; this is not *exactly* true. The aorist doesn't have respect to time.

To illustrate the idea behind the aorist, I could say, "I had coffee this morning." Saying that does not tell you if I downed a cup in ten seconds, or if I slowly drank a pot of coffee over the course of the morning. The tense of the verb "had" doesn't tell you about the duration, and the statement "I had coffee this morning," would be true whether it took me ten seconds, or three hours. The aorist for "eats" in the verse above is the same, and it must be taken to mean that if anyone "eats" this bread (which is to receive Christ into himself through faith) at any point in time (whether it was continual or not), he will live forever. Someone who will live forever cannot die, and if this were not sufficient He has just said that he will "not die." If anything could cause him to lose that life, even if it were by his own choice, Jesus' statement would be false.

Jesus makes an even more compelling argument in John 10:27-30:

> My sheep hear My voice, and I know them, and they follow Me. And I give them eternal life, and they shall never perish; neither shall anyone snatch them out of My hand. My Father, who has given them to Me, is greater than all; and no one is

able to snatch them out of My Father's hand. I and My Father are one.

In the Greek, the phrase "they shall never perish" is in the middle voice, which is not part of English grammar. The middle voice is used when the subject performs an action that has an effect on itself. This is significant because it means that Jesus is saying, "they shall never cause themselves to perish" by anything they could do. The illustration of Christ as the Good Shepherd in this context adds to this illustration. Part of a shepherd's job is to keep his sheep from doing something stupid and causing themselves to die. Sheep need a great deal of help there.

Furthermore, Jesus adds, "neither shall anyone snatch them out of My hand," and even more, "no one is able to snatch them out of My Father's hand." The picture here is of Christ holding us firmly in His hand, and the Father's hand coming over the top of Christ's hand to offer extra security. Jesus concludes this illustration with, "I and My Father are one" to further emphasize that both He and the Father share the same purpose in keeping us secure.

Finally, what does the word *everlasting* in the term "everlasting life" even mean if it can end?

If Jesus was trying to communicate that the one who believes in Him is eternally secure, how else could He have said it? He has covered this truth from every conceivable angle, and has said it all in plain language.

PAUL ON ETERNAL SECURITY

Paul echoes Jesus' clarity when he adds, "For the gifts and the calling of God are irrevocable" (Rom 11:29). Irrevocable, by definition, means something cannot be taken away. The context is regarding God's promises to Israel (their restoration and kingdom blessing), but the broad language used in the verse applies that sureness to all of the promises of God.

Likewise, Rom 8:35-39 clearly states the believer's security:

Who shall separate us from the love of Christ? Shall tribulation, or distress, or persecution, or famine, or nakedness, or peril, or sword? As it is written: "FOR YOUR SAKE WE ARE KILLED ALL DAY LONG; WE ARE ACCOUNTED AS SHEEP FOR THE SLAUGHTER." Yet in all these things we are more than conquerors through Him who loved us. For I am persuaded that neither death nor life, nor angels nor principalities nor powers, nor things present nor things to come, nor height nor depth, nor any other created thing, shall be able to separate us from the love of God which is in Christ Jesus our Lord.

This blessed truth is not only wonderful to know, it is foundational to the Christian life. That's why God says it so plainly and leaves no room to wiggle out of it. The one who believes in Jesus cannot ever be separated from God, no matter what.

ASSURANCE

This brings us to a separate, but related topic of the believer's assurance. To have assurance of eternal salvation is to be 100% sure that you are justified before God, have eternal life, and will spend eternity with God. A believer can be secure and still not have assurance, but God's intention is that we would have both.

Assurance of salvation is vital. Many Bible teachers think that without fear of the lake of fire, the believer will not pursue holiness. But God has many ways to motivate His people, and He doesn't need one like this that is so contrary to His purposes. It is a terrible burden to spend your life wracked with guilt and fear. Not knowing where we will spend eternity is not the light burden Jesus promised us. Furthermore, one of God's expressed purposes in our salvation is to release us from the bondage of the fear of death (Heb 2:14-15). Those who would bring the believer back into that bondage are working against God's expressed purpose. The person who believes in Christ has no legitimate reason to fear where he will spend eternity because his place with God in the New Heaven and New Earth is guaranteed.

While there are those who believe that they must call people's identity as Christians into question to motivate them towards Christian maturity, God's way is to start with the believer's secure identity as a child of God and work towards obedience from there.[100] A wonderful example of this is found in 1 Cor 6:18-20:

Flee sexual immorality. Every sin that a man does is outside the body, but he who commits sexual immorality sins against his own body. Or do you not know that *your body is the temple of the Holy Spirit who is in you*, whom you have from God, and you are not your own? For you were bought at a price;

---

[100] See Hodges, *The Gospel Under Siege*, pp. 52-53.

therefore glorify God in your body and in your spirit, *which are God's.* (Emphasis added.)

Paul does not say here that if they don't flee sexual immorality, they aren't Christians. In fact, the very reason they should flee sexual immorality is *because they are Christians.* They are the dwelling place of God, and they belong to Him. If the reality of their identity in Christ is in question, Paul's entire point is meaningless.

Reversing God's principle of working from security rather than towards it, assumes the seemingly reasonable belief that fear of the lake of fire and desire for the glories of heaven are powerful motivators. But all this kind of motivation can lead to are oppressive, legalistic attempts at self-willed obedience. Even worse, this perspective often brings about harsh, judgmental attitudes and societal attempts at suppressing the sin nature. The end results are oppression and wickedness, rather than freedom and holiness. This was certainly the case for the Medieval Catholic Church and the Puritans. It is likewise the case for world religions that use this kind of motivation like Hinduism and fundamental Islam.

The Bible often speaks of God as our Father and believers as His children. In fact, the family is one of the most common illustrations used to describe God's relationship with His people. If we apply this backward motivation to family life, the absurdity of having to prove our identity through works becomes obvious. If I were to tell my little boy, "If you don't behave, that just proves you were never my son to begin with, and I'll throw you out on the street," no doubt CPS would soon be knocking at my door. That isn't the way I discipline my son, and it isn't God's way either. God is not interested in participating in that kind of spiritual abuse. In fact, it is a complete reversal of God's method of spurring on obedience.

Paul told the Ephesian church:

> I, therefore, the prisoner of the Lord, beseech you to walk worthy of the calling with which you were called, with all lowliness and gentleness, with longsuffering, bearing with one another in love, endeavoring to keep the unity of the Spirit in the bond of peace. There is one body and one Spirit, just as you were called in one hope of your calling; one Lord, one faith, one baptism; one God and Father of all, who is above all, and through all, and in you all. (Eph 4:1-6)

Rather than questioning their calling as children of God, Paul uses the sure reality of that calling, the commonality they share in the Holy Spirit, and the very reality of God indwelling all of them ("and in you all"), as the basis for his plea that they "walk worthy of the calling with which [they] were called." Even the plea itself reaffirms their calling. What's even more telling is that Paul has just spent three chapters outlining all the blessings they share by virtue of their being "in Christ." While we have only been through a couple of examples, seemingly every page in the New Testament shows us that the reality of our position as children of God and the surety of the blessings that we have in Christ are the foundation of the kind of obedience that God is looking for. Those who suggest otherwise are missing the value of a great wealth of Scripture.

NO BOASTING: EPHESIANS 1–2

This leads us to an important point. Whether it comes to our initial reception of eternal life, or our ongoing assurance, Jesus Christ, His work, and His promises are the only firm foundation. God set it up that way to exclude boasting entirely so that He gets all the glory.

In Paul's prayer beginning in Eph 1:16, he prays for the Ephesians to gain a knowledge of several things. A couple of these things, which I will cover here, should give us pause. The first of these is that Paul prays that the Ephesians would know "…what are the riches of the glory of [Christ's] inheritance in the saints" (1:18), and the second is as he continues praying for things he wants the Ephesians to know, he comes to this, "And He put all things under His feet, and gave Him to be head over all things to the church, which is His body, the fullness of Him who fills all in all" (Eph 1:22-23). Paul speaks here of the riches of the glory of *Christ's* inheritance in *us*—we are His rich and glorious inheritance. Moreover, that we, the Church, are His fullness. In other words, the *Church* fills up *Christ*.

Now, as people who recognize that everything good we have comes from God and every spiritual blessing we have is found in Christ, how can we reconcile this reality with Paul's insistence that we are a glorious inheritance for Him and that we fill Him up? Was *He*, who is before all things and in whom all things consist (Col 1:17), lacking in *anything*? How could that be? And how could *we* complete Him?

Paul anticipates these questions and goes on to answer them. But it is easy to miss the point Paul is making because of a couple of factors. First, the chapter break which comes after 1:23 gives the impression that Paul is moving on to another point with the beginning of chapter 2. But the chapter breaks were added centuries after Paul wrote his letter. Secondly, the NKJV translation (and several other translations) seems to miss the point Paul is making in looking back to what he has been discussing in chapter 1 and adjust the translation to look exclusively forward. In 2:1, the NKJV reads, "And you *He made alive*, who were dead in trespasses and sins" (italics are from the NKJV). The words in italics, "*He made alive*" have been supplied by the translators for reading clarity and are not in the original Greek. In this case, the addition is incorrect. But "And you who were dead in trespasses and sins" doesn't make sense, so the addition is understandable. However, in this instance, the Greek word *kai* which is translated "and" should be translated "even" (the word can be used to mean either), and the verse should read, "...even you who were dead in trespasses and sins."

Putting this into the context, the passage is much clearer:

> Therefore I also, after I heard of your faith in the Lord Jesus and your love for all the saints, do not cease to give thanks for you, making mention of you in my prayers: that the God of our Lord Jesus Christ, the Father of glory, may give to you the spirit of wisdom and revelation in the knowledge of Him, the eyes of your understanding being enlightened; that you may know what is the hope of His calling, what are the riches of the glory of His inheritance in the saints, and what is the exceeding greatness of His power toward us who believe, according to the working of His mighty power which He worked in Christ when He raised Him from the dead and seated Him at His right hand in the heavenly places, far above all principality and power and might and dominion, and every name that is named, not only in this age but also in that which is to come. And He put all things under His feet, and gave Him to be head over all things to the church, which is His body, the fullness of Him who fills all in all, even you who were dead in trespasses and sins... (Eph 1:15-2:1)

Paul is not confused. He isn't forgetting the fact that the people he is writing to came from sin and spiritual deadness. He is not forgetting that these believers had been living their lives in obedience to Satan (2:2) or that they had been "by nature children of wrath" (2:4). In fact, that's exactly Paul's point. It isn't about who they were, it is about what God has done.

One of the most incredible descriptions of the beauty of God's grace follows:

> But God, who is rich in mercy, because of His great love with which He loved us, even when we were dead in trespasses, made us alive together with Christ (by grace you have been saved), and raised us up together, and made us sit together in the heavenly places in Christ Jesus, that in the ages to come He might show the exceeding riches of His grace in His kindness toward us in Christ Jesus. For by grace you have been saved through faith, and that not of yourselves; it is the gift of God, not of works, lest anyone should boast. (Eph 2:4-9)

So how does this equate to our being Christ's fullness? As the perfect God and perfect Man, He is complete in Himself; however, His love and grace cannot be fully demonstrated without an unworthy bunch like us in whom He can show His exceeding riches of grace and kindness.

Verse 10 presents another translation issue. The NKJV and several other translations use the word *workmanship*, which is problematic for two reasons. First, *workmanship* in English can be either singular or plural, and people often erroneously tend toward an individualistic view when interpreting Scripture. But the Greek word behind it is singular, so the discussion is not about the individual Christian, but the Church. Secondly, the word *workmanship* misses the beauty that is being expressed here. The Greek word is *poiēma*, from which we get our English word *poem*, and it means *masterpiece*. This word is only used one other time in Scripture. Romans 1:20 uses it to describe God's masterpiece of the created universe, through which He reveals His attributes.

Paul is saying that we together are God's *masterpiece*. "For we are His masterpiece, created in Christ Jesus for good works, which God prepared beforehand, that we should walk in them." And this is all based upon the amazing thing that God has done in taking this shabby group of individuals, living in bondage to the Adversary, and by grace creating from them the very Body of Christ (Eph 2:6, 15-16), the dwelling place of the living God (2:21-22).

So when Paul writes, "For by grace you have been saved through faith, and that not of yourselves; it is the gift of God, not of works, lest anyone should boast," the absolute bankruptcy of the idea that our works could play any role in our new birth should be apparent. God did this great thing, so that we would be able to do the good works He has prepared (2:10b). But our works can play no role in our salvation, so that God can have the full glory which is due for creating His greatest masterpiece—the Body of Christ.

PRACTICE

1) In the passages above (John 6:37, 39-40, 49-51a; and 10:27-30), what ten things does Jesus say that reinforce our security in Him?

2) Read Rom 6:1-14. How does assurance of salvation relate to the command: "reckon yourselves dead indeed to sin but alive to God..." in v 11?

3) How does Gal 3:1-5 relate to the doctrine of assurance?

DISCUSS

1) Is it accurate to say that mixing works and grace for eternal life diminishes God's glory? Why or why not?

2) Read Heb 2:14-15. Whose work is being done if believers are made to fear death, i.e., if their assurance is undermined? What practical steps can be taken to help believers who have this fear?

3) Does it make sense to you that the Apostle Paul would reinforce the security of the Corinthians in 1 Cor 6:18-20 to encourage them toward holy living? Why or why not?

4) Does acknowledging the existence of carnal Christians have an impact on assurance? Why or why not?

5) Calvinism teaches that all believers persevere in faith and holiness until the end of life. If this were true, how would it affect assurance?

The Judgment Seat of Christ

"For we must all appear before the judgment seat of Christ, that each one may receive the things done in the body, according to what he has done, whether good or bad." *Second Corinthians 5:10*

LESSON OBJECTIVES

1. To introduce the Judgment Seat of Christ
2. To explain how the doctrine of rewards is essential to a right understanding of Free Grace

INTRODUCTION

Every human being will face judgment for his or her works. In Isa 45:23, the Lord said, "to Me every knee shall bow, every tongue shall take an oath." This is universal in scope, and no human being will escape it, including those who believe in Jesus.

There are two seats of judgment mentioned in Scripture, the *Bema*,[101] and the *Thronos* (throne). D.M. Panton observed: "The tribunal, before which disciples appear, is peculiar. It is a *Bema*, not a Thronos ; [*sic*] a judgment seat for the investigation of disciples, not a throne for the arraignment of rebels."[102] *Bema* is a word used for the seat on which judges of athletic games would sit to give out prizes to athletes who won

---

[101] *Bema* is a Greek word meaning *judgment seat.*

[102] D.M. Panton, *The Judgment Seat of Christ* (Hayesville, NC: Schoettle Publishing Co., Inc. 1984), pp. 14-15.

their events in the games. The *Bema* will occur before the Millennial kingdom (Matt 16:27), and the *Thronos*, the judgment for unbelievers, will occur after the Millennium (Rev 20:7, 11-15).

The judgment that believers will face is called the Judgment Seat of Christ, or the *Bema*. This is what Paul was referring to when he wrote to his fellow believers in Corinth:

> Therefore we make it our aim, whether present or absent, to be well pleasing to Him. For we must all appear before the judgment seat of Christ, that each one may receive the things done in the body, according to what he has done, whether good or bad. (2 Cor 5:9-10)

Christ will not judge believers at the *Bema* based upon His own righteousness, or upon His own works. This is not a place for grace and receiving free gifts. It is a place for receiving wages for work done. At the *Bema*, the truth of Paul's statement, "Do not be deceived, God is not mocked; for whatever a man sows, that he will also reap" (Gal 6:7), will be apparent.

Throughout the New Testament, the Judgment Seat of Christ takes center stage, and references and allusions to it occur on almost every page (one notable exception is the Gospel of John[103]). Because every book in the New Testament—outside of the Gospel of John—was written to believers, it makes sense that each writer would be working to prepare his readers for the judgment of their life's work.

THE JUDGMENT SEAT OF CHRIST IS NOT FOR DETERMINING ETERNAL DESTINY

The Judgment Seat of Christ is not to determine eternal destiny. Believers cannot enter into that kind of judgment: "Most assuredly, I say to you, he who hears My word and believes in Him who sent Me has everlasting life, and shall not come into judgment, but has passed from death into life" (John 5:24). The *Bema* is for the determining of rewards.

In Luke 19:11-27, the Lord gives us a picture of the *Bema* in a parable:

> Now as they heard these things, He spoke another parable, because He was near Jerusalem and because they [His disciples] thought the kingdom of God would appear immediately. Therefore He said: "A certain nobleman went into a far country

---

[103] Philemon also contains no references to the Bema in its 25 verses.

to receive for himself a kingdom and to return. So he called ten of his servants, delivered to them ten minas, and said to them, 'Do business till I come.' But his citizens hated him, and sent a delegation after him, saying, 'We will not have this man to reign over us.' And so it was that when he returned, having received the kingdom, he then commanded these servants, to whom he had given the money, to be called to him, that he might know how much every man had gained by trading. Then came the first, saying, 'Master, your mina has earned ten minas.' And he said to him, 'Well done, good servant; because you were faithful in a very little, have authority over ten cities.' And the second came, saying, 'Master, your mina has earned five minas.' Likewise he said to him, 'You also be over five cities.' Then another came, saying, 'Master, here is your mina, which I have kept put away in a handkerchief. For I feared you, because you are an austere man. You collect what you did not deposit, and reap what you did not sow.' And he said to him, 'Out of your own mouth I will judge you, you wicked servant. You knew that I was an austere man, collecting what I did not deposit and reaping what I did not sow. Why then did you not put my money in the bank, that at my coming I might have collected it with interest?' And he said to those who stood by, 'Take the mina from him, and give it to him who has ten minas.' (But they said to him, 'Master, he has ten minas.') 'For I say to you, that to everyone who has will be given; and from him who does not have, even what he has will be taken away from him. But bring here those enemies of mine, who did not want me to reign over them, and slay them before me.'"

In this parable, there are two broad categories of people—servants, and enemies. The king goes away to a far country to receive a kingdom, and in the meantime, his servants are each given one mina (about one fourth of a year's wages for an agricultural worker) and told to do business with it until he returns.

Upon the king's return, he speaks with each servant to find out the return on his investment. We only see three examples of these ten servants, probably because they are representative of the three main kinds of servants. There are those whose work is very fruitful, like the servant who earned ten minas with the one he was given. There are those whose service is fruitful, but not as much as it could be, like the one who earned five. And there are those who do nothing at all.

Interestingly, it was a legalistic mindset that drove the unfaithful servant to unfruitfulness. He said, "Master, here is your mina, which I have kept put away in a handkerchief. For I feared you, because you are an austere man. You collect what you did not deposit, and reap what you did not sow." Ironically, the truth about Christ's character is exactly the opposite. As the Lord said to the Israelites, "I have given you a land for which you did not labor, and cities which you did not build, and you dwell in them; you eat of the vineyards and olive groves which you did not plant" (Josh 24:13). Even the mina this servant had to work with was a gift from the king.

But the king judges this lazy servant based upon the false standard the servant had ascribed to his king: "Out of your own mouth I will judge you."

The minas here represent responsibility. We are each given responsibility in this life. We are enabled and charged to work, using the spiritual enablement Christ has given us, to build up the Body of Christ. If we are faithful with this small task, we will be given much more responsibility upon Christ's return. This responsibility will be in proportion to our labors now, though the reward is exceedingly generous (i.e., authority over ten cities for producing two and a half years' worth of a poor worker's wages). On the other hand, if we do nothing with what we are given, we will not receive any responsibility at that time, and even the responsibility we have now will be taken away:

> "Take the mina from him, and give it to him who has ten minas." (But they said to him, "Master, he has ten minas.") "For I say to you, that to everyone who has will be given; and from him who does not have, even what he has will be taken away from him."

Christ will not entrust the administration of His kingdom to those who are unfaithful with what He has given them now.

But even with this picture of a negative judgment, this wicked servant is contrasted with the king's enemies: "But bring here those enemies of mine, who did not want me to reign over them, and slay them before me" (Luke 19:27). This refers back to his citizens who hated him in 19:14. The enemies are not even present when the servants are judged. It is after the judgment that the king says, "bring here those enemies of mine."

So, while we must all be presented before Christ to be judged, the issue is not our eternal destiny. The issue is the determining of rewards.

THE JUDGMENT SEAT OF CHRIST IS FOUNDATIONAL TO FREE GRACE

The Judgment Seat of Christ is a foundational doctrine to Free Grace. All over the Bible, it is clear that there is a prize to be won, wages to be earned, and loss ahead if we fall away. When scholars do not give rightful place to the *Bema*, and instead join the two separate judgments—the one for believers only and the one for unbelievers—into one, they end up with believers before the *Thronos*, being judged to determine their eternal destiny. The prize and the gift get confused, and Bible interpreters have to go through a great deal of trouble to make words like *wages* and *free gift* mean the same thing. In the end, the free gift is presented as anything but free. Likewise, the very real accountability we have is softened, and the Judgment Seat of Christ becomes little more than an afterthought.

Free Grace naturally grows out of Dispensationalism, and both depend on recognizing distinctions, "rightly dividing the word of truth" (2 Tim 2:15). Below is a small chart of contrasts between the free gift and the prize:

The Free Gift	The Prize
For by grace you have been saved through faith, and that not of yourselves; it is the gift of God, not of works, lest anyone should boast. (Eph 2:8-9)	For the Son of Man will come in the glory of His Father with His angels, and then He will reward each according to his works. (Matt 16:27)
Jesus answered and said to her, "If you knew the gift of God, and who it is who says to you, 'Give Me a drink,' you would have asked Him, and He would have given you living water." (John 4:10)	And he who overcomes, and keeps my works until the end, to him I will give power over the nations. (Rev 2:26)

The Free Gift	The Prize
...not by works of righteousness which we have done, but according to His mercy He saved us, through the washing of regeneration and renewing of the Holy Spirit. (Titus 3:5)	Do you not know that those who run in a race all run, but one receives the prize? Run in such a way that you may obtain it. And everyone who competes for the prize is temperate in all things. Now they do it to obtain a perishable crown, but we for an imperishable crown. Therefore I run thus: not with uncertainty. Thus I fight: not as one who beats the air. But I discipline my body and bring it into subjection, lest, when I have preached to others, I myself should become disqualified. (1 Cor 9:24-27)
...being justified freely by His grace through the redemption that is in Christ Jesus. (Rom 3:24)	And let us not grow weary while doing good, for in due season we shall reap if we do not lose heart. (Gal 6:9)
And the Spirit and the bride say, "Come!" And let him who hears say, "Come!" And let him who thirsts come. Whoever desires, let him take the water of life freely. (Rev 22:17)	And behold, I am coming quickly, and My reward is with Me, to give to every one according to his work. (Rev 22:12)

One passage in particular discusses the gift and the prize together, clearly making a distinction:

> For we are God's fellow workers; you are God's field, you are God's building. According to the grace of God which was given to me, as a wise master builder I have laid the foundation, and another builds on it. But let each one take heed how he builds on it. For no other foundation can anyone lay than that which is laid, which is Jesus Christ. Now if anyone builds on this foundation with gold, silver, precious stones, wood, hay, straw, each one's work will become clear; for the Day will declare it, because it will be revealed by fire; and the fire will test each one's work, of what sort it is. If anyone's work which he has built on it endures, he will receive a reward. If anyone's work is burned, he will suffer loss; but he himself will be saved, yet so as through fire. (1 Cor 3:9-15)

The Greek word for "burned" is *katakaiō*, which essentially means *to burn to the ground* or *to burn up completely*. This depicts someone whose work is entirely burned up, meaning that he receives no reward at all. "But," Paul says, "he himself will be saved, yet so as through fire" (1 Cor 3:15). The picture here is someone escaping a burning house. His house is destroyed, but he escapes with his life.

This means that even if a believer has no rewardable works in his life as a Christian, his or her eternal destiny is secure. So, rightly understanding that we will face a very real judgment with a very real possibility of receiving no reward at all, helps us to keep the grace of God in perspective. We need not fear the lake of fire, but the accountability so clearly laid out in Scripture still applies to us.

CONCLUSION—A WORD ABOUT REWARDS

The rewards we can receive at the *Bema* for service in this life primarily deal with ruling with Christ in His kingdom. But desiring to rule with Christ is not like the struggle for power that we see in the world today. Christ's rule will be the greatest service that He can yet give the world. By His rule, He will serve the world with strength and compassion, and He will right all of the injustices of the present age. (For more on the kingdom, see Section 5.)

God didn't keep rewards a secret; this is because He wants us to be motivated by them. They are one of many significant motivators He has given us.

Many have the mistaken idea that seeking rewards is selfish. But wanting to rule with Christ is not about a lust for power, it is about wanting greater opportunity to serve. If we love Christ and His people, of course we will want every opportunity to serve them forever. Those whom He finds faithful in the very little tasks of service we have been given now will be rewarded with greater opportunities to serve forever in His kingdom. And there is nothing at all wrong with wanting our Lord to be pleased with us and wanting to hear from Him, "Well done!"

PRACTICE

1) Read Matt 6:28-34. What should we be doing instead of worrying about things like food and clothing?

2) Read 2 Cor 11:22-28; 4:17-18; and Rom 8:18. What do these passages tell us about rewards?

3) Read 2 Tim 4:6-8, written shortly before Paul was beheaded by Emperor Nero. What does this passage tell you about the importance of rewards in Paul's life?

4) In 1 Cor 3:9-15, what is the building? What does this mean regarding what we are judged for, according to this passage?

5) In Phil 4:1, the Apostle Paul calls the Philippians, "My joy and crown." Why do you suppose he uses these terms for them?

DISCUSS

1) The Apostle Paul was excited about rewards. The doctrine had taken hold of him. How can we let the prospect of these future blessings motivate us the way it motivated him?

2) How does it help to know that the One who will judge us loves us and can sympathize with our weakness (Heb 4:15)?

3) James 2:13 says, "For judgment is without mercy to the one who has shown no mercy. Mercy triumphs over judgment." This lets us know that if we are merciful to others, Christ will be more merciful to us at the *Bema*. How can we do better at showing mercy to others?

4) Will we be rewarded for works done legalistically? Why or why not?

5) It is difficult to discern from Scripture whether or not our sins will be brought up at the *Bema*. But, even if they are not, how can our personal holiness, or lack of it, affect our ministry, and therefore affect our rewards?

Answering the Five Points of Calvinism

"We don't have the right to twist the meaning of the Five Points of Calvinism to our liking and then call ourselves Calvinists" – Earl Radmacher[104]

LESSON OBJECTIVES

1. To briefly explain each of the Five Points of Calvinism
2. To show how the Bible addresses each of the Five Points of Calvinism

INTRODUCTION

This lesson is not meant to be a comprehensive refutation of Calvinism. George Bryson's *The Dark Side of Calvinism*,[105] and Anthony Badger's *Confronting Calvinism*[106] are good resources for further study. The student may also find Bryson's shorter work, *The Five Points of Calvinism: Weighed and Found Wanting* useful, especially for sharing with others.

---

[104] Told to me in personal conversation.

[105] George Bryson, *The Dark Side of Calvinism: The Calvinist Caste System* (Santa Ana, CA: Calvary Chapel Publishing, 2004).

[106] Anthony Badger, *Confronting Calvinism: A Free Grace Refutation and Biblical Resolution of Radical Reformed Soteriology* (Place Unknown: Anthony B. Badger, 2013).

For an invaluable lexical study of many key words in the Calvinism debate (predestined, elect, foreknowledge, etc.), see Gordon Olson's books, *Getting the Gospel Right*[107] and *Beyond Calvinism and Arminianism*.[108]

This lesson will also not argue from a philosophical or theological standpoint, and is not intended to refute the proof texts used by Calvinists. Applying the hermeneutical principles learned in Section 1 should be sufficient to address each of those passages. This lesson is merely to show that each of the Five Points of Calvinism goes against the plain teaching of Scripture, and because the Bible does not contradict itself, Calvinism must be false.

It should be noted that Arminianism is also unbiblical, but a refutation of Arminianism is inherent in Lessons 9-12.

THE FIVE POINTS OF CALVINISM EXPLAINED

The Synod of Dort was a group of Reformed clergy that met in the town of Dordrecht in The Netherlands to author a definition of their theology (Calvinism) and a refutation of Arminianism. The five points they decided upon form the acronym, TULIP—Total Depravity, Unconditional Election, Limited Atonement, Irresistible Grace, and Perseverance of the Saints. Each of the Five Points of Calvinism is explained briefly below.

TOTAL DEPRAVITY

Total Depravity is the doctrine that because the unregenerate[109] are dead in sins, they cannot do anything of spiritual value, even believe in Christ, without first being regenerated. In other words, *Total Depravity* states that an unbeliever is made alive in Christ before ever coming to faith in Christ. Another distinctive of *Total Depravity* is the teaching that faith is a gift of God and not the responsibility of man.

---

[107] Gordon Olson, *Getting the Gospel Right: A Balanced View of Salvation Truth* (Cedar Knolls, NJ: Global Gospel Publishers, 2005).

[108] Olson, *Beyond Calvinism and Arminianism: An Inductive, Mediate Theology of Salvation* (Cedar Knolls, NJ: Global Gospel Publishers, 2002).

[109] An unregenerate person is one who has yet to receive the free gift of eternal life.

UNCONDITIONAL ELECTION

Unconditional Election is the doctrine that God arbitrarily (i.e. without reference to any foreseen quality, belief, or action on the part of the individual) chose in eternity past each individual whom He would save and each individual whom He would reprobate (destine for the lake of fire). This choice was not based on merit, nor on foreknowledge of those individuals' faith in Christ.

LIMITED ATONEMENT

Limited Atonement is the doctrine that Christ did not die for the whole world, but only for those whom God predestined to eternal salvation. Additionally, this doctrine contends that Christ's death effects salvation in all those for whom He died.

IRRESISTIBLE GRACE

Irresistible Grace is the doctrine that a genuine offer of salvation cannot be resisted by the elect.

PERSEVERANCE OF THE SAINTS

Perseverance of the Saints is the belief that all of the elect will necessarily persevere in faith and good works until the end of life. The one who does not persevere proves he or she was not elected to eternal salvation.

This doctrine is often confused with the doctrine of eternal security, but is actually in conflict with it.

THE FIVE POINTS OF CALVINISM CONTRASTED WITH SCRIPTURE

Below I have demonstrated how each of the Five Points of Calvinism contrasts with plain statements in Scripture.

TOTAL DEPRAVITY

While it is Biblically true that apart from Christ, the unregenerate (along with the regenerate[110]) can do nothing to merit God's favor, faith is not meritorious, and the Bible clearly teaches that regeneration[111] is the result of faith, not the other way around.

Ephesians 2:8-9 is a common go-to passage for teaching that faith is a gift, but the Greek grammar makes this extremely unlikely, and the passage actually teaches the opposite.

The verse reads: "For by grace you have been saved through faith, and that not of yourselves; it is the gift of God, not of works, lest anyone should boast."

This passage clearly teaches that salvation comes through faith "by grace you have been saved through faith." In this context, the word "saved" refers to regeneration. In verse 5, Paul writes, "[God] even when we were dead in trespasses, made us alive together with Christ (by grace you have been saved)." The parenthetical clause Paul added to the end of his reference to regeneration is repeated in verse 8, "…by grace you have been saved." This lets us know that Paul means to refer back to the regeneration he just described.[112]

If Calvinistic Total Depravity were true, faith would come through salvation, not the other way around.

Calvinism also teaches that the word "that" in verse 8 refers back to the word "faith," i.e. "For by grace you have been saved through faith, and that [faith] not of yourselves; it is the gift of God." But this is extremely unlikely when the Greek grammar is taken into account.

In Greek, pronouns take on the gender of the noun to which they refer. Faith is a feminine noun. Thus, if Paul were teaching that faith is not of ourselves, he would have to use the feminine form for the pronoun "that." But Paul did not use a feminine pronoun, he used a neuter pronoun. Neuter pronouns do not refer to feminine nouns.

The neuter is often used, however, to refer to broader concepts, and not directly to specific nouns in the immediate context. In this case, "that" refers to salvation. The phrase "you have been saved" is translated from a Greek verb, which does not have gender. The correct way to understand

---

[110] The regenerate are those who possess eternal life.

[111] Regeneration is the reception of eternal life.

[112] For a helpful discussion, see Frank Tyler's article, "For God Made Us Alive Together with Christ Through Faith" in *Grace in Focus*, July-August, 2012.

the passage is, "For by grace you have been saved through faith, and that [salvation] not of yourselves; it is the gift of God, not of works, lest anyone should boast."

So, Eph 2:8-9 does not teach that regeneration comes before faith; it teaches just the opposite.

The phrase "Jesus, the author and finisher of our faith," from Heb 12:2, has also been taken to suggest that God causes us to believe. But the faith in view is the set of beliefs we have, not our personally believing them. This is a very common use of the word "faith" in scripture. Jesus is the author and finisher of our faith in the sense that He writes and completes the content of our faith.

We may also note Rom 10:17: "So then faith comes by hearing, and hearing by the word of God." Clearly here, faith comes by hearing the Word of God, not as a result of regeneration.

Lastly, in Acts 10, God sent Peter to Cornelius as a response to Cornelius' seeking God while still an unbeliever. This should be impossible according to the Calvinistic doctrine of Total Depravity.

It is true that Jesus said, "No one can come to Me unless the Father who sent Me draws him; and I will raise him up at the last day" (John 6:44). But He also said, "And I, if I am lifted up from the earth [i.e. at the cross], I will draw all to Myself" (author's translation). He also promised that the Holy Spirit would "convict the world of sin, and of righteousness, and of judgment" concerning Christ (see John 16:8-11).

Man would never seek God on his own (Rom 3:11), but God has not left anyone on his own. He is in the world working to draw all to Himself. Those who respond by believing in Jesus are born again.

UNCONDITIONAL ELECTION

The essential proposition behind the Calvinistic doctrine of Unconditional Election is that God decreed from eternity past some specific people who would be eternally saved and others who would not.

In this system, there is not a legitimate offer of eternal salvation to those who are not elect. If God indeed loves all men and desires all men to be eternally saved, Unconditional Election cannot be true.

First Timothy 2:3-6 says explicitly that God's desire is for "all men to be saved and come to the knowledge of the truth." The full passage reads:

> For this is good and acceptable in the sight of God our Savior, who desires all men to be saved and to come to the knowledge of the truth. For there is one God and one Mediator between God and men, the Man Christ Jesus, who gave Himself a ransom for all, to be testified in due time.

The argument is often made that God's decreed will (what He will decree to happen) and His desired will (what He wants to happen) are not necessarily the same. This is true. However, God's decreed will and His desired will never come into direct conflict. God is free to do as He chooses regarding man's salvation, so He would not decree something that frustrates His greater desire. If Unconditional Election were true, God's decreed will and His desired will would be in direct conflict.

The Calvinistic view here is primarily based upon an incorrect understanding of the meaning of the word "elect" as it is used in Scripture. Election is not about the salvation of the elect. For a fuller discussion, see Lesson 24 in this curriculum.

LIMITED ATONEMENT

Christ did not only die for the elect, but for the whole world. 1 John 2:2: "And He Himself is the propitiation for our sins, and not for ours only but also for the whole world." See also John 1:29; 3:16; 2 Cor 5:14-15; 1 Tim 2:3-6. The Calvinistic doctrine of Limited Atonement directly contradicts these passages.

Second Peter 2:1 also does away with either Limited Atonement or Perseverance of the Saints. It says, "But there were also false prophets among the people, even as there will be false teachers among you, who will secretly bring in destructive heresies, *even denying the Lord who bought them*, and bring on themselves swift destruction" (Emphasis added). This verse either speaks of genuine Christians who are denying the Lord and bringing in destructive heresies, or it affirms that the Lord bought (i.e. died for) these unbelieving people.

Furthermore, in the New Testament the word *atonement* (essentially, to cover) is never used of Christ's death. The words *propitiation* (satisfactory, complete payment) and *takes away* (compare 1 John 2:2 and John 1:29 with Heb 10:4) are used instead. These are much stronger words. Christ's blood not only covers the sins of the whole world, it completely pays for them and takes them away.

IRRESISTIBLE GRACE

The doctrine of Irresistible Grace assumes that all those who reject the offer of salvation were not given a genuine offer to begin with. This is logically deduced from the other points of Calvinism, and if they are not true, the logical basis for this point is not there.

In many of the passages in which eternal life is offered and rejected, there is no clear indicator about whether or not the offer was genuine (though it seems disingenuous to make a non-genuine offer); but Acts 13:46 clearly shows an outright rejection of a genuine offer of eternal life.

PERSEVERANCE OF THE SAINTS

The New Testament abounds with warnings and encouragements given to genuine Christians that they should persevere in the face of persecution and temptations. If every genuine believer would necessarily persevere in holiness and faith no matter what, these warnings and encouragements would be unnecessary.

It is possible for a true believer in Christ to fail to persevere in holiness and good works (such a person is still secure in his or her eternal salvation). Second Peter 1:1-9 demonstrates this so clearly that we would have to read it away entirely to escape this truth. It says:

> Simon Peter, a bondservant and apostle of Jesus Christ, *To those who have obtained like precious faith with us* by the righteousness of our God and Savior Jesus Christ: Grace and peace be multiplied to you in the knowledge of God and of Jesus our Lord, as His divine power has given to us all things that pertain to life and godliness, through the knowledge of Him who called us by glory and virtue, by which have been given to us exceedingly great and precious promises, that through these you may be partakers of the divine nature, having escaped the corruption that is in the world through lust. But also for this very reason, giving all diligence, *add to your faith* virtue, to virtue knowledge, to knowledge self-control, to self-control *perseverance*, to perseverance godliness, to godliness brotherly kindness, and to brotherly kindness love. For if these things

are yours and abound, you will be neither barren nor unfruit-
ful in the knowledge of our Lord Jesus Christ. For *he who lacks*
these things is shortsighted, even to blindness, and has forgotten that *he was cleansed from his old sins.* (Emphasis added.)

Peter is writing to fellow believers in Jesus Christ, "to those who have
obtained like precious faith with us." Even those who would suggest that
not all faith in Christ is sufficient must admit that "like precious faith
with us" has to be referring to genuine saving faith.[113] Yet Peter does not
assume that faith will naturally result in: virtue, knowledge, self-control,
perseverance, godliness, brotherly kindness, and love. On the contrary,
he urges them toward adding those things to their faith, and continues,
"he who lacks these things is shortsighted, even to blindness, and has
forgotten that he was cleansed from his old sins." If it were impossible for
a true believer to lack perseverance, Peter would not be able to affirm that
someone who lacks it (along with all the other virtues mentioned) "was
cleansed from his old sins." Peter says this person has forgotten that fact,
not that it wasn't true.

The same truth can be seen in Matt 13:1-8, 18-23; 2 Tim 2:11-13; Heb
6:4-6, and countless other places in the New Testament.

Lastly, there are specific examples in the Bible of believers who did not
persevere to the end of life. Some of the clearest examples:

1. Solomon (1 Kings 11:1-10)

2. Saul (compare 1 Sam 10:6-13; 11:13-14; and chapters 13–21)

3. The believers in Corinth who had died because of their selfish
    gluttony and winebibbing at the Lord's Supper meetings (1 Cor
    11:17-34)

4. Hymenaeus and Alexander (1 Tim 1:19-20)

5. Hymenaeus and Philetus (2 Tim 2:17-18; this could be the same
    Hymenaeus)

6. Possibly Simon Magus (Acts 8:12-24, though we do not know if
    he lived faithfully later)

7. Possibly John the Baptist (compare John 1:29; Matt 11:1-6; and
    13:20-21; see Greek *skandalizō* in 11:6 and 13:21). John the
    Baptist is often mistaken for being a martyr for Christ; however,
    he died not for Christ but for the law (Mark 6:14-28).

---

[113] I am using the language of the Calvinists here when I say "saving faith." Faith does not save,
Christ saves through faith.

If there is even one genuine believer who does not persevere in faith and holiness, the doctrine of the Perseverance of the Saints is not true. The Bible has many examples.

PRACTICAL CONCERNS WITH PERSEVERANCE OF THE SAINTS

Perseverance of the Saints teaches that none of the exhortations to persevere or warnings against failing to persevere, are applicable to true believers.

There are two possible reactions if this proposition is accepted:

1. "I am a true believer, so none of these passages apply to me."

This eliminates large portions of the New Testament as practical to the believer.

2. "I can't know if I will persevere, so there is no way that I can know if I am a true believer until I am on my deathbed."

    1. This eliminates the "your works should reflect your secure identity" motivation. See Eph 4:1-6; 1 Cor 6:18-20; Romans 6–8.
    2. This removes the perception of security and the peace that comes with it, and reinstates the bondage that comes with "fear of death" (Heb 2:14-15).
    3. This encourages unhealthy comparison with others.
    4. This misunderstands grace.

Calvinistic teachers, especially those who hold to Lordship Salvation, tend to encourage both reactions. This is described as a pendulum of motivation, with comfort on one side and fear on the other. By contrast, the Bible speaks of grace as a sure possession, something to rest upon, something that should encourage us toward obedience because it *is* sure.

PRACTICE

1) How does 1 Cor 3:9-15 address the issue of Perseverance of the Saints?

2) Is 1 Cor 9:24-27 about eternal salvation or about reward? Why?

3) Read 1 Kings 11:1-10. What does this say about Perseverance of the Saints?

4) Read 2 Cor 5:12-21. What does this passage teach about the purpose of God's work in Christ's death?

5) Read 1 Tim 2:3-7. What does this passage teach relative to Calvinistic doctrines?

DISCUSS

1) Does 1 Cor 3:1-4 teach that there are carnal Christians? Why or why not?

2) What points of the Five Points of Calvinism are refuted by John 3:16?

3) Does it make sense that 2 Pet 2:1 contradicts either Limited Atonement or Perseverance of the Saints? Which do you think it is refuting? Why?

4) Read Heb 6:4-5. Is there any way the Author of Hebrews could have been clearer regarding the regenerate status of these people?

5) How are Perseverance of the Saints and Eternal Security at odds?

Tough Texts Part 1, James 2:14-26

"James says that the key to a useful, living faith is good works. He does not say a living faith is the key to good works. So the issue in James is not whether faith exists in a person, but how it becomes profitable or useful to the Christian." *Charlie Bing*[114]

LESSON OBJECTIVE

1. To equip the student to understand and communicate the meaning of Jas 2:14-26

INTRODUCTION[115]

James 2:14-26 is perhaps the most commonly cited objection to the doctrine of justification by faith alone apart from works. For this reason, this passage will receive a more extended treatment than other tough texts. The entire passage in question is below:

> What does it profit, my brethren, if someone says he has faith but does not have works? Can faith save him? If a brother or sister is naked and destitute of daily food, and one of you says to them, "Depart in peace, be warmed and filled," but you do not give them the things which are needed for the body, what

---

[114] Bing, *Lordship Salvation*, p. 36.

[115] Though there are some differences, this lesson is largely adapted from Zane Hodges' commentary, *The Epistle of James: Proven Character Through Testing* (Denton: Grace Evangelical Society, 2009) pp. 59-75. See also Fred R. Lybrand, *Back to Faith: Reclaiming Gospel Clarity in an Age of Incongruence* (NP: Xulon Press, 2009) pp. 101-109.

does it profit? Thus also faith by itself, if it does not have works, is dead. But someone will say, "You have faith, and I have works." Show me your faith without your works, and I will show you my faith by my works. You believe that there is one God. You do well. Even the demons believe—and tremble!

But do you want to know, O foolish man, that faith without works is dead? Was not Abraham our father justified by works when he offered Isaac his son on the altar? Do you see that faith was working together with his works, and by works faith was made perfect? And the Scripture was fulfilled which says, "ABRAHAM BELIEVED GOD, AND IT WAS ACCOUNTED TO HIM FOR RIGHTEOUSNESS." And he was called the friend of God. You see then that a man is justified by works, and not by faith only. Likewise, was not Rahab the harlot also justified by works when she received the messengers and sent them out another way? For as the body without the spirit is dead, so faith without works is dead also.

The exchange between James and the objector as it is translated here (by the NKJV) is actually nonsensical in places. In Greek literature, it is common to introduce an objector with a phrase like, "But someone will say," as here in v 18 (see, for example, Rom 6:1, 15; 9:14, 19; 1 Cor 15:35). This is done in anticipation of an objection that the reader may have. As translated here, the objection is simply, "You have faith, and I have works." This is no objection at all. In addition, James' response, in this translation, treats the situation as if it were reversed, as if the objector had said, "You have works, and I have faith." The result is an objector objecting against nothing, making no point, and then James arguing against the opposite of what the objector said.

All modern translations similarly struggle with making sense of this passage. But the passage, though admittedly requiring great care to understand, is not beyond comprehension. I hope to make the meaning clear in this lesson.

A FEW OBSERVATIONS

There are a few things to note before we get started talking about what the text means.

1. James confirms that his audience is made up of believers only (see 1:18; 2:12-13, only believers are judged by the law of liberty, and

that at the Judgment Seat of Christ to determine rewards, not eternal destiny). Fifteen times James refers to his audience as his brothers (Jas 1:2, 16, 19; 2:1, 5, 14; 3:1, 10, 12; 4:11; 5:7, 9, 10, 12, 19). These people have eternal life which can never be lost, thus there is no danger for them regarding their eternal destiny.

2. Some translations read, "Can *such* faith save him?" in v 14. The word *such* (and any word like it) is absent in the Greek text.

3. In Greek, a writer can let the reader know whether he expects a "yes" or a "no" to a rhetorical question. By using *mē* instead of *ou* to introduce the question, James clues us in that he is expecting an answer of "no" to the question, "Can faith save him?" But in this context, salvation at the Judgment Seat of Christ is in view (see 2:13 and 3:1). It may help to read the question as Hodges suggests, "Faith can't save him, can it?"[116]

4. The Greek adverb *kalōs*, translated in v 19 as "you do well," is often used to express the idea of doing good works (see Matt 12:12; Luke 6:27; Jas 2:8 for good examples). My translation below uses "you do good" in v 19 to make it clearer to the English reader that doing good works is in view.

5. In the original Greek texts, there were no quotation marks, so the positioning of the quotes is up to the translators. The objector's quote, starting in v 18 should continue all the way to the end of v 19. James' comment, "But do you want to know, o foolish man..." marks the beginning of James' response. This too is common in Greek rhetoric. The objector's main point is in v 19, in which he is attempting to show that there is no connection between faith and works. Faith in James produces good works "you do well;" the same faith in the demons merely produces "trembling." A more accurate translation of this verse and the rest of the passage is below.

6. In v 24, the word "only" in the Greek is an adverb and cannot modify "faith" (a noun), as the English text suggests. The verse should read, "You see then that a man is justified by works, and not *only* [justified] by faith."

---

[116] Hodges, *James*, p. 60.

A PROPOSED TRANSLATION

With a few modifications to reflect the points above and adjustment to reflect the majority of Greek manuscripts and more literally express the words of the Greek text, the passage becomes clearer. Before continuing, read the translation below carefully:

> What does it profit, my brethren, if someone says he has faith but does not have works? Faith cannot save him, can it? If a brother or sister is naked and destitute of daily food, and one of you says to them, "Depart in peace, be warmed and filled," but you do not give them the things which are needed for the body, what does it profit? Thus also faith by itself, if it does not have works, is dead.

> But someone will say, "You have faith, and I have works. Show me your faith from your works, and I will show you from my works, my faith.[117] You believe that there is one God and you do good, and the demons believe—and tremble!"

> But do you want to know, O foolish man, that faith without works is dead? Was not Abraham our father justified by works when he offered Isaac his son on the altar? Do you see that faith was working together with his works, and by works faith was made perfect? And the Scripture was fulfilled which says, "ABRAHAM BELIEVED GOD, AND IT WAS ACCOUNTED TO HIM FOR RIGHTEOUSNESS." And he was called the friend of God. You see then that a man is justified by works, and not only [justified] by faith. Likewise, was not Rahab the harlot also justified by works when she received the messengers and sent them out another way? For as the body without the spirit is dead, so faith without works is dead also.

While the passage is still difficult with this translation, this translation better reflects the meaning of the Greek and corrects the nonsensical exchange from the NKJV and other translations.

---

[117] You may notice that the objector is suggesting that both he and James demonstrate what they believe by their works. The difference is the starting point. The objector is speaking facetiously, trying to claim that it is just as absurd to start from faith and demonstrate what one believes by working as it is to start with works and demonstrate what one believes through those works. This is difficult to convey in English.

JUSTIFICATION BY WORKS

Those who hold to Lordship Salvation read this passage as if it is teaching justification by faith, but that the faith which justifies must be a working faith. However, while James does acknowledge justification by faith (Jas 2:24, though, see below), justification by faith is not the subject of the passage. Rather, James focuses on justification by works. Three times James uses the phrase "justified by works," and all three times we are to understand that justification by works is exactly what he means. Much damage has been done by interpreters not wanting to admit this.

So how does this not contradict the Apostle Paul's doctrine of justification by faith alone apart from works? James is not talking about justification by works *before God*. He is talking about justification by works before men. Justification before God has always been by faith apart from works, as Paul's quotation of Gen 15:6 in Romans 4 shows. Because men cannot see faith without works, for our faith to be seen as valuable to others, it must manifest itself in works. A Christian who does not put his faith to work brings ridicule and scorn to God.

In our world, Christianity is coming under attack. The primary tool the atheists use to attack Christianity is actually the atheist's perception of his own moral superiority. These attacks would be more obviously ridiculous if Christians were better at following the example set by James (in feeding and clothing the needy 2:15-17), and by Peter in doing good:

> ...having your conduct honorable among the Gentiles, that when they speak against you as evildoers, they may, by your good works which they observe, glorify God in the day of visitation. ... For this is the will of God, that by doing good you may put to silence the ignorance of foolish men—as free, yet not using liberty as a cloak for vice, but as bondservants of God." (1 Pet 2:12, 15-16)

As it is, the Church appears to outsiders to obsess over squabbles, and seems to care only about keeping a list of pharisaical dos and don'ts and collecting offerings rather than caring for the needy. In the end, Christ is dishonored, and our witness suffers because our faith has not been justified before men by our actions.

This is where James' references to the Judgment Seat of Christ in 2:13 and 3:1 come in. Our positive judgment at the *Bema* requires that we show mercy to others (2:15-17) and that we have an effective witness (2:18-26).

ABRAHAM AND RAHAB

The example of Abraham shows us that James is speaking of justification before men, not before God. This is plain because of *when* James says Abraham is justified. James points to his offering of Isaac (Genesis 22), which occurred thirty-three years after Paul says that Abraham was justified before God in Genesis 15. Paul says:

> What then shall we say that Abraham our father has found according to the flesh? For if Abraham was justified by works, he has something to boast about, but not before God. For what does the Scripture say? "ABRAHAM BELIEVED GOD, AND IT WAS ACCOUNTED TO HIM FOR RIGHTEOUSNESS." Now to him who works, the wages are not counted as grace but as debt. But to him who does not work but believes on Him who justifies the ungodly, his faith is accounted for righteousness. (Rom 4:1-5)

If the same justification is in view in both passages, these passages present an irreconcilable contradiction. Justification before God cannot happen twice, thirty-three years apart from each other. Justification before God is a once-for-all declaration of righteousness. And justification before God cannot be both by grace through faith apart from works, and by works.

Having eliminated justification before God as the subject of James 2, how then do we know that James is talking about justification before men? The phrase "and he was called the friend of God" makes this clear. Who called Abraham the friend of God? Other men. In fact, he is known by that name amongst Jews, Christians, and Muslims—nearly half of the world's population.

Likewise, the example of Rahab the Harlot in v 25 shows that justification before men was in view. Rahab was a resident of Jericho when the Israelites were coming to seize and raze the city. Because of Rahab's fear of God, she hid the Jewish spies that came to her, and told the Jericho guards that they had gone in another direction. Because she saved the lives of the Jewish spies, she was spared by the Israelites when they overtook the city. Clearly she was justified before men through her actions.

WORKS ANIMATE FAITH

Lordship Salvation teachers must take James to be saying that true faith necessarily animates works. This reverses James' principle. James is saying that works animate faith. This point is most clearly explained in James' final statement, "For as the body without the spirit is dead, so faith without works is dead also." Charlie Bing observes:

> James ends his discussion with an analogy that illustrates and repeats his theses: "For as the body without the spirit is dead, so faith without works is dead (*nekra*) also" (v. 26). While most assume that the analogy teaches true faith animates works, James' point is the opposite because the animating principle in the analogy is not faith, but works. It is works which vitalizes or makes faith useful.[118]

James' point is backed up by experience. When we go out and serve the needy, our faith is enlivened and becomes useful to others as a result.

CONCLUSION

While a superficial reading of Jas 2:14-26 seems to support Lordship Salvation, it really doesn't. Many of James' points must be manipulated to keep the passage in line with Lordship thought. James is not talking about the kind of faith that saves, versus the kind that does not. James says plainly that faith cannot save (2:14) in the sense he is discussing. James is not talking about justification by faith that has a working quality; he is discussing justification by works. And James is not calling his readers to have a better faith, one that works. He is calling them to put the faith they do have to work, so that their faith can profit the needy, that their faith can be enlivened, and that they will be justified in the eyes of men, so Christ will be honored.

James is not in conflict with Paul. It isn't even that we need to keep them in balance with one another. They are in complete harmony; James just needs to be taken for what he says.

---

[118] Bing, *Lordship Salvation*, p. 36.

PRACTICE

1) Practice talking through James 2 with someone from your study group. You may use this lesson as an aid in your discussion.

DISCUSS

1) What does James mean when he says, "But do you want to know, O foolish man, that faith without works is dead?" How does this answer the objector's point in verse 19?

2) It is sometimes said that "dead faith is no faith." How does the illustration in v 26 refute this?

3) What does Jas 2:15-17 teach us about helping brothers in need?

4) Paul says in Rom 4:1-5 that if justification before God is by works, we would be able to boast before God. How so? See also Eph 2:8-9.

5) Do works strengthen our faith? If so, how?

Tough Texts Part 2

"Everyone who believes that Jesus is the
Christ is born of God..." *First John 5:1*

LESSON OBJECTIVE

1. To offer simple solutions to some of the most commonly used
   works-based salvation proof texts

INTRODUCTION

There are many passages used to support works-oriented soteriol-
ogies. Most of these verses plainly have to do with the Judgment
Seat of Christ, and for the sake of brevity I will not cover those here.
Below are some of the other passages that can be confusing for one
reason or another.

FIRST JOHN[119]

First John is perhaps the most debated book amongst scholars on the
topic of salvation. As noted in previous lessons, much of the confusion
comes from misdiagnosing the purpose statement for the book. When
the structure of the book is taken into account, the purpose statement
reveals itself as 1:3-4:

> [T]hat which we have seen and heard we declare to you, that
> you also may have fellowship with us; and truly our fellowship

---

[119] For a fuller description of the passages cited, along with a capable exegesis of the entire epistle,
see Zane Hodges, *The Epistles of John: Walking in the Light of God's Love* (Denton, TX: Grace
Evangelical Society, 1999) and Dave Anderson, *Maximum Joy* (Irving, TX: Grace Evangelical
Society, 2005).

is with the Father and with His Son Jesus Christ. And these things we write to you that your joy may be full.

Once again, the audience for the book is made up of believers in Christ. John wrote:

> I write to you, little children,
>> Because your sins are forgiven you for His name's sake.
> I write to you, fathers,
>> Because you have known Him who is from the beginning.
> I write to you, young men,
>> Because you have overcome the wicked one.
> I write to you, little children,
>> Because you have known the Father.
> I have written to you, fathers,
>> Because you have known Him who is from the beginning.
> I have written to you, young men,
>> Because you are strong, and the word of God abides in
> you,
>> And you have overcome the wicked one.
>> (1 John 2:12-14; see also 2:21; 3:1-2; 4:4)

These believers were in no way in danger of the lake of fire. But for them to experience the fellowship and joy that John was writing about, they needed to allow Christ to manifest His life in them. This would result in loving one another and clinging to the truth.

First John can be difficult if we do not grasp these two concepts: 1) the Greek word *ginōskō*, "to know," implies great intimacy which goes beyond believing in Jesus, and 2) the concept of abiding in Christ also expresses intimacy. To abide in Christ, and to let Him abide in us means to rest in unity with Him and to allow His life to manifest itself in us, not just to be in Him positionally.

KNOWING GOD

First John 2:3 reads:

> Now by this we know that we know Him, if we keep His commandments. He who says, "I know Him," and does not keep His commandments, is a liar, and the truth is not in him.

This verse is often taken to imply that we must look to our works to determine whether or not we believe. But the Lord's interaction with Martha in John 11:25-27 shows us that we can know what we believe at the moment of faith, not by observing over time how our behavior changes. We know we believe because that's part of what believing means, not because of works. But our works do tell us if we have an intimate relationship with God.

Zane Hodges's comments on this verse are excellent:

> First John 2:3 is not talking about the *saving* knowledge of Christ, but a *fellowship* knowledge. While it is true that all believers do know God and Christ at a fundamental level, all believers may *not* know them at the level of communication and fellowship (cf. the interaction between Philip and Jesus in John 14:7-9). First John 2:3 refers not to the *saving* knowledge of God, but of [*sic*] the *experiential* knowledge of God.[120]

In John's writings, knowing God is an intimate thing, and that relationship is manifested by works.

ABIDING IN CHRIST

First John 3:24 reads:

> Now he who keeps His commandments abides in Him, and He in him. And by this we know that He abides in us, by the Spirit whom He has given us.

This verse is not saying that we know by keeping His commandments if we are saved. But that we know we are resting in unity with Him and allowing His life to be manifested in us if we keep His commandments (see 3:23). Jesus said to His believing disciples, "You are already clean because of the word which I have spoken to you. Abide in Me, and I in you. As the branch cannot bear fruit of itself, unless it abides in the vine, neither can you, unless you abide in Me" (John 15:3-4). In the context of both 1 John 3 and John 15, love for the brethren is in focus.

If we don't love the brethren, we know we aren't abiding in Him (see also 1 John 2:3-11).

FIRST JOHN 3:9

First John 3:9 has baffled many interpreters from a variety of theological perspectives. It reads, "Whoever has been born of God does not sin,

---

[120] Zane Hodges, "The First Epistle of John," *The Grace New Testament Commentary* Vol. 2 (Denton, TX: Grace Evangelical Society, 2010), p. 1198. Emphasis in original.

for His seed remains in him; and he cannot sin, because he has been born of God." The phrases "does not sin" and "he cannot sin" are absolute statements in the Greek.

Recognizing that believers do sin, but still viewing this verse as a test of whether or not one is a believer, Lordship Salvation proponents have often added "continually" to the verse, so that it reads, "Whoever has been born of God does not sin *continually...*"

The addition of "continually" in some English translations is defended by looking to the present tense in the Greek. It is said that the present tense denotes continual action. In reality, the Greek present tense is a "zero tense" and does not express continuation, as is commonly thought. This is especially true outside of the indicative mood (which is the case here). Outside the indicative mood, the present tense doesn't say anything about time at all. And even within the indicative mood, the Greek present tense does not say whether or not an action is continual, but just that it is currently occurring. The Greek word *phagō* is in the present tense in this form, and it means "I am eating." But the Greek reader would not assume that I meant I am continually eating for years; he would assume that I mean I am eating now.

Those who would claim that the present tense means the action is ongoing are also ignoring the fact that the present tense is also used in 1:8, "If we say that we have [present tense] no sin, we deceive ourselves, and the truth is not in us." If the Greek present tense expresses continual action, there is an irreconcilable contradiction between these verses. Appealing to the supposed continual nature of the present tense in 1 John 3:9, but not in 1:8, is special pleading.

This verse teaches that the one who is born again is unable to sin *at all*. But, of course, believers do sin. What this is teaching is that when the believer is expressing the life of Christ within him, he is unable to sin. 1 John 3:6 expresses a similar point. This concept will be further discussed in Section 3: Life and Liberty.

Throughout First John, the theme of abiding in Christ and letting His life manifest itself in us is expressed in many ways. If we are resting in Him, holding fast to the truth, and living in intimate relationship with Him, sin and hatred for our brothers and sisters in Christ will be far from our experience. God is love, and the one who knows Him intimately lives in love.

MATTHEW 5-7

The Sermon on the Mount in Matthew will be discussed more in Section 5: The Kingdom. But for now, a few observations will suffice.

1. While others are present, Jesus is speaking to His disciples (5:1-2). Jesus is not speaking to unbelievers.

2. Jesus affirms sixteen times that God is their Father in these three chapters.

3. The subject of the Sermon on the Mount is "the gospel of the kingdom" (see 4:17, 23), which is related to kingdom rewards, not the free gift of eternal life.

4. The phrase "you will know them by their fruits" in 7:15-20 is about knowing false prophets by the words they speak, not knowing who is and is not a believer by his works. See Matt 12:33-35.

CALLS TO DISCIPLESHIP IN THE SYNOPTIC GOSPELS

There are many calls to discipleship in the Synoptic Gospels (Matthew, Mark, and Luke). All of these calls clearly involve sacrifice on the part of the one who wishes to be a disciple of Jesus. Luke 14:26-33 is representative:

> If anyone comes to Me and does not hate his father and mother, wife and children, brothers and sisters, yes, and his own life also, he cannot be My disciple. And whoever does not bear his cross and come after Me cannot be My disciple. For which of you, intending to build a tower, does not sit down first and count the cost, whether he has enough to finish it— lest, after he has laid the foundation, and is not able to finish, all who see it begin to mock him, saying, 'This man began to build and was not able to finish'? Or what king, going to make war against another king, does not sit down first and consider whether he is able with ten thousand to meet him who comes against him with twenty thousand? Or else, while the other is still a great way off, he sends a delegation and asks conditions of peace. So likewise, whoever of you does not forsake all that he has cannot be My disciple.

First we should note that to "hate" in Scripture usually does not mean to despise, but to neglect by comparison. Jesus is not calling these potential disciples to hate their families and their own life, but not to put them before Christ.

Nevertheless, this is a heavy cost to pay to be Jesus' disciple. To take up our cross is to bear shame and death. And Jesus calls us to count the cost and weigh it carefully. This is hardly "tak[ing] of the water of life freely" (Rev 22:17).

The words *disciple* and *believer* are not synonyms. To be a disciple is to be a devoted learner. When Jesus made calls to discipleship, He was calling people to leave everything in a literal sense and travel with Him so that they might learn from Him. He was a traveling Rabbi, and they didn't have podcasts. If someone wanted to follow Him, he had to let go of everything else in a very literal way to do so.

John 8:30-32 teaches the difference between being a believer and being a disciple:

> As He spoke these words, many believed in Him. Then Jesus said to those Jews who believed Him, "If you abide in My word, you are My disciples indeed. And you shall know the truth, and the truth shall make you free."

All believers have everlasting life, but only disciples experience all of the blessings that are available in this life and in the kingdom to come.

HEBREWS 6

Hebrews 6:4-8 is one of those passages that convinced me of the error of the Calvinistic doctrine of Perseverance of the Saints. Verses 4-5 are as robust a description of believers as any in Scripture: "...those who were once enlightened, and have tasted the heavenly gift, and have become partakers of the Holy Spirit, and have tasted the good word of God and the powers of the age to come," yet the possibility of their falling away is also affirmed.

Arminians take this verse as an argument against eternal security, claiming that people can fall away not only from faith and faithfulness, but from a place of security to one of damnation. This view is forced. The passage does not mention damnation, or even hint at it (see notes on v 8 below). Anyone who ever believes in Jesus is eternally secure no matter what (John 5:24; 6:39-40, 51; 10:27-30; 11:25-26; Rom 11:29; Eph 1:13-14).

Calvinists tend to take this one of three ways. The first common way Calvinists take this passage is that this describes an impossible hypothetical. The "if" of "if they fall away" is taken to mean "if (though it can never happen)."

There are two main problems with this view. Firstly, there is no "if" in the Greek phrase "if they fall away." In fact, it simply adds "and have fallen away" to the list of descriptions in vv 4-5. Secondly, were this accurate, this passage would lose all force. Why would this passage even exist if it describes an impossible situation? God does not warn us of impossible hypotheticals in Scripture.

The second Calvinistic view is that this describes the believer who has "temporary faith." This was the dominant view for centuries but is less common today. The doctrine of temporary faith states that someone may have what he and others believe to be genuine faith (a faith which is actually a gift from God in this view) and produces what seems to be genuine spiritual fruit, but does not persevere until the end of life. The only difference between this faith and genuine faith, according to this doctrine, is that it does not continue until the end of life. This supposedly proves that this person was reprobate (predestined to the lake of fire).

Someone who falls away in this way is seen as the only type of person who can be sure of his eternal destiny before death, namely that he cannot escape the lake of fire, no matter what. Many Reformed Calvinists have considered themselves to be part of this group and have therefore despaired of their eternal destiny. This view paints God as a cruel teaser and has led many into deep depression and even suicide.

Several factors in the text make this view impossible: First, the Bible itself, with the authority of God, calls these people "holy brethren" (3:1). Second, the use of "we" in v 3 strongly implies that the Author of Hebrews considers this warning to apply to himself as well. Third, anyone who believes in Jesus has everlasting life (John 6:47; Acts 16:31; note the aorist tense of "believe") and will not come into judgment to determine his eternal destiny (John 5:24). This would include people with temporary faith. It is our life that is eternal, not necessarily our faith.

The third Calvinistic view is that verses 4-5 do not describe a true believer. This view is very weak because it describes a believer as well as any other passage in the Bible. Someone who is "enlightened" cannot be left in darkness. Someone who has "tasted of the heavenly gift" has received eternal life and the Holy Spirit. (See the same word for "taste" in Heb 2:9 in which the author of Hebrews said Jesus "taste[d] death for everyone." This cannot describe anything but a full experience.) Someone who has "tasted the good word of God and the powers of the age to come" not only receives God's truth, but even has an experience of the power he will have in full in the age to come, the kingdom (compare 2 Cor 3:18 with 1 John 3:2). Yet these believers have fallen away. Fallen away from what? From the basic doctrines described in vv 1-2, especially in this case, forgetting their Christian liberty and their kingdom hope. The eternal destiny of these believers is never mentioned in the passage and is simply not the point. All believers are secure in their eternal destiny, no matter what (John 6:39-40; Rom 11:29).

But it is impossible to renew these brothers to repentance (turning from dead works toward faith in God, see v 1). The word "impossible" here has the place of emphasis in the Greek and is the emphasis of the passage. This is not describing something that is impossible with God, however (nothing is, Matt 19:26), but something that is impossible for us to do. If a brother falls away from grace into legalism, we cannot convince him to return to grace. Only God can do that, and it must come through chastisement (v 7-8).

The phrase "since they crucify again for themselves the Son of God, and put Him to an open shame" from v 6 refers to the fact that by returning to law and denying a future kingdom, they are actually denying the value of Christ's crucifixion and "insult[ing] the spirit of grace" (Heb 10:29). This shames the Son of God. Because of this, falling into legalism is one of the most destructive sins a believer can commit.

Hebrews 6:7-8 is describing by illustration the experience of the believer described in vv 4-6. That believer is like the earth drinking in the rain, and actually bearing useful herbs, and receiving blessing from God, yet still going on later to bear thorns and briers (useless plants that choke out the good). Like that field, this believer needs drastic measures to recover it. The Greek word translated "end" here does not mean eternity, but the "conclusion of an act or state." The state of falling away is concluded with chastisement. A field is not burned in order to destroy the field, but to return it to productivity. This is an illustration of chastisement for the good of the fallen believer. A parallel concept is found in First Corinthians 5.

HEBREWS 10:23-39[121]

No doubt the language used in this passage is scary. God's judgment is a scary thing, but the judgment we are in danger of is not concerning our eternal destiny. It is impossible that we would ever come into that kind of judgment (John 5:24).

The author of Hebrews is again writing to a believing audience, and in this passage, he again includes himself as a recipient of the warning (see "we" in v 26).

Verse 26 alludes to Num 15:30-31, where the Mosaic Law provided no sacrifice to atone for sinning "presumptuously" or, literally "with a high hand." This is significant because of the specific sin that the Author of Hebrews was warning against. These believers were being pressured to abandon Christ and return to the Law of Moses. The Author of Hebrews is warning these believers that the Law of Moses offers no safety for them. To return to the law is to sin presumptuously, an act that carries the penalty of death under the law.

In other words, the Author of Hebrews was saying that if they would put themselves back under the law, they will find no help in the law's sacrifices, but only judgment.

What is the punishment worse than death (v 29)? The Author is intentionally vague about what this may entail. However, the focus on the passage is losing kingdom inheritance (see vv 35-36), which is certainly a punishment worse than death. I for one would much rather die early than miss out on ruling with Christ in His kingdom.

In verse 39, the word for *perdition* simply means destruction and can involve many kinds of destruction. Destruction in the lake of fire should not be assumed when the word *perdition* is used. In addition, "saving of the soul" in this context has to do with having a fulfilled purpose. Kingdom reward is the focus throughout the passage.

SECOND CORINTHIANS 13:5

Paul has affirmed that the people he is writing to are believers throughout the epistle (See 1:1-2, 21; 8:7; and especially 6:14-20—no unbelievers are a part of the "temple of the living God").

---

[121] See J. Paul Tanner, "Hebrews" in *The Grace New Testament Commentary*, Vol 2 (Denton, TX: Grace Evangelical Society, 2010), pp. 1074-75.

The immediate context also shows that Paul is not talking about the Corinthians' need to test themselves to see whether or not they are believers, but to see whether or not Jesus is dynamically working in them. False teachers had been questioning that fact concerning Paul (2 Cor 13:3), and Paul asks the Corinthians to test themselves so that they can affirm that Jesus is working in them. If Paul's ministry resulted in Jesus dynamically living in them, this is proof that Jesus is also active in Paul.

What does "in the faith" mean? In the New Testament, the phrase "in the faith" is consistently used to mean believing and practicing truth (see Acts 14:22; 1 Cor 16:13; Col 2:6-7 and elsewhere). It is appropriate for us believers to test ourselves to see whether or not we are believing and practicing truth. It is not appropriate for believers to test themselves to see whether or not they are eternally saved. For that we are to look only to Jesus.

What does "disqualified" mean? The basic meaning of disqualified is *disapproved*. It simply means not to have God's approval in a practical sense. While every believer stands righteous before God and is adopted into His family, not every believer is living in a way that pleases God and invites His blessing.

For more discussion on these and many other passages related to the Lordship Salvation controversy, see *The Gospel Under Siege* by Zane Hodges, available at www.faithalone.org.

PRACTICE

1) From the Ephesians 1–3 list of things God has done that you made in Lesson 8: Bible Study Method and Application, which of these apply practically to your Christian life? Can you walk by faith, knowing all of those blessings are true if you doubt your salvation? Based on this, is it right that Christians need to be unsure of their eternal salvation to live the Christian life?

2) Read Luke 14:26-33. How can this be reconciled with Rev 22:17?

3) How can John 14:23-24 be reconciled with Rom 3:21-26?

4) What result could the disciple expect from keeping the beatitudes in Matt 5:3-12?

5) Write a paragraph explaining John 8:30-32 in your own words.

DISCUSS

1) How does 1 John 3:9 apply to us when temptation arises?

2) If faith is believing what is true, and we are called to live by faith in the power of the indwelling Christ, how would this be affected by doubts about our salvation?

3) How can we know if we are "in the faith" (2 Cor 13:5)?

4) Can a works-salvation mindset ever lead to holy living? Why or why not?

5) Paul was slandered by people saying his gospel encourages sin. What does this say about the true gospel? (See Rom 3:8).

Life and Liberty

SECTION GOALS

1. To teach the believer about his freedom in Christ and all that implies

2. To help the believer understand the meaning and value of Christ living in him or her

3. To help the believer to discern between spirit and flesh

4. To teach the reader to trust in Christ, not in self

INTRODUCTION

When I was younger I was taught that the Christian life basically comes down to trying really hard and being disciplined. If I was struggling, I wasn't trying hard enough. This never gave me victory over sin, and because I was also taught Lordship Salvation, I was paralyzed by worries about my own salvation. No matter how hard I tried, I failed.

About a year and a half after I learned about Free Grace, I sat in a church service in which my pastor, Dale Taliaferro, explained the Christian life from a Biblical perspective. I was gripped by his message as I had never been before. I learned that I failed because I was trying to do the impossible. I was trying to do what only Christ can do. Instead of trying harder—I tried *really* hard—I needed to quit trying on my own and instead to trust Him.

This had a radical and immediate impact, especially in that I wasn't so miserable all the time. The transformation has continued over the last decade, and I still see that there is too much of me and that there's a great deal more of Him to experience. It gets sweeter all the time, but it's a journey, not a destination.

This section is here to help you get started on that journey if that is what you need, or to continue on from where you are. In short, what this section boils down to is this: Christians are not called to a *changed* life, but to an *exchanged* life. We are not to conform to a certain standard, but to be transformed. When we trust in Him, Christ in us becomes for us everything we need for life and godliness. Through faith, Christ becomes for us the strength, the love, the joy, the peace, the humility, and the holiness we need to live every day in a fallen world. This truth is not merely academic, but real, practical and sufficient for all of our needs.

HELPFUL BOOKS ON LIFE AND LIBERTY

Title	Author	Audience
The Christian's Secret of a Happy Life[121]	Hannah Whitall Smith	All
The Normal Christian Life[122]	Watchman Nee	Intermediate
Sit, Walk, Stand[123]	Watchman Nee	All
What Shall This Man Do?[124]	Watchman Nee	Intermediate
The Overcoming Life[125]	Watchman Nee	All
Humility[126]	Andrew Murray	All
He That is Spiritual[127]	Lewis Sperry Chafer	Intermediate
The Complete Green Letters[128] (this is an excellent work, but be mindful of the influence of Calvinism)	Miles Stanford	Intermediate
The Mystery of Godliness[129]	Major Ian Thomas	All

[122] Hannah Whitall Smith, *The Christian's Secret of a Happy Life* (Uhrichsville, OH: Barbour Publishing, Inc., 1998). Originally published in 1875.

[123] Watchman Nee, *The Collected Works of Watchman Nee: Set 2, Vol. 33, The Normal Christian Life* (Anaheim: Living Stream Ministry, 1993).

[124] Nee, *Sit, Walk, Stand* (Bombay: Gospel Literature Service, 1957).

[125] Nee, *What Shall This Man Do?* (Great Britain: Victory Press, 1961, 1965, 1968).

[126] Nee, *The Overcoming Life* (Anaheim, CA: Living Stream Ministry, 1997).

[127] Andrew Murray, *Humility* (Springdale, PA: Whitaker House, 1982).

[128] Lewis Sperry Chafer, *He That Is Spiritual: A Classic Study of the Biblical Doctrine of Spirituality*, Chafer Memorial Edition (Grand Rapids, MI: Zondervan, 1918, 1967).

[129] Miles Stanford, *The Complete Green Letters* (Grand Rapids, MI: Zondervan, 1975, 1983).

[130] Major Ian Thomas, *The Mystery of Godliness* (Grand Rapids, MI: Zondervan, 1964).

Our Inability, His Ability

"Man's chief care, his highest virtue, and his only happiness, now and through all eternity, is to present himself as an empty vessel in which God can dwell and manifest His power and goodness." *Andrew Murray*[131]

LESSON OBJECTIVES

1. To show that we are incapable of living in a way that pleases God on our own

2. To show that through Christ living in us, we can do all things

3. To show how God accomplished this through our death and resurrection with Christ

INTRODUCTION

The Christian life can be summed up with two phrases from the Bible, "…without Me [Jesus], you can do nothing" (John 15:5), and "I can do all things through Christ who strengthens me" (Phil 4:13).

OUR INABILITY

Believers in Christ are partakers of the Divine nature (2 Pet 1:4). We have been freed from sin as a necessary master (Rom 6:1-14). We have the Almighty God living within (Gal 2:20; Col 1:27). But that does not mean

---

[131] Andrew Murray, *Humility* (Springdale, PA: Whitaker House, 1982), p. 10.

that we are unable to sin or even that we are inherently good. Christians, like everyone else, have sin indwelling their bodies (Rom 7:17) and have nothing good in their flesh (Rom 7:18).

It was to Christians, the eleven faithful disciples, that Jesus said, "... without Me, you can do nothing" (John 15:5). Peter denied Christ a total of six times on the night of His crucifixion.[132] And after raising the dead and healing the sick, he effectively denied the gospel for a time by separating from the Gentile believers in Antioch (Gal 2:11-21).

The fact is, apart from dependence on Christ for His empowering, Christians are not above the description of human corruption in Rom 3:10-18:

As it is written:

"THERE IS NONE RIGHTEOUS, NO, NOT ONE;

THERE IS NONE WHO UNDERSTANDS; THERE IS NONE WHO SEEKS AFTER GOD.

THEY HAVE ALL TURNED ASIDE; THEY HAVE TOGETHER BECOME UNPROFITABLE;

THERE IS NONE WHO DOES GOOD, NO, NOT ONE."

"THEIR THROAT IS AN OPEN TOMB;

WITH THEIR TONGUES THEY HAVE PRACTICED DECEIT";

"THE POISON OF ASPS IS UNDER THEIR LIPS";

"WHOSE MOUTH IS FULL OF CURSING AND BITTERNESS."

"THEIR FEET ARE SWIFT TO SHED BLOOD;

DESTRUCTION AND MISERY ARE IN THEIR WAYS;

AND THE WAY OF PEACE THEY HAVE NOT KNOWN."

"THERE IS NO FEAR OF GOD BEFORE THEIR EYES."

---

[132] When the Gospels are compared, it is clear that Peter denied Christ three times before the rooster crowed once, and three more times before it crowed a second time. See Johnston Cheney, *The Life of Christ in Stereo: The Four Gospels Combined as One* (Portland, OR: Western Baptist Seminary Press, 1969).

Because we are weak and sinful on our own, we could never live in a way that pleases God if we were left to our own strength. In fact, on our own we can't even think in a way that is pleasing to God. This is what Paul meant when he said, "Because the carnal [fleshly] mind is enmity against God; for it is not subject to the law of God, nor indeed can be" (Rom 8:7).

This presents a problem, because the life that we are called to is infinitely higher than the righteousness of the law. We are called to love one another in the way that Christ has loved us (John 13:34). How can we who are selfish, love with a selfless love? We simply don't have the strength.

HIS ABILITY

The good news is that we aren't left to our own strength. In fact, God doesn't expect us to do anything in our own strength. Christ is our strength. He is our love, He is our joy, our peace, our self-control, our sound mind, and everything else we need to live this life in overwhelming victory.

Nothing is too difficult for God, and He cares deeply for you. Jesus told the disciples, "These things I have spoken to you, that in Me you may have peace. In the world you will have tribulation; but be of good cheer, I have overcome the world" (John 16:33). Out of context, this verse might seem unusual in that Jesus was telling the disciples to be of good cheer because He has overcome the world. How does this help them in this situation? But Jesus had just spent three chapters describing and illustrating that after His ascension and the sending of the Holy Spirit, they would be united with Him. He would indwell them and empower them to live this life by His victory.

A few verses from these chapters stand out:

John 14:16-17

> And I will pray the Father, and He will give you another Helper, that He may abide with you forever—the Spirit of truth, whom the world cannot receive, because it neither sees Him nor knows Him; but you know Him, for He dwells with you and will be in you.

14:20

> At that day you will know that I am in My Father, and you in Me, and I in you.

14:21

> He who has My commandments and keeps them, it is he who loves Me. And he who loves Me will be loved by My Father, and I will love him and manifest Myself to him."

14:27

> Peace I leave with you, My peace I give to you; not as the world gives do I give to you. Let not your heart be troubled, neither let it be afraid.

15:5

> "I am the vine, you are the branches. He who abides in Me, and I in him, bears much fruit; for without Me you can do nothing.

16:7

> Nevertheless I tell you the truth. It is to your advantage that I go away; for if I do not go away, the Helper will not come to you; but if I depart, I will send Him to you.

16:13-14

> However, when He, the Spirit of truth, has come, He will guide you into all truth; for He will not speak on His own authority, but whatever He hears He will speak; and He will tell you things to come. He will glorify Me, for He will take of what is Mine and declare it to you.

Christ is the only Person who ever lived a life that was pleasing to God, and only He can do it today. It is our unity with Christ that gives us access to His unlimited holiness, righteousness, love, and power. He becomes for us everything that we need for life and godliness. In ourselves we are nothing; in Him, we lack nothing.

DYING TO SELF

When Christ died on the cross, He took us all with Him. By the cross, God declared that the old creation is done as far as spiritual things are concerned. What this means is that God is not working in us to reform our old self, but to declare it dead and replace it with His Son. This is good news for us, because we are so helpless on our own.

In John 12:24-25, Jesus makes the call for us to die to self: "Most assuredly, I say to you, unless a grain of wheat falls into the ground and dies, it remains alone; but if it dies, it produces much grain. He who loves his life [Greek: *psuchē*] will lose it, and he who hates his life [*psuchē*] in this world will keep it for eternal life [*zoē*]." The word *psuchē* in the Bible is often used to describe the natural life, natural abilities, and natural desires. This is the case here.

If we give up dependence on our natural abilities, we experience Christ's abilities. If we give up our natural desires and desire instead the Lord, He fulfills that desire (Psalm 37:4). When we give up our own lives, we gain an experience of His life (Gal 2:20). This theme of losing self to gain Christ is prevalent throughout the New Testament.

Who can deny that those who love their own minds often descend into some of the stupidest ideas that one can imagine? Nazi Germany was the most educated society in history. Or that those who love their emotions live roller coaster emotional lives? See the high rate of suicide and substance abuse among Hollywood actors. Or that those who live to please their own desires find themselves unfulfilled? "I can't get no satisfaction."

By reckoning ourselves dead to self and alive in Christ, we can experience His life instead of ours.

DEAD TO SIN

If you worked for Bear Stearns in 2007 and the CEO of the company called and said he needed you to come in on Saturday to work, you would be there on time and ready to work until the task he gave you was done. When the CEO calls, you do what he or she says. In 2008, Bear Stearns collapsed. After that, if the same CEO called you and asked you to come in to work on Saturday, you could reply, "I don't work for you anymore" or you could simply not answer the phone. You are free from his demands.

In Rom 6:1-7, Paul makes a similar point regarding our freedom from sin. One quick note about the translation of verse 6: the phrase "done away with" is better translated "rendered unemployed."

> What shall we say then? Shall we continue in sin that grace may abound? Certainly not! How shall we who died to sin live any longer in it? Or do you not know that as many of us as were baptized into Christ Jesus were baptized into His death? Therefore we were buried with Him through baptism

into death, that just as Christ was raised from the dead by the glory of the Father, even so we also should walk in newness of life. For if we have been united together in the likeness of His death, certainly we also shall be in the likeness of His resurrection, knowing this, that our old man was crucified with Him, that the body of sin might be done away with [rendered unemployed], that we should no longer be slaves of sin. For he who has died has been freed from sin.

There are three entities at play: our old man, the body of sin, and sin. There is a hierarchy here that looks like this:

Before the Cross	After the Cross
Sin *is the boss of* ⇩	Sin is the boss of *no one* because ⇩
The old man, *the boss of* ⇩	The old man was *crucified* therefore ⇩
The body of sin	The body of sin is *unemployed*

As this chart shows, the body of sin no longer has a necessary master in sin because the middle man, our old man, was crucified. Because we have been crucified with Christ, we are freed from sin as a necessary master. This is true whether it feels that way or not.

The power of this truth is found when we put Rom 6:6 together with Rom 6:11. It says, "knowing this [all this stuff we've been covering]… reckon yourselves to be dead indeed to sin, but alive to God in Christ Jesus our Lord." We know it's true that we have been crucified with Christ. We must reckon it so.

To reckon means we accept the fact as true and we proceed on that basis. We have died to sin, that is a true fact and we must proceed upon the basis of that truth. We have died to sin. What this means is that with the knowledge that you are freed from sin, you "do not let sin reign in your mortal body, that you should obey it in its lusts. And do not present your members as instruments of unrighteousness to sin, but present yourselves as instruments of righteousness to God" (Rom 6:12-13a).

Before you were in Christ, you had no choice when sin called. Before your reconciliation with God, you were an enemy of God (Rom 5:10) and therefore incapable of pleasing Him (Rom 8:8). Sin was your master and you could do nothing but obey. Now you have a choice and sin is only your master if you let it reign over you. Because we have died, we are free from sin. But we can still walk right up to sin and present ourselves as its slave. Sin is a hard-hearted master who only wants to destroy you and make you miserable. You don't have to serve sin ever again. You have died and you are now free, reckon it so.

ALIVE IN CHRIST

Galatians 2:20 is one of the most potent verses dealing with the Christian life.

> I have been crucified with Christ; it is no longer I who live, but Christ lives in me; and the life which I now live in the flesh I live by faith in the Son of God, who loved me and gave Himself for me.

In this context, freedom from the law is in view; however, this verse does establish a broader principle. We have died with Christ and He is alive in us. This is the power of resurrection by which we are placed into an organic union with Him. Because of this, Paul can say, "Blessed be the God and Father of our Lord Jesus Christ, who has [already] blessed us with every spiritual blessing in the heavenly places in Christ" (Eph 1:3).

In Christ, God has provided for something better than merely struggling through life, pushing all our sinful desires deep down inside, and hoping they do not erupt. He provided for a life which cannot help but please God and overflow with love, joy, peace, longsuffering, kindness, goodness, faithfulness, gentleness, and self-control (Gal 5:22-23). This is what Christ meant when He said, "I have come that they may have life, and that they may have it more abundantly" (John 10:10b). Instead of merely suppressing the sin within us, God wants us to be freed from it entirely and to be able to express the life of Christ within us freely.

A Christian is essentially a vessel for the life of Jesus Christ. Paul says, "we have this treasure in earthen vessels..." (2 Cor 4:7). It isn't that the vessels are any better than they used to be; that is simply not the point. What matters is what is on the inside. Peter says it like this:

> Grace and peace be multiplied to you in the knowledge of God and of Jesus our Lord, as His divine power has given to us all things that pertain to life and godliness, through the knowledge of Him who called us by glory and virtue, by which have been given to us exceedingly great and precious promises, that through these you may be partakers of the divine nature, having escaped the corruption that is in the world through lust. (2 Pet 1:2-4)

You, my brother, my sister, are a partaker of the divine nature. Our natural tendency when we hear that statement is to try to read it away, make it out to be merely "positional" truth rather than "experiential" truth. But God's intention is for us to experience this truth to the fullest. The very life of God is welling up inside you, waiting for you to let it out.

This is not a question of maturity; it's a question of dependence. Do we depend on the natural elements of our being, or do we depend on Jesus Christ Who is alive in us and incapable of even the smallest sin (1 John 3:9)? To depend on Christ takes a completely different way of going about things than what you may have experienced in your life, but that difference is the difference between a heavy burden and an easy yoke. It's all by God's grace. If you believe in Christ to be your love, His love will be expressed. If you believe in Him to be your peace, He will be your peace. The same is true with everything that a godly life requires, because the Lord has not given to us a *part* of the Spirit, but the whole Person, complete with everything we could ever need for life and godliness.

PRACTICE

1) Read 2 Cor 12:9. Do you also rejoice in your weakness?

2) Why can't we just live the best way we know how, trying hard to live according to the Bible's ethical standard? See John 15:5; Romans 7.

3) Read 2 Cor 3:18. What image are we being transformed into? By what power is it done? What is our part in the process?

4) What is the essential truth about receiving God's strength for living as taught by Isa 40:29-31. Is this true for us today?

5) What kind of baptism is being spoken about in Rom 6:1-6, spiritual or water? What impact does this make for our Christian life?

DISCUSS

1) Read John 1:1-3; Col 1:15-18; Hebrews 1; Rev 1:8, 17-18; and
4:8-11. How does knowing that this is the One who lives in
you and offers His whole being to you affect your view of your
personal problems?

2) What does "partakers of the divine nature" (2 Pet 1:4) mean?

3) Billy Graham and Bill Bright are both known to have said, "95%
of Christians live defeated lives." Is this true? Why or why not?

4) I have often heard things like, "If so-and-so were a Christian, he
would make a huge impact." What is wrong with this thinking?
See 1 Cor 1:26-31.

5) *How* do we live by God's power instead of our own?

Liberty

*"Stand fast therefore in the liberty
by which Christ has made us free,
and do not be entangled again with
a yoke of bondage." Galatians 5:1*

LESSON OBJECTIVES

1. To show the contrast between the principles of law and grace
2. To show the believer's personal freedom from the Mosaic Law
   and man-made religious laws

INTRODUCTION

Because we have died to the law, we are no longer bound by it in any way (Rom 7:1-4). This is, as much as anything, a pillar of Paul's gospel. This freedom from the law is not just for justification (our righteous standing before God) but also for sanctification (our walk with the Lord as justified saints). This freedom is not only related to the Law of Moses, but also man-made religious laws.

A quote from Dr. Alva McClain is helpful:

> The Word of God condemns unsparingly all attempts to put the Christian believer "under the law." The Holy Spirit through the Apostle Paul gave to the church the book of Galatians for the very purpose of dealing with this heresy. Read this epistle over and over, noting carefully the precise error with which the writer deals. It is not a total rejection of the gospel of God's grace and a turning back to a total legalism. It is rather the error of saying that the Christian life, having begun by simple faith in Christ, must thereafter continue under the law

or some part of it. This is clear from the apostle's indignant charge: "This only would I learn of you, Received ye the Spirit by the works of the law, or by the hearing of faith? Are ye so foolish? having begun in the Spirit, are ye now made perfect in the flesh?" ([Gal] 3:2-3). Little wonder that he begins the chapter with a cry of astonishment, "O foolish Galatians, who hath bewitched you, that ye should not obey the truth . . .?" ([Gal] 3:1).[133]

FREEDOM FROM THE LAW OF MOSES

As Christians, we have nothing to do with the Law of Moses—including the Ten Commandments (see 2 Cor 3:3-8). We were justified by faith apart from the works of the law (Rom 3:19-24; Gal 2:16), and we are being sanctified apart from the law as well. The reason for this is that the law and grace work by contradictory principles. It should be noted here that the problem is not with the law itself, but with the weakness of the flesh, highlighted by the law. The chart below illustrates this difference.

Law	Grace
Live by Works (Gal 3:12)	Live by Faith (Gal 2:19-21)
Produces Defeat (Rom 7:5-25)	Produces Victory (Rom 6:14)
Weak and Beggarly (Gal 4:9)	Powerful (Heb 7:16) Made Heirs (Gal 4:7)
A Curse (Gal 3:10)	A Blessing (Gal 3:9)
Produces Works of the Flesh (Gal 5:19-21)	Produces Fruit of the Spirit (Gal 5:22-23)
Bondage (Gal 5:1)	Freedom (Gal 5:1)
Estrangement from Christ (Gal 5:4)	Unity with Christ (Eph 2:11-22)
Enmity Between Men (Gal 2:11-14; Eph 2:11-15)	Unity Between Brothers (Gal 3:28; Eph 2:14-15)
Fear of God (Exod 19:17–20:19)	Intimacy with God (John 17:20-26; 1 John 4:18)
Death (Rom 8:6)	Life (Rom 8:2-6)

The Bible could not be clearer that the Christian is not under law, and that the law was indeed *abolished* through the crucifixion of Christ. Some of the more notable passages on this subject are below:

---

[133] McClain, *Law and Grace*, pp. 51-52.

Acts 10:10-16

Then [Peter] became very hungry and wanted to eat; but while they made ready, he fell into a trance and saw heaven opened and an object like a great sheet bound at the four corners, descending to him and let down to the earth. In it were all kinds of four-footed animals of the earth, wild beasts, creeping things, and birds of the air. And a voice came to him, "Rise, Peter; kill and eat." But Peter said, "Not so, Lord! For I have never eaten anything common or unclean." And a voice spoke to him again the second time, "What God has cleansed you must not call common." This was done three times. And the object was taken up into heaven again.

Acts 15:5-12

But some of the sect of the Pharisees who believed rose up, saying, "It is necessary to circumcise them [the Gentile Christians], and to command them to keep the law of Moses." Now the apostles and elders came together to consider this matter. And when there had been much dispute, Peter rose up and said to them: "Men and brethren, you know that a good while ago God chose among us, that by my mouth the Gentiles should hear the word of the gospel and believe. So God, who knows the heart, acknowledged them by giving them the Holy Spirit, just as He did to us, and made no distinction between us and them, purifying their hearts by faith. Now therefore, why do you test God by putting a yoke on the neck of the disciples which neither our fathers nor we were able to bear? But we believe that through the grace of the Lord Jesus Christ we shall be saved in the same manner as they." Then all the multitude kept silent and listened to Barnabas and Paul declaring how many miracles and wonders God had worked through them among the Gentiles.

Romans 6:14

For sin shall not have dominion over you, for you are not under law but under grace.

Romans 7:4-6

Therefore, my brethren, you also have become dead to the law through the body of Christ, that you may be married to another—to Him who was raised from the dead, that we should bear fruit to God. For when we were in the flesh, the sinful passions which were aroused by the law were at work in our members to bear fruit to death. But now we have been delivered from the law, having died to what we were held by, so that we should serve in the newness of the Spirit and not in the oldness of the letter.

Romans 8:2-4

For the law of the Spirit of life in Christ Jesus has made me free from the law of sin and death. For what the law could not do in that it was weak through the flesh, God did by sending His own Son in the likeness of sinful flesh, on account of sin: He condemned sin in the flesh, that the righteous requirement of the law might be fulfilled in us who do not walk according to the flesh but according to the Spirit.

Galatians 2:19–3:5

For I through the law died to the law that I might live to God. I have been crucified with Christ; it is no longer I who live, but Christ lives in me; and the life which I now live in the flesh I live by faith in the Son of God, who loved me and gave Himself for me. I do not set aside the grace of God; for if righteousness comes through the law, then Christ died in vain. O foolish Galatians! Who has bewitched you that you should not obey the truth, before whose eyes Jesus Christ was clearly portrayed among you as crucified? This only I want to learn from you: Did you receive the Spirit by the works of the law, or by the hearing of faith?—Are you so foolish? Having begun in the Spirit, are you now being made perfect by the flesh? Have you suffered so many things in vain—if indeed it was in vain? Therefore He who supplies the Spirit to you and works miracles among you, does He do it by the works of the law, or by the hearing of faith?

Galatians 3:21-25

Is the law then against the promises of God? Certainly not! For if there had been a law given which could have given life, truly righteousness would have been by the law. But the Scripture has confined all under sin, that the promise by faith in Jesus Christ might be given to those who believe. But before faith came, we were kept under guard by the law, kept for the faith which would afterward be revealed. Therefore the law was our tutor to bring us to Christ, that we might be justified by faith. But after faith has come, we are no longer under a tutor.

Galatians 5:1

Stand fast therefore in the liberty by which Christ has made us free, and do not be entangled again with a yoke of bondage.

Galatians 6:15

For in Christ Jesus neither circumcision nor uncircumcision avails anything, but a new creation.

Ephesians 2:14-15

For He Himself is our peace, who has made both [Jews and Gentiles] one, and has broken down the middle wall of separation, having abolished in His flesh the enmity, that is, the law of commandments contained in ordinances, so as to create in Himself one new man from the two, thus making peace.

Colossians 2:13-15

And you, being dead in your trespasses and the uncircumcision of your flesh, He has made alive together with Him, having forgiven you all trespasses, having wiped out the handwriting of requirements that was against us, which was contrary to us. And He has taken it out of the way, having nailed it to the cross. Having disarmed principalities and powers, He made a public spectacle of them, triumphing over them in it.

The list could be extended seemingly forever.

THE PURPOSE OF THE LAW

What then is the purpose of the law? There are several verses that address this question, but I am only going to deal with a few.

Galatians 3:19 (author's translation)

Why, then, the law? It was added with a view toward transgressions, until the Seed should come to whom the promise was made...

This verse is teaching that the law was brought in to bring in transgressions. Sins exist still when there is no law, but when laws are broken, sins become transgressions. In other words, the law was given to make sinners more guilty.

Romans 3:19-20

> Now we know that whatever the law says, it says to those who are under the law, that every mouth may be stopped, and all the world may become guilty before God. Therefore by the deeds of the law no flesh will be justified in His sight, *for by the law is the knowledge of sin.* (Emphasis added.)

This passage teaches that through the law, man's guilt becomes obvious. This is similar to the point made in Gal 3:19. But here Paul adds something important, "by the law is the knowledge of sin." Sin, when it appears in the singular, usually refers not to sins committed, but to the sin which indwells man—the thing within us that drives us toward sinning. The law was given to awaken that monster so that we could know (experientially) the power of indwelling sin.

This is expanded upon in Rom 7:5-8

> For when we were in the flesh, the sinful passions which were aroused by the law were at work in our members to bear fruit to death. But now we have been delivered from the law, having died to what we were held by, so that we should serve in the newness of the Spirit and not in the oldness of the letter. What shall we say then? Is the law sin? Certainly not! On the contrary, I would not have known sin except through the law. For I would not have known covetousness unless the law had said, "YOU SHALL NOT COVET." But sin, taking opportunity by the commandment, produced in me all manner of evil desire. For apart from the law sin was dead.

This passage further explains the purpose of the law in arousing indwelling sin. In the example given, when the law told Paul, "don't covet," coveting all of a sudden became a problem. I call this the "don't touch the cookies" principle. As soon as someone says, "don't touch the cookies," we have cookies on the mind and if we're hungry we are probably going to be hungry for cookies. Indwelling sin makes whatever we can't have attractive to us.

In other words, the law was given to make us more guilty, to condemn, to kill (see Second Corinthians 3). Why is this a good thing? Because it leads us to Jesus and His grace. By the cross we have all been condemned and killed, therefore the law has already fulfilled its purpose. Jesus can now give us justification, eternal life, and complete freedom from self, sin, and law. The law was given so that we could be fully set free through the cross.

This is what Paul meant by, "For I through the law died to the law that I might live to God" (Gal 2:19). The law fulfilled its purpose in him completely and he was utterly dead to it. Now he could instead "live to God."

THE LAW OF CHRIST

Because of the common translation of 1 Cor 9:19-21 (reflected in the NASB), some confusion has arisen about the law of Christ:

> For though I am free from all men, I have made myself a slave to all, so that I may win more. To the Jews I became as a Jew, so that I might win Jews; to those who are under the Law, as under the Law though not being myself under the Law, so that I might win those who are under the Law; to those who are without law, as without law, though not being without the law of God *but under the law of Christ*, so that I might win those who are without law. (NASB, emphasis added)

The phrase "but under the law of Christ" is incorrectly translated. In verse 20, Paul uses the phrase *hupo nomos*, meaning "under law," three times expressing the fact that he is not under law, but he lives as if he were when doing so helps him reach his Jewish brethren (according to the flesh). But when discussing the law of Christ, Paul does not use the phrase *hupo nomos*, but *ennomos Christou* meaning "lawful with respect to Christ." This is an important distinction. Paul makes several strong statements that the Christian is not *under* law—any law.[134] He wrote, "If you are led by the Spirit (and you are), you are not under law" (Gal 5:18, literal translation), and "For sin shall not have dominion over you, for you are not under law but under grace" (Rom 6:14). He does not use the definite article, "the," because he is not referring to the Law of Moses only, but to law as a principle of life.

Paul also says, "For the law of the spirit of life in Christ Jesus has made me free from the law of sin and death" (Rom 8:2), and "Bear one another's burdens, and so fulfill the law of Christ" (Gal 6:2). And James says we are to speak and do "as those who will be judged by the law of liberty" (Jas 2:12). So, "the law of Christ," or "the law of the spirit of life in Christ Jesus" and "the law of liberty" apply to us, but in what way, and what is it?

---

[134] Of course, this discussion is not about civil and criminal laws, but religious ones. Christians are to obey the governing authorities as long as those laws don't come into direct conflict with God's will.

Many take these phrases to refer to all of the commands given to the Church, but this definition is not in keeping with the context in which these phrases appear. Galatians 6:2 calls the spiritual people in the church to restore the sinning brethren, bearing their burdens. James 2:12 refers to recognizing our guilt under the Law of Moses and granting mercy to others rather than condemning them (see 2:10-13). Romans 8:2 is a separate category altogether, referring to natural laws, not commandments. There is a natural law within Paul that he is bent toward sinning despite his best efforts (Rom 7:14-24), but by the Spirit of life in Christ Jesus, he can break free from that natural law and have victory over sin.

So, what is the law of Christ? Simply put, it is the commandments given and expounded upon by Jesus in the Upper Room Discourse in John 13–17. The first is found in 13:34, "A new commandment I give to you, that you love one another; as I have loved you, that you also love one another." The second is, "Let not your heart be troubled; you believe in God, believe also in Me" (John 14:1), in other words, we are to rest in Christ through faith. Jesus puts it another way elsewhere in the sermon, saying, "abide in Me."

Jesus labors to communicate throughout the sermon that loving others the way Christ has loved us is impossible on our own, but by keeping the second commandment, to abide in Him, we will find that commandment not to be burdensome. This is summed up in John 15:5: "I am the vine, you are the branches. He who abides in Me, and I in him, bears much fruit; for without Me you can do nothing."

Loving one another the way Christ has loved us is expressed in many ways, but a couple of these ways are found in the passages which discuss the law of Christ, i.e. the law of liberty. We are to bear one another's burdens in restoring others to a right relationship with God and the Church (Gal 6:1-2) and we are to be merciful to one another (Jas 2:12-13). Both of these passages also treat this as the right outworking of faith (see Gal 5:22-25 and Jas 2:14-17).

John also discusses Christ's commandments in his first epistle. It is a constant theme throughout, but it is summed up in 1 John 3:23: "And this is His commandment: that we should believe on the name of His Son Jesus Christ and love one another, as He gave us commandment." This is precisely what Jesus said in His discourse in John 13–17.

HOW SHOULD WE VIEW THE COMMANDS GIVEN TO THE CHURCH?

This brings us to an important question: how should we view the commands given to the Church, knowing that law as a principle of living leads to being under sin's dominion? If we want to obey God, we must do so by the Spirit, in freedom, and from the heart. We cannot do that if we turn the New Testament into a checklist, a list of laws to live by. Paul labors to communicate the fact that when we view obedience legalistically we are inevitably limited to "the flesh" as a source of power and therefore doomed to fail (see Rom 6:14; 7:5-6; 8:3-8). Victory over sin only comes through the Spirit, and the Spirit works in liberty, "...where the Spirit of the Lord is, there is liberty" (2 Cor 3:17).

So how do we reconcile this with the fact that the New Testament is full of commands? The first thing that we need to understand is that just because something is a command grammatically doesn't mean it's a law. Exhortations are given with the same grammar as a law would be. In the New Testament epistles, commands (grammatically) are always given based upon the truth of our identity in Christ and are intended to point us to walk in a way that is consistent with the fact that we are united with Christ. In the Old Testament Law, this was not the case. Old Testament believers were not united with Christ and these commandments were given without promise of spiritual aid in keeping them.

Colossians 3:9-10 is an excellent example of an exhortation based upon our union with Christ, "Do not lie to one another, since you have put off the old man with his deeds, and have put on the new man who is renewed in knowledge..." Usually the identity truth is established in the first part of the book and the exhortations come after. For example, the exhortation in Eph 4:1-3 is based upon the truth of our unity in Christ which is established in chapters 1–3 and the exhortations in Phil 4:1-3 are based upon what Paul established in chapters 2–3, seen especially in Phil 3:20-21. Taken together, Phil 3:20-4:3 reads:

> For our citizenship is in heaven, from which we also eagerly wait for the Savior, the Lord Jesus Christ, who will transform our lowly body that it may be conformed to His glorious body, according to the working by which He is able even to subdue all things to Himself. Therefore, my beloved and longed-for brethren, my joy and crown, so stand fast in the Lord, beloved. I implore Euodia and I implore Syntyche to be of the same mind in the Lord. And I urge you also, true companion, help

these women who labored with me in the gospel, with Clement also, and the rest of my fellow workers, whose names are in the Book of Life.

The difference between a law and an exhortation is the difference between "do this and live" (cf. Gal 3:12) and "as you are living out the life of Christ, direct it this way." It is the difference between doing something to be right with God and doing something because He has set us right. It is the difference between a responsibility we must meet, and something we must trust God to meet in us. This is a subtle difference, but it is a difference that divides defeat and victory.

As an illustration, try to obey the command "be anxious for nothing" (Phil 4:6) as a law and you will find that you are not only anxious generally but that you are anxious about being anxious. But if we understand that Paul was seeking to comfort us by pointing us to the fact that in reality, because of our union with Christ, we really have nothing to be anxious about, the anxiety falls away, replaced by the peace of God which surpasses all understanding.

WHAT ABOUT OTHER LAWS?

If man is free from the law that God gave, of course we are free from the religious laws that men make as well. We are not only free from the Mosaic Law, but from law as a principle of life. The principle of law means working in our own strength to try to please God. We are free from that entirely. We are instead to live by faith and allow Christ to live His life out in us as we live in freedom. The result is the fruit of the spirit from Gal 5:22-23, "against such there is no law" anyway.

And an honest assessment of religious laws would have to bring in the conclusion that they simply don't work. This is what Paul meant when he said, "These things indeed have an appearance of wisdom in self-imposed religion, [self-imposed] humility, and [self-imposed] neglect of the body, but are of no value against the indulgence of the flesh" (Col 2:23, author's edit).

Life under law simply doesn't work, but life in the Spirit does, overwhelmingly so. Some people may be able to condemn a lifestyle of freedom from law *in principle*, but no one will ever be able to condemn the free life of the Spirit as it is lived out. Why? Because it is a righteous and happy life—it's the kind of life that people long for.

CONCLUSION

I hope that you can say with me that you love God's ways, you love everything about Him and want to live the way He wants you to live. The only way to accomplish that is to walk in the Spirit, by faith, in freedom.

If it makes you nervous to let go of the checklist of laws and walk in true freedom, remember these few things: 1) God is the One who is at work in you "to will and to do for His good pleasure" (Phil 2:13). 2) There is no law against the fruit of the Spirit (Gal 5:22-23). 3) Love is the fulfillment of the law (Rom 13:8, 10; Gal 5:14).

The proof of the doctrine is in the pudding. Peter tells us, "For this is the will of God, that by doing good you may put to silence the ignorance of foolish men—as free, yet not using liberty as a cloak for vice, but as bondservants of God" (1 Pet 2:15-16). Live in freedom, but serve God with a pure heart, demonstrating to the world that the Spirit of Christ is powerful to produce right living.

PRACTICE

1) Read Exod 19:17–20:19, Heb 4:15-16 and 10:20-22. What contrasts do you see?

2) Read Col 2:11-23. What practical points do you see? How do you apply it?

3) Read Gal 2:11-16 and Eph 2:11-18. What effect does the law have upon communities?

4) Read Rom 8:3-4 and Rom 13:8, 10. Based upon this, could someone fulfill the righteous requirement of the law at any time while not being under law?

5) Read Gal 3:22-25. What does this passage mean on a practical level?

DISCUSS

1) Read Gal 5:12. Should we be this bold when defending the Christian's freedom from the law? Why or why not? How does this balance with our call to gentleness?

2) Can law ever produce holiness? Why or why not? See Rom 7:14-25; Col 2:20-23.

3) Why do you suppose people associate holiness with law rather than freedom? How can you help that problem?

4) How can you promote a lifestyle of freedom and righteousness in your church family?

5) How are the two aspects of the Law of Christ (1 John 3:23) related? See John 15:5.

Spirit, Soul, & Body

"Once I met a young brother—young, that is to say, in years, but who had learned a good deal of the Lord. God had brought him through much tribulation to gain that knowledge of Himself. As I was talking with him I said, 'Brother, what has the Lord been teaching you these days?' He replied, 'Only one thing: that I can do nothing apart from Him.' 'Do you really *mean*,' I asked, 'that you can do nothing?' 'Well, no,' he said. 'Of course I *can* do many things! In fact that has been just my trouble. Oh, you know, I have always been so confident in myself. I know I am well able to do lots of things.' So I asked, 'What then do you mean when you say you can do nothing apart from Him?' He answered, 'The Lord has shown me that I *can* do anything, but that *He* has said, 'Apart from me ye can do nothing.' So it comes to this, that everything I have done and can still do apart from Him *is nothing*!" *Watchman Nee*[135]

LESSON OBJECTIVES

1. To describe the human body, soul, and spirit
2. To distinguish between the functions of the soul and spirit
3. To show how this relates to walking in the spirit

---

[135] *The Normal Christian Life*, p. 160-61 [italics in original].

INTRODUCTION

Several times in the New Testament, and at key places in discussions about living the Christian life, we are encouraged to be "led by the Spirit" and to "walk in the spirit" and the like. Yet it's difficult to find Bible teachers with a clear explanation of what that is. Many will say it simply means to try to obey God's rules, but its use in Gal 3:3 makes it clear that this explanation is inadequate.

To understand these phrases, we need to restore the Biblical concept of man. By far the most common view both inside and outside of Christianity is that man is in two parts—material (body) and immaterial (soul/spirit). This is called a bipartite view of man.

The Biblical concept, however, is that man is tripartite, made up of three distinct parts: spirit, soul, and body. There are many verses in the Bible that express this view, and we will cover many of them, but the most obvious examples are:

First Corinthians 2:14-15

> But the natural [Greek: soulish] man does not receive the things of the Spirit of God, for they are foolishness to him; nor can he know them, because they are spiritually discerned. But he who is spiritual judges all things, yet he himself is rightly judged by no one.

First Corinthians 15:44-45

> It is sown a natural [Greek: soulical[136]] body, it is raised a spiritual body. There is a natural [Greek: soulical] body, and there is a spiritual body. And so it is written, "THE FIRST MAN ADAM BECAME A LIVING BEING [Greek: soul]." The last Adam became a life-giving spirit.

First Thessalonians 5:23

> "Now may the God of peace Himself sanctify you completely; and may your whole spirit, soul, and body be preserved blameless at the coming of our Lord Jesus Christ."

Hebrews 4:12

> For the word of God is living and powerful, and sharper than any two-edged sword, piercing even to the division of soul

---

[136] I use "soulical" here and "soulish" in 1 Cor 2:14 above in order to distinguish that which is properly of the soul (as here) with that which is improperly of the soul (as in 1 Cor 2:14).

and spirit, and of joints and marrow, and is a discerner of the thoughts and intents of the heart.

Clearly a distinction between soul and spirit is made in these passages. In addition to the soul and spirit being distinguished in 1 Thess 5:23 and Heb 4:12, Paul's contrast of the two in 1 Cor 2:14 and 15:44-45 would not make sense if they were the same thing.

Here is a simple chart to help us understand this makeup:

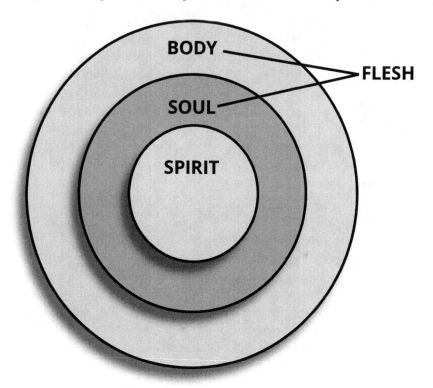

So why do so many consider man to be bipartite? A big part of the problem, as is often the case, is tradition. Because of Augustine's heavy reliance on Plato[137] and Plotinus (a disciple of Plato), and his Manichean[138] background, a bipartite concept of man permeated his writings. Augustine was extremely influential in both the Roman Catholic Church and the

---

[137] Augustine considered Plato's writings to be divinely inspired.

[138] Manicheanism is a heresy similar to Gnosticism in many ways. Augustine was a Manichean before converting to Christianity. Gnosticism also divided man into two parts, material and immaterial.

Reformation.[139] Thomas Aquinas did hold to a form of tripartite man, but this came 800 years later and did not see man as spirit, soul, and body, but rather as body and soul; he believed that the soul contained the animal life or the animating aspect of life, and the intellect. No place was given for a separate spirit. The bipartite view is also supportive of Calvinism, and Calvinism has dominated academic literature for hundreds of years.

Another source of confusion is that in the Bible, the word *soul* (Hebrew: *nephesh*, Greek: *psuchē*) can refer simply to a person (1 Pet 3:20) or to his or her physical life (Jas 5:20). Likewise, the word *spirit* (Hebrew: *ruah*, Greek: *pneuma*) can sometimes be used to refer generally to the immaterial part of man (John 19:30; Jas 2:26). Though some have thought so, this does not mean that they are the same thing. Both are essential parts of the immaterial part of man, and both are essential to human life. If I said someone's heart gave out and that another person's lungs stopped working, you would know that I meant that these people died physically, but you would not assume then that I was saying the heart and the lungs were the same thing.

Dr. Charles Ryrie, a true gentleman and world-class scholar to whom I am indebted a great deal, holds to a Bipartite Unity view. His book *Basic Theology*[140] has a chapter devoted to explaining and defending this view. Unfortunately, his arguments are not in response to the best representation of the tripartite view. Namely, he responds to the possible tripartite view that the spirit is superior to the soul, which is superior to the body. However, the Biblical tripartite view is not that the soul and body are inherently inferior to the spirit, but that they are still awaiting redemption. In the resurrection, sin will be eradicated in us, and we will live as three-part, unified beings with spirit, soul, and body working together in holy unity.

Dr. Ryrie also responds to the tripartite idea that we cannot love the Lord with our soul, but this is also not the best representation of the tripartite view. It is not that the body and soul cannot be holy or love God, but that they cannot be holy or love God on this side of the resurrection *unless they are brought into subjection to the spirit.*

Dr. Ryrie rejects the tripartite view because of the analogy many tripartite believers have expressed—that the three aspects of man reflect the

---

[139] See David R. Anderson, "Another Tale of Two Cities" *Journal of the Grace Evangelical Society* Fall, 2005. Available online at http://faithalone.org/journal/2005ii/anderson.pdf

[140] Charles C. Ryrie, *Basic Theology: A Popular Systematic Guide to Understanding Biblical Truth* (Chicago, IL: Moody Press) 1986, 1999.

Trinity. This is at least partly because he sees the tripartite view as holding that the body and soul are inferior to the spirit. Dr. Ryrie's objection is that this would make one member of the Trinity inferior to another. Both views agree that one member of the Trinity is not inferior to another. That there is a proper chain of command does not suggest inferiority. Within the Trinity, the Spirit is subject to Christ, Who is subject to the Father. Likewise, in man, a chain of command does not suggest inferiority.

Practical experience confirms the Bible's teaching that man is tripartite. If our entire immaterial makeup were one and the Holy Spirit indwells that part of us, we would never have wrong thinking, inner turmoil, pride, or any other sin that emanates from within. Our only struggles would be temptations from the outside which play upon our physical senses.

Failing to recognize the distinction between the spirit and the soul has led to great confusion about the concept of walking in the spirit. If we are to walk in the spirit, and the spirit is equated with our soul (our natural mind, will, and emotion), how is this any different than how the more civilized unbeliever walks? Returning to a Biblical, tripartite concept of man will help us to understand what it is to walk in the spirit.

Because the discussion is often based upon terminology, we miss the real, crucial element to this discussion. The Bible teaches that our bodies and our natural mind, will, and emotions are unreliable, weak, and bent toward sin, and that they must be brought into subjection to the will of God through the power of the indwelling Christ (John 14–16; Rom 3:9-18; 7:11–8:7; 1 Cor 2:9-16; 2 Cor 10:5; Phil 4:6-9; 1 Pet 3:11). Whether a believer holds to a tripartite or bipartite view of man is less important than the recognition of this principle.

Accepting the tripartite nature of man is humbling. To accept it, we must admit that we truly are dependent upon Christ for everything, including being able to think clearly.

As discussed in Lesson 16, Jesus said in John 12:25, "He who loves his [soul] life [Greek, *psuchē*] will lose it, and he who hates his life [*psuchē*] in this world will keep it for eternal [spiritual] life [*zoē*]." I take this to mean that love of our natural abilities—mind, will, and emotion—will lead to losing the very thing we love. Societies that have exalted these aspects have proven this point. No society in the history of the world was more educated than Nazi Germany. Likewise, our emotionally driven society in America today has led to all kinds of social problems and emotional instability.

From my own experience, I can say that when I stopped trusting in my own mind, my thinking became much clearer and the Bible began to make a lot more sense.

I'm convinced that much of the confusion in Bible scholarship today is the result of interpreters trusting in themselves. Paul confirms this in Gal 5:19-20 when he calls "dissentions" and "heresies," "works of the flesh." This is why theological error is nearly always supportive of prideful boasting, even if subtly so. Lordship Salvation is a good example (see Eph 2:8-9); the health, wealth, and prosperity gospel[141] is another.

WHAT IS THE BODY?

The body is the material part of man, and it is the means by which we interact with the world. The body senses and responds to all kinds of physical stimuli. Touch, taste, smell, sight, and hearing are senses by which we take in those stimuli.

The body is indwelt by sin (Rom 7:17, 23), and sin uses these stimuli, along with the body's natural needs (food, shelter, sexual satisfaction, etc.) to create external temptation.

THE HUMAN SOUL

The simplest way to describe the soul is that the soul is the self-life. This can be seen in many passages in which the word *psuchē* is used (Matt 10:39; Mark 8:35; John 12:24-25). All of your natural abilities and talents (other than the physical ones) are functions of the soul.

It should be noted here that the word *flesh* (Greek, *sarx*) or *carnal* (the related Greek word, *sarkos*) sometimes refers not to the body alone, but to the soul as well. This is especially true with regards to the natural mind. One example is Rom 8:7: "Because the carnal [Greek, *sarkos*] mind is enmity against God; for it is not subject to the law of God, nor indeed can be." Our bodies have a brain, but they do not have a mind, so the phrase "carnal mind" is a reference to this aspect of the soul.

The soul's function can be divided into three main parts: mind, will, and emotion.

---

[141] The health, wealth, and prosperity gospel is the false teaching that Christians will definitely be blessed with material things if they exhibit faith.

Mind: Lamentations 3:20; John 10:24; Phil 1:27 (the word *psuchē* is translated as mind here); Jas 3:15 (The word translated "sensual" here is literally "soulish.")

Will: Job 7:15; Psalms 27:12; 35:25 (LXX); Rev 18:14

Emotion: Mark 14:34; Acts 2:43

The natural mind is especially distrusted in the Bible. James 3:14-15 is one clear example:

> But if you have bitter envy and self-seeking in your hearts, do not boast and lie against the truth. This wisdom does not descend from above, but is earthly, sensual (Greek: *soulish*), demonic.

This is written to Christians, so we must understand by this that even in believers the soul's "wisdom" is geared toward "bitter envy" and "self-seeking," and is associated with earthly and demonic wisdom.

In 1 Cor 2:14, Paul says that "the [soulish] man cannot receive the things of the Spirit of God, for they are foolishness to him; nor can he know them, because they are spiritually discerned." Commentators often limit this to a description of unbelievers, but this is not the most natural reading of the Greek and is based largely on the English translation "natural" which is a bit forced, but common here. Only a few short verses later, the Corinthian believers are described as "carnal," which is clearly a close synonym for "soulish" (this can be seen in their inability to receive spiritual truths, see 1 Cor 3:1-2, compare 1 Cor 2:14 above). Paul uses "soulish" in 2:14 because he is distinguishing between the functions of soul and spirit, and he uses "carnal" in 3:1-4 because it is a broader description (a person can also be carnal by being driven by their physical desires).

The reason "the soulish man cannot receive the things of the Spirit of God" is because the Spirit of God humbles us and glorifies Christ. Our soul, our natural selves, puffs up at the suggestion.

The natural self can only be brought into subjection to the will of God through the power of the indwelling Holy Spirit, and the Holy Spirit is never in the Bible said to indwell a person's soul—nor is the impression ever given that there is any close association between the two.

THE HUMAN SPIRIT

The believer's human spirit is the dwelling place of the Holy Spirit (Rom 8:9-16; 1 Cor 3:16; 6:17, 19; Gal 3:2-3) and has the basic functions of conscience, spiritual leading, and communion.

CONSCIENCE (ACTS 17:16; ROM 8:16; 9:1):

Conscience is essentially knowing that a moral action is wrong without needing to reason why it is wrong. Some who recognize the tripartite nature of man consider the conscience to be a function of the soul because the conscience can be "weak" (1 Cor 8:7-12). However, a comparison of Rom 8:16 and 9:1 along with Acts 17:16 seems to suggest that the conscience is a function of the spirit. Either way, we are always to obey our conscience because we cannot be walking in faith and disobeying our conscience at the same time (Rom 14:23).

The proper function of conscience for believers is very different from guilt. Conscience is the conviction of what needs to be done and a warning against wrong. Conscience also leads us to confession of sins and looking to Christ for forgiveness. Guilt remains after the sin has been properly dealt with and prolongs interruption in fellowship with God. Guilt is not from God.

SPIRITUAL LEADING (MARK 2:8, JOHN 11:33; ACTS 16:6-7; 18:5; 20:22-23; 1 COR 2:9-16):

One of the functions of the human spirit is to receive leading from the Holy Spirit. When the Bible does not speak to a specific issue or circumstance, yet the Lord has a preference for us, He communicates that to us spiritually. This has been called leading by impression or intuition, but these phrases are problematic because they fail to distinguish between the Spirit's leading and emotions or instinctual impressions. The Bible uses the phrase "led by the Spirit [or spirit]" (Matt 4:1; Luke 4:1; Rom 8:14; Gal 5:18), so I prefer the term *spiritual leading*.

Acts 16:6-7 and 20:22-23 form great examples of spiritual leading. There are some questions about how often the Holy Spirit leads in this way; some say it is rare in the life of the believer, some say that it is a regular occurrence, some say that this no longer occurs at all. This question is addressed in Gal 5:25, "If we live in the Spirit, let us also walk in the

Spirit." This verse uses a special word for "walk" which essentially means *to march in step*. This suggests that life in the Spirit is an ongoing and constant, step-by-step thing.

Some have the concern that dependence on the Spirit's leading puts the believer in danger of being led by his emotions. No doubt many people attribute their emotional ups and downs to the Spirit's leading. However, spiritual leading and emotion are actually quite different and abuses of truth should not lead us to reject that truth. Essentially, the Spirit leads us toward certain actions that are within our liberty in Christ by conviction that a certain action is needed. My mentor and former pastor told me of a time when he was teaching as a guest Bible study teacher and he had a conviction not to tell a certain joke that he often told and ignored that conviction. It turns out that the joke was perceived to make light of a serious situation that group had just gone through. As a result, the class was emotionally disturbed and had a difficult time learning from him. The Holy Spirit knew what my mentor could not have known, so He gave him a conviction. As you can see, this is not an emotional process at all and it was related to directing him within an area of Christian liberty, not an area to which the Bible had already spoken.

Related to this is spiritual discernment. This is essentially having a conviction about the truth or error of something without having full knowledge of why something is true or false.

All conservative scholars agree that the Holy Spirit is working in the world to convict the world of certain truths, namely that they are not rightly related to God in areas of sin, righteousness, and judgment because they don't believe in Jesus (John 16:7-8). But not all agree that the Holy Spirit works in the *believer* to convict him of truths. First Corinthians 2:9-16 seems to teach that the Holy Spirit likewise communicates with believers spiritually.

First Corinthians 2:14 is mentioned above, but it is helpful to look at 2:12-15 together:

> Now we have received, not the spirit of the world, but the Spirit who is from God, that we might know the things that have been freely given to us by God. These things we also speak, not in words which man's wisdom teaches but which the Holy Spirit teaches, comparing spiritual things with spiritual. But the natural man does not receive the things of the Spirit of God, for they are foolishness to him; nor can he know them,

because they are spiritually discerned. But he who is spiritual judges all things, yet he himself is rightly judged by no one.

The Greek phrase translated here as "comparing spiritual things with spiritual" is a bit enigmatic. It is, most literally, "combining spiritual spiritual." And it is probably expressing the idea of communicating spiritual things with spiritual people. This is especially likely because verse 12 expressly says that the Holy Spirit was given so "that we might know the things that have been freely given to us by God."

This also seems to match experience. All who interact regularly with teachers about Biblical things have had experiences when a teacher has made a statement regarding some spiritual thing and they either know that it is true or that it is false, even if they can't explain why. The Holy Spirit simply convicts those people regarding truth. For example, when I first heard of Free Grace through Zane Hodges, I was reluctant because of many social pressures and internal confusion, but I had a conviction that it was true. Likewise, when I was younger and was ambushed by Church of Christ teachers who wanted to convince me of baptismal regeneration,[142] I had a strong conviction that what they said was false, even though I couldn't explain why. I didn't yet have the training, but the Lord was protecting me. The Bible confirms those convictions.

When we have such an impression that something is either true or false, Scripture is still the final say and we need to be diligent workers, rightly dividing the truth. The Spirit never leads us in a way that is inconsistent with the Bible. But if we have a conviction that something is true, we should search the Scripture to see if it is so. When we have a conviction that a proposition is false, we should search the Scripture to test that proposition.

Spiritual discernment is the reason why some fundamental truths elicit such an emotional response from some believers who are caught in error. If there were no conviction of its truth, those people could respond calmly. Instead, because they are held captive by Satan with regard to that issue (2 Tim 2:23-26), emotions well up to crowd out the conviction. This is one reason we must get our emotions under the control of the Spirit. See the following lesson for a Biblical understanding of how to do that.

Spiritual leading is a very important part of God's dealing with us because we have a limited scope of knowledge. We do not know the circumstances of others' lives, or how they will respond to different statements, but God does. If a conviction comes in saying, "don't tell that joke

---

[142] Baptismal regeneration is the false teaching that water baptism is required for regeneration.

right now" or "use this verse instead of that one to encourage this person," unless the Bible says otherwise, follow the conviction.

A note of caution: waiting on the Spirit's leading is often used as an excuse not to do a good thing when the Bible has already told us God's will. The Spirit is not given to encourage inaction. If the Bible says to do something, or if it is a clear opportunity to do good to someone that does not conflict with other present opportunities, just do it. There is no reason to wait on a spiritual conviction when the Lord has already revealed His will. "Therefore, as we have opportunity, let us do good to all, especially to those who are of the household of faith" (Gal 6:10).

COMMUNION (LUKE 1:47; JOHN 4:23; ROM 1:9; 7:6; 1 COR 14:15):

The Father, the Son, and the Spirit are persons, not impersonal forces or collections of attributes. The function of communion is essentially fellowship with, and worship of, God. It is experiencing a relationship with the Persons of the Godhead. It is a simple concept, but the depth of its experience cannot be exhausted.

CONCLUSION

Walking in the spirit is often placed in contrast to law-living in the Bible (Rom 7:5-6; Gal 3:1-3; 5:16-25 and many other places). This is because law-living is a dependence on your natural abilities to obey God. To walk in the spirit, by contrast, is to place no confidence in yourself and place all confidence in God to guide you every step of the way.

What it all boils down to is this: don't trust in yourself, trust in God. Knowing ourselves so that we have a good understanding of what is of us and what is of God helps us to be able to place our confidence only in God.

Even if you are smart, don't trust your mind simply because it is of yourself. Smart people, even smart people who spend all their time studying the Word, can still think really stupid things. The "bitter envy" and "self-seeking" described in Jas 3:14-15 is plainly evident in more than a little bit of theological discourse, where name-calling, misrepresenting and demonizing others, and arrogance are commonplace. Nearly everyone who participates in this sort of theological discourse is both intelligent and versed in Scripture, and the dark side of it should serve as a warning.

If you typically desire to do good, don't trust your will to bring about the performance of that good (Rom 7:14-25).

If you typically have warm and pleasant emotions toward others, don't trust in that either because feelings can be greatly changed by circumstances.

PRACTICE

1) Throughout history, people have worked to develop communion with God through asceticism, chanting, and saying certain phrases. These are all attempts at using physical means to control spiritual things. By contrast, how does Rom 8:3-7 teach us to live according to the spirit?

2) Though the phrase "in the spirit" doesn't appear in John 14:21 or Eph 3:14-19, how do these passages relate to walking in the spirit? What do they teach we must do to walk in the spirit?

3) Read John 4:23. Why does Jesus mention both spirit and truth as necessary for true worship?

4) Why are regulations "of no value against the indulgence of the flesh" (Col 2:20-23)? (Hint, see Rom 7:5–8:7.)

5) Read Acts 1:8; 11:11-12; 13:1-4; 16:6-10; and 19:21. What do we learn from the circumstances in which the Spirit led in these verses?

DISCUSS

1) Why are law-living and spirit-living contrasted in Scripture?

2) Read Gal 5:18-25. Why does our freedom from law discussed in this passage flow out from our being led by the Spirit?

3) How can you discern between the Spirit and your own natural mind?

4) How can you discern between the Spirit and your emotions?

5) Read John 14:21. Does this verse teach us anything about living in the spirit? (Hint: see Practice, Question 5.)

Emotions

"Let not your heart be troubled..." John 14:1

LESSON OBJECTIVE

1. To show in the Bible how God delivers us from troubled hearts and gives us peace and joy

INTRODUCTION

Emotions are probably the one area of life in which most Christians find their biggest struggle, and even fail miserably.

Some believers have no idea that God even cares about our emotional lives. Others think that they are on their own when it comes to trying to keep their hearts under control. Both seem to have their emotional lives driven by circumstance.

But, in John 13–17, on the night before Jesus was crucified, He was greatly concerned with His disciples' emotional well-being.

THE SETTING OF THE PASSOVER MEAL

Let's put ourselves in the disciples' place for a moment, and see what was going on from their perspective.

The disciples have all left everything to follow Jesus.

The disciples have been kicked out of the synagogue for confessing that Jesus is the Christ (John 9:22; 12:42). The synagogue is the social hub of the culture as well as the religious hub, so they are significantly cut off from society.

Their lives are threatened by the religious leaders (John 11:8-16).

This, however was all okay because they are expecting Jesus to set up the kingdom right then. He had already come into Jerusalem, riding on a donkey's colt (see Zech 9:9) to shouts of "Hosanna! 'BLESSED IS HE WHO COMES IN THE NAME OF THE LORD!' The King of Israel!" (John 12:13). To the Jews, these were signs that the kingdom was coming immediately.

THE PASSOVER MEAL

This brings us to the Passover meal. After washing the disciples' feet, Jesus says something the disciples did not expect. "Most assuredly, I say to you, one of you will betray Me" (John 13:21). Each of the disciples asked, "Lord, is it I?" (Matt 26:22).

Then Jesus added to it by saying that He is going away and that they cannot follow Him (John 13:33-36). What else did they have from a circumstantial perspective? They had nothing and nowhere to go, and even their safety was in jeopardy.

Lastly, Jesus said that the leader among the disciples, Peter, would deny Him that very night.

Peter believed that his commitment was absolute, that he was willing to lay down his life for Jesus. But the reality was, at least for the moment, far from it. His denial would be direct and repeated. In fact, comparing the various accounts in the gospels shows that Peter denied Jesus a total of six times that night, three before the rooster crowed once, and three more times before it crowed again. What a crushing thought.

The very next words out of the Lord's mouth didn't reflect disappointment or anger at Peter's upcoming denial. Jesus was concerned with Peter's and the rest of the disciples' emotional well-being. "Let not your heart be troubled," He said (14:1).

This is a command.

But Jesus did not leave them with a command only, but left them with every help they would need to obey it. And how ridiculous would it be to tell a group, "stop being upset" as their whole lives come crashing down around them and not help them to overcome those feelings?

THE SOLUTION

So if the disciples were not called to wrestle their own emotions down, what was their responsibility? Jesus spent the next four chapters talking about what He would do to help them, but He summed up their responsibility in the next phrase: "you believe in God, believe also in Me" (John 14:1). We know that the eleven faithful disciples who made up Jesus' audience were already believers (John 2:11, 13:30) who already possessed eternal life. Jesus' focus here was a continued and matured belief in Jesus to meet all of their spiritual needs.

No passage of the Bible describes in detail the attributes, character, and desires of all three Persons of the Trinity like John 13–17. Twenty-three times in John 14 alone, Jesus uses the word "Father." Jesus' unity with the Father and the Holy Spirit is stressed (John 14:7, 9-11, 16-20; 15:23; 16:13-15, 27, 32; 17:5-10, 21-26). This unity is especially manifested in the Godhead's unending love for the disciples.

Furthermore, the unity that is described between Father, Son, and Holy Spirit is offered to the disciples as well (every believer in Christ has God living within [Rom 8:9, Col 2:6]; the focus of this passage is an experience of that fact):

John 14:20-21

> "At that day you will know that I am in My Father, and you in Me, and I in you. He who has My commandments and keeps them, it is he who loves Me. And he who loves Me will be loved by My Father, and I will love him and manifest Myself to him."

John 15:5

> "I am the vine, you are the branches [a vine and its branches are united—where does a vine end and its branches begin?]. He who abides in Me, and I in him, bears much fruit; for without Me you can do nothing."

John 17:20-26

> "I do not pray for these alone, but also for those who will believe in Me through their word; that they all may be one, as You, Father, are in Me, and I in You; that they also may be one in Us, that the world may believe that You sent Me. And the glory which You gave Me I have given them, that they may be one just as We are one: I in them, and You in Me; that they

may be made perfect in one, and that the world may know that You have sent Me, and have loved them as You have loved Me. Father, I desire that they also whom You gave Me may be with Me where I am, that they may behold My glory which You have given Me; for You loved Me before the foundation of the world. O righteous Father! The world has not known You, but I have known You; and these have known that You sent Me. And I have declared to them Your name, and will declare it, that the love with which You loved Me may be in them, and I in them."

The disciples can be united with God and one with each other in God.

For this reason, I interpret John 14:2, "In My Father's house are many mansions [literally, dwellings]; if it were not so, I would have told you. I go to prepare a place for you," differently than many others. One other time in John, the phrase "My Father's house" appears, and it is not about heaven. In 2:16, the phrase "My Father's house" refers to the temple, which we later learn is His body (v 21). Are we promised a place in heaven? Of course we are. But this is not something new to the disciples (John 6:39). Jesus was speaking about their place in His Body, the Church. This is the focus of the entire Upper Room Discourse in John (chapters 13–17). His unity with them, not the promise of heaven, is the answer to the disciples' troubled hearts.

Some have pointed to 14:3, "And if I go and prepare a place for you, I will come again and receive you to Myself; that where I am, there you may be also," as evidence that heaven is intended, assuming that Jesus is referring to His return to take His throne in the kingdom. But 14:16-18 show us that Jesus is referring to coming to them by sending His Spirit:

And I will pray the Father, and He will give you another Helper, that He may abide with you forever—the Spirit of truth, whom the world cannot receive, because it neither sees Him nor knows Him; but you know Him, for He dwells with you and will be in you. I will not leave you orphans; I will come to you.

Jesus will return physically, and bring His disciples (and all believers) into glory, but that is not the focus of this passage. Jesus is focusing on His indwelling their hearts through the Holy Spirit.

Jesus says explicitly, "Peace I leave with you, My peace I give to you; not as the world gives do I give to you. Let not your heart be troubled, neither let it be afraid." (14:27), letting us know that the answer to the disciples' troubled hearts is not a circumstantial change, the only way the world gives peace. The answer is that He will give them His peace, by giving them Himself.

Jesus said, "It is to your advantage that I go away, for if I do not go away, the Helper will not come to you" (John 16:7). If your view of the Christian life doesn't see the indwelling Holy Spirit as an advantage over having Christ Himself walking around with you daily, then you are not recognizing the value of our oneness with Christ through the Spirit.

This brings us to the fruit of the Spirit in Gal 5:22-23: "But the fruit of the Spirit is love, joy, peace, longsuffering, kindness, goodness, faithfulness, gentleness, self-control..." All of these things describe the nature of God, and if we live by the Spirit, letting Christ replace us, His life, full of love, joy, and peace, becomes ours. This is how Christ can promise His peace (John 14:27), love (15:5-12), and joy (15:11; 17:13) to the disciples despite their unbelievably bad circumstances.

Paul reflects the very same phenomenon in 2 Cor 1:3-7:

> Blessed be the God and Father of our Lord Jesus Christ, the Father of mercies and God of all comfort, who comforts us in all our tribulation, that we may be able to comfort those who are in any trouble, with the comfort with which we ourselves are comforted by God. For as the sufferings of Christ abound in us, so our consolation also abounds through Christ. Now if we are afflicted, it is for your consolation and salvation, which is effective for enduring the same sufferings which we also suffer. Or if we are comforted, it is for your consolation and salvation. And our hope for you is steadfast, because we know that as you are partakers of the sufferings, so also you will partake of the consolation.

In the Greek, the words for comfort (*paraklēsis*), suffer (*pathēma*), and tribulation (*thlipsis*) appear redundant, so the translators have tried to add variety by using words like consolation, and trouble. Repeatedly, Paul shows that suffering and tribulation bring in comfort. Not because suffering is desirable, but because through suffering we find ourselves in greater dependence on Christ and in that we find the fullness of joy.

THE VINE AND THE VINEDRESSER[143]

This brings us to the True Vine analogy in John 15:1-12. This analogy has been badly butchered by people trying to read a justification context into it. Only the eleven faithful disciples are present and there is no possibility of their losing eternal life. Furthermore, Jesus' focus is helping them to not have a troubled heart and threatening them with the lake of fire would be counter-productive to say the least.

In verse 2, "Every branch in Me that does not bear fruit He takes away; and every branch that bears fruit He prunes, that it may bear more fruit," the word for "takes away" is the Greek *airō,* "I lift up," not *aireō,* "I take away." A better translation of the verse is found in the marginal reading of the NKJV: "Every branch in Me that does not bear fruit He lifts up; and every branch that bears fruit He prunes, that it may bear more fruit."

This also matches the viticulture practices in the Middle East (both now and in ancient times), where, due to extreme temperatures, grapevines grow on the ground, rather than on raised wires. This is usually an effective way for grapes to grow. However, some branches send out small, thin roots that dig shallowly into the ground. These branches cease to depend on the main vine for sustenance, and live instead on what nutrients they can get directly from the ground. The result is either no fruit, or small, bitter grapes. The vinedresser then goes and props up those branches using a rock and a stick so that the branch must depend on the vine for nutrients. This results in a much greater production of fruit.

The question, then, is what does it mean to be lifted up? Many believe that this means to be encouraged, and this certainly may be the case. However, when we compare the analogy to the historical situation another possible interpretation arises. The problem that is being corrected by lifting up the branches is that the branches that do not bear fruit are depending on the earth's insufficient sustenance. The possibility of this is then removed so that the main vine's life could flow freely.

Likewise, the disciples had all of their connections with the world removed so that no source of comfort would remain other than the life of Christ. If this is what the analogy means, we can see that the disciples' terrible circumstances were actually the loving care of the Vinedresser.

The cares of the world are hindrances to our love, joy, and peace. When something in our lives keeps us from depending on Christ, many times

---

[143] For more information and a slightly different perspective, see Gary Derickson, "Viticulture and John 15:1-6" *Journal of the Grace Evangelical Society* (Spring 2005).

the very best thing that God can do for us is to remove it. I have an old friend who made a fortune in foreign stocks and later lost it all. He is one of the most humble and sweet-spirited men I have ever known, and his loss of the world's treasures was one experience God used to build that aspect of Christ's life into him. Thank God for loss when it means we gain Christ. It is far better to live in a cardboard box or in a Roman prison and have Christ's perfect love, joy, and peace manifested in us, than to live in a fancy mansion, dependent upon circumstances for happiness.

And it is even better when love, joy, and peace drive us to an effective mission.

EMOTIONS AND MISSION

We do not belong to ourselves. We have been given a mission to share Christ with the world. This is to be done through active sharing (Acts 1:8), through demonstration of doing good (1 Pet 2:15), and through perfect love being shared among brothers (John 13:35; 17:23). Jesus focuses on the latter in the Upper Room. The first reference is John 13:35, "By this all will know that you are My disciples, if you have love for one another." The other reference is 17:23, "I in them, and You in Me; that they may be made perfect in one, and that the world may know that You have sent Me, and have loved them as You have loved Me." Oneness among brethren demonstrates Christ to the world.

As I mentioned earlier, a troubled heart can keep us from our mission. Perhaps the most prevalent way this is so, is that we can often let a troubled heart wreck relationships. Nothing is more devastating to the perceived validity of the gospel than Christians bickering. And nothing is more powerful as proof of the gospel than brothers doing what people don't do—putting others before themselves and humbling themselves in order to build, maintain, and repair relationships.

But in order to do this, we need to take hold of the provision God has made for comforting our troubled hearts. Troubled hearts keep us focused upon ourselves, our problems, our needs, our rights being violated. But in peace, we can see the needs of others and truly love them as Christ has loved us.

CONCLUSION

Christ commands us not to let our hearts be troubled, but, as always, His command comes with the full provision we need to accomplish it. No matter the circumstances, Christ's provision for joy and peace is ours because circumstances cannot change the fact that Christ Himself is within us.

When our circumstances seem crazy and out of control, it may very well be the Father's loving and careful hand lifting us as a vinedresser lifts a vine to cause it to depend upon the main vine for sustenance. This is good for us. Take comfort that this Vinedresser loves you as He works.

Lastly, we need to consider this command, to receive God's comfort, as being of great importance. The effectiveness of our mission depends upon it.

PRACTICE

1) What are some other passages that let us know that God cares about our emotional lives?

2) Are you holding onto bitterness, anger, unforgiveness, worry, or some other emotional turmoil? If so, pray for Christ's empowerment to overcome those feelings, knowing that He cares for you and wants you to cast your cares on Him (1 Pet 5:7).

3) How does 2 Cor 11:22-28 help us to understand 2 Cor 1:3-7?

4) Given Christ's love for the Apostles, why do you suppose they all suffered so much?

5) How do the deeds of the flesh in Gal 5:19-21 illustrate the need to let go of our troubled hearts?

DISCUSS

1) Is it better to suffer with joy or to be comfortable and miss out on His joy? Why?

2) Is it sometimes difficult to realize that it is better to have the indwelling Holy Spirit than having Christ physically with us? Why or why not?

3) How do troubled hearts keep us from fulfilling our mission?

4) Love is not an emotion. Love is humbly putting others before yourself (1 Cor 13:4-8a). But how might having a troubled heart keep us from loving others?

5) Has God ever led you to more peace through loss?

Humility

"For who is greater, he who sits at the table, or he who serves? Is it not he who sits at the table? Yet I am among you as the One who serves." Luke 22:27

LESSON OBJECTIVES

1. To show that God is humble
2. To define humility
3. To show that we should also be humble

INTRODUCTION

People do not usually think of God as humble. In fact, many Christian teachers argue forcefully that He is not and that He should not be. However, John 1:14 and 18 tell us, "And the Word became flesh and dwelt among us, and we beheld His glory, the glory as of the only begotten of the Father, full of grace and truth," and, "No one has seen God at any time. The only begotten Son, who is in the bosom of the Father, He has declared Him." By this we know that Jesus Christ was in the world manifesting and declaring God's true nature in such a way that can be understood by men.

Thus, if the Bible teaches that Jesus Christ is humble, God is humble.

HUMILITY IN THE TRINITY

For all of eternity, the Three Persons of the Blessed Trinity have lived in humble love toward one another: the Father seeking the glory of the

Holy Spirit and the Son; the Son seeking the glory of the Father and the Spirit, and the Holy Spirit seeking the glory of the Father and the Son.

That the Father wants to glorify the Son is revealed in that Christ is preeminent over all things:

> He is the image of the invisible God, the firstborn over all creation. For by Him all things were created that are in heaven and that are on earth, visible and invisible, whether thrones or dominions or principalities or powers. All things were created through Him and for Him. And He is before all things, and in Him all things consist. And He is the head of the body, the church, who is the beginning, the firstborn from the dead, that in all things He may have the preeminence. (Col 1:15-18)

In the creations, both old and new (the New Creation is the Church), and in God's plan for the ages, God's desire to exalt the Son is plainly revealed. In Heb 1:2, we learn that the Father made the ages (Greek *aiōnas*) through Christ.

Yet, though the Father's desire is to exalt the Son, the Son sought to exalt the Father through His humble submission. Philippians 2:5-11a says:

> Let this mind be in you which was also in Christ Jesus, who, being in the form of God, did not consider it robbery to be equal with God, but made Himself of no reputation, taking the form of a bondservant, and coming in the likeness of men. And being found in appearance as a man, He humbled Himself and became obedient to the point of death, even the death of the cross. Therefore God also has highly exalted Him and given Him the name which is above every name, that at the name of Jesus every knee should bow, of those in heaven, and of those on earth, and of those under the earth, and that every tongue should confess that Jesus Christ is Lord...

Though Christ was for eternity equal with the Father, He became obedient to Him, and made Himself a servant. In turn, the Father has assured that Jesus will be given "the name which is above every name" and that every creature everywhere will confess His lordship. And yet, even this is "to the glory of God the Father" (2:11b). Through humble submission, the Son gives the Father opportunity to express His humble love. In so doing, the Father is exalted as well.

GOD'S HUMILITY EXPRESSED IN JESUS

It is not merely God's power and holiness that we see in Jesus, but also His love and humility.

Humility is expressed in loving others and putting them ahead of ourselves (this is the natural outworking of looking to God and not at ourselves). This is the easiest way for us to see how Christ modeled humility for us.

Luke 2:22-24 says:

> Now when the days of her [Mary's] purification according to the law of Moses were completed, they [Mary and Joseph] brought Him to Jerusalem to present Him to the Lord (as it is written in the law of the Lord, "Every male who opens the womb shall be called holy to the LORD"), and to offer a sacrifice according to what is said in the law of the Lord, "A pair of turtledoves or two young pigeons."

The normal sacrifice for presenting a child in the temple was a lamb, but provision was made for poor families to bring "two turtledoves or two young pigeons" (Lev 12:8). The fact that Mary and Joseph offered a "pair of turtledoves or two young pigeons" when they presented Jesus in the temple shows us that when Christ came into the world, He was born into a poor family. Normally, we do not get to choose who our parents are, but God did choose Jesus' earthly mother and step-father. Jesus could have come as the Son of a queen or a wealthy dignitary, but He came into a family that couldn't even afford to offer a lamb as a sacrifice. From the moment Jesus was conceived, He was already choosing humility.

When Jesus was led by the Holy Spirit into the wilderness to be tempted by Satan, He fasted for forty days and forty nights. Certainly Jesus had a right to eat, yet He gave up His rights and obeyed God instead. And when Satan tempted Jesus, he tempted Him by offering Him things that were rightfully His—food, angelic protection, revelation of Who He is, and the world as His kingdom. But Jesus was not seeking His own rights. He was seeking only God's will.

On the night before Jesus' crucifixion, while the disciples were arguing amongst themselves about who is the greatest (Luke 22:24), Jesus took off His outer garment (appearing as a slave), girded Himself with a towel, bent down, and washed the disciples' feet (John 13). The One who spoke their feet into existence, Who upholds them by the power of His might, Who was born to be King of the universe, became a servant of His creation. Furthermore, He washed the feet of His betrayer. Love endures all things, and love "...does not take into account a wrong suffered" (1 Cor 13:5, NASB).

The ultimate expression of Christ's humility is His accepting a humiliating and painful criminal's death without defending Himself, all because He loved us more than He loved His own rights.

GOD IS LOVE

All of the world's religions either have a multitude of selfish gods vying for power over each other and struggling for territory on earth, or a single prideful god. The true God is not that way, and much harm has been done to the Church by people who are presenting God as if He were essentially no different than the Muslim god, wholly selfish, toying with men. Does God have a right to toy with us and do with us what He likes? Of course He does. He can do whatever He desires with His creation. Does He choose to do this? No. God has chosen love, and love is inseparable from humility.

First Corinthians 13:4-8a says:

> Love suffers long and is kind; love does not envy; love does not parade itself, is not puffed up; does not behave rudely, does not seek its own, is not provoked, thinks no evil; does not rejoice in iniquity, but rejoices in the truth; bears all things, believes all things, hopes all things, endures all things. Love never fails.

Every aspect of this beautiful description of love is dependent on humility. God Himself *is* love (1 John 4:7-8), so God is also humble.

HUMILITY DEFINED

Regarding humility, John Nelson Darby said:

> It is better to be thinking of what God is than of what we are. This looking at ourselves, at the bottom is really pride, a want of the thorough consciousness that we are *good for nothing*. Till we see this we never look quite away from self to God. In looking to Christ, it is our privilege to forget ourselves. *True humility does not so much consist in thinking badly of ourselves, as in not thinking of ourselves at all. I am too bad to be worth*

thinking about. What I want is, to forget myself and to look to God, who is indeed worth all my thoughts.[144]

In the context he is talking about our need to look to God and His promises alone for our assurance of salvation, and never to ourselves or to our works. But this applies to every area of our lives. In looking to God alone, not thinking of ourselves at all, we find humility.

Humility recognizes that the description of man in Rom 3:10-18 applies to us, then recognizes that it doesn't matter at all because of who God is.

It was not humble for Moses to say, "O my Lord, I am not eloquent, neither before nor since You have spoken to Your servant; but I am slow of speech and slow of tongue" (Exod 4:10), when God sent him as His voice to the Egyptians. The Lord's response, "Who has made man's mouth?" (4:11) shows what the humble perspective would have been.

It does not matter if you are not eloquent. It does not matter if you get nervous when you share the gospel. God does not get nervous. God does not struggle to find His words. And God Himself is within you: "For God has not given us a spirit of fear, but of power and of love and of a sound mind" (2 Tim 1:7). Who you are in yourself makes no difference at all. All that matters is who God is in you. As Paul said, "But we have this treasure in earthen vessels, that the excellence of the power may be of God and not of us" (2 Cor 4:7).

CAST YOUR CARES ON JESUS

First Peter 5:6-7 says, "Therefore humble yourselves under the mighty hand of God, that He may exalt you in due time, casting all your care upon Him, for He cares for you." What is clear in the Greek but can get lost in the English translation is that "casting all your care upon Him" fulfills the clause, "humble yourselves under the mighty hand of God" in the previous verse. In other words, humility is accomplished in casting all our care upon Jesus.

When we have great burdens that we attempt to carry ourselves, we are saying in pride, "God I don't need You," denying Jesus' statement "without Me you can do nothing" (John 15:5). But the humble person depends upon Jesus to care for him.

---

[144] John Nelson Darby, "A Voice From the Past: The True Grace of God in Which You Stand" *Journal of the Grace Evangelical Society*, Vol. 8:15, Autumn, 1995. Available online at www.faithalone.org/journal. Emphasis added.

God is not limited, so no request is too small or too big for Him. Our seeking His help in prayer is His desire and it honors Him by recognizing His ability and His love for us.

GOD WILL EXALT THE HUMBLE

Seeking to exalt ourselves is short-sighted. One point from 1 Pet 5:6 not discussed above is the principle that God exalts the humble one "in due time." Likewise, James says, "Humble yourselves in the sight of the Lord, and He will lift you up" (Jas 4:10), and Jesus said, "everyone who exalts himself will be humbled, and he who humbles himself will be exalted" (Luke 18:14; see also Luke 14:11).

A person who gets upset at a lack of recognition from men is forgetting that God will give all the recognition due a person at the Judgment Seat of Christ. But if we exalt ourselves and demand praise now, we will miss out on this praise and reward then:

> Take heed that you do not do your charitable deeds before men, to be seen by them. Otherwise you have no reward from your Father in heaven. Therefore, when you do a charitable deed, do not sound a trumpet before you as the hypocrites do in the synagogues and in the streets, that they may have glory from men. Assuredly, I say to you, they have their reward. But when you do a charitable deed, do not let your left hand know what your right hand is doing, that your charitable deed may be in secret; and your Father who sees in secret will Himself reward you openly. (Matt 6:1-4).

Humbling ourselves before God and casting our care upon Him means that we let Him decide when and where to give praise.

CONCLUSION

If Jesus, the Creator and Sustainer of the world and the ages, the One for whom everything was made, and the rightful King of the universe, could choose to humble Himself, we should too. We can do so, trusting that He, the Righteous Judge, will handle the exalting and will do it perfectly. We must not seek the praise of men, because it's fleeting and will cause us to compromise God's will for the will of others. Humility is always the better choice.

This presents a difficulty because we are prideful by nature. Add to this the fact that the god of this world (Satan) is prideful to the core and we are thus bombarded daily with the "glories" of pride, and the deck might seem stacked against us. How can we, prideful as we are, be humble?

Our need for humility is one more care that we must cast upon Jesus. He is able. The most humble One of all lives within us, making Himself available to us. We simply need to trust Him to manifest Himself in us in that way.

PRACTICE

1) Read 1 Cor 9:1-18. How does Paul show humility here?

2) Is there any relationship in your life that could benefit by your humbling yourself? If so, pray for the Lord's enablement for you to do just that.

3) Is there any burden in your life that you are carrying yourself instead of casting on Jesus? If so, pray for the Lord to take care of it.

4) What effect does humility have on rewards?

5) Read Daniel 6. In what ways did Daniel show humility?

DISCUSS

1) How can you encourage humility in your church family without judgment?

2) Is boasting always wrong?

3) What other ways did Jesus and His apostles show humility?

4) How does humility play a role in healthy marriages and other relationships?

5) What keeps us from letting arguments go and making peace?

6) If your whole local church family worked to encourage and build up one another, what would this do for the expression of humility in the church?

Prayer

"Far be it from me that I should sin against the LORD in ceasing to pray for you" *1 Samuel 12:23*

LESSON OBJECTIVES

1. To introduce some fundamental concepts about prayer
2. To encourage the student toward a Biblical prayer life

INTRODUCTION

When the temple made of stones still stood during Jesus' earthly ministry, someone entering the temple would go through a gate in a large wall to reach the Court of the Gentiles. Here, anyone who wanted to come and worship the Lord could come. If this person were Jewish, he or she could pass through the beautiful gate and enter the Women's Court. All Jewish people, both male and female, could enter this area. Through one more gate was the Court of Israel, where all Jewish men were allowed to go. This is where the Brazen Altar was, and where the priests would perform sacrifices. Through another large gate, the men of Israel, who were also of the tribe of Levi, who were also descended from Aaron, and whose lots had been cast that day could enter. This was the Holy Place. But still, even these could not go past the three-inch (7.5cm) thick, intricately woven fabric that set the Holy of Holies apart.

The Holy of Holies was where God's Shekinah glory was manifested. God resided above the Mercy Seat (Heb 9:5). In the Holy of Holies, between the wings of the large angelic images, the Ark of the Covenant sat. The Ark of the Covenant was an ornate box which contained the golden pot full of manna, Aaron's rod that budded, and the stone tablets on which God inscribed the Ten Commandments (Heb 9:4).

There was one person who *could* go into the Holy of Holies. The High Priest could enter once per year on the Day of Atonement, but not without blood to sprinkle onto the Mercy Seat, and before he entered he had to fill the Holy of Holies with the smoke of incense so that he could not see the Shekinah glory undimmed. The Mercy Seat was the top of the Ark, where the High Priest would sprinkle the blood of an unblemished lamb. So, between the Ten Commandments, which were constantly broken, and the Shekinah glory of God, was the atoning blood. There was no provision in the Bible for cleaning the Ark, so year after year, the Ark would have been covered with more and more blood.

If the High Priest did anything incorrectly as he went in on this one day, he would be struck dead. If he died, the other priests would not be able to go in to retrieve his body or they too would be struck dead. So, the High Priest would wear a rope with bells so that people could periodically make sure he was still alive and pull him out if not.

When Jesus died on the cross, the veil in the temple closing off the Holy of Holies was torn from top to bottom (Matt 27:51). The way inside was now open to all.

The author of Hebrews wrote:

> This hope we have as an anchor of the soul, both sure and steadfast, and which enters the Presence behind the veil, where the forerunner has entered for us, even Jesus, having become High Priest forever according to the order of Melchizedek. (Heb 6:19-20)

And,

> Therefore, brethren, having boldness to enter the Holiest by the blood of Jesus, by a new and living way which He consecrated for us, through the veil, that is, His flesh, and having a High Priest over the house of God, let us draw near with a true heart in full assurance of faith, having our hearts sprinkled from an evil conscience and our bodies washed with pure water. (Heb 10:19-21)

Wall after wall after wall, and then a thick veil and the fear of death separated the people from God—but no more. Because Jesus died for us, He has opened the way to freely enter into God's presence any time we need His help with anything: "Let us therefore come boldly to the throne of grace, that we may obtain mercy and find grace to help in time of need" (Heb 4:16). In fact, His temple now is our very body and His glory resides in our own spirit (1 Cor 6:17-19), so nothing separates us from Him. Because of His abundant grace toward us, there are no walls or gates or veils, just full and free access into His presence (Rom 5:2).

Knowing that this access we have is based upon what Christ has done, not what we have done should impact our prayers. Sometimes it feels like we cannot approach God when we are very aware of our sins, or that when we have had a good day, spiritually, we have more confidence in prayer. But this misunderstands both the value of Christ's blood and the purpose of prayer. Our ability to come boldly to the throne of grace isn't based upon our merits and we cannot demerit our way out of that access. Prayer is part of the process of cleansing the sin out of our lives, and we cannot wait until we clean ourselves up to approach God. He has removed all barriers, we should not reconstruct them.

What does this mean, practically? People have always been able to pray to God. But because of Jesus' sacrifice, the distance created by sin is gone. Know confidently that you are welcome in the Lord's presence, not because of anything you have done, but because of what Jesus has done. And know that He delights in giving you every truly good thing.

PRAYING IN JESUS' NAME

Jesus told His disciples, "If you ask anything in my name, I will do it" (John 14:14). This verse is the reason many people say, "in Jesus' name" at the end of their prayers. There's nothing wrong with saying that, in fact, I usually do. But this verse means much more than that. In 1 John 5:14-15, John writes, "Now this is the confidence that we have in Him, that if we ask anything according to His will, He hears us. And if we know that He hears us, whatever we ask, we know that we have the petitions that we have asked of Him." This is a parallel verse to John 14:14 and it lets us know that to pray in Jesus' name is to pray according to His will.

A person's name is closely associated with who he is, his character, integrity, and will. And God has revealed in His word everything we need in order to pray in Jesus' name. His character and integrity—perfect. His will—holiness, righteousness, love. When we pray in His perfect name, we aren't praying for our own selfish desires (though that doesn't exclude our good, which He desires), we are praying for His will to be done with the knowledge that we can fully trust Him to handle any circumstance.

This should help us understand that prayer is not begging or bargaining. Whenever I hear a prayer on TV, there's usually an "if you do this, I will promise to..." and the word "please" is used as often as if someone were asking his sibling for a favor. Matthew 6:7-8 teaches us a great principle about prayer. The Lord said, "when you pray, do not use vain repetitions as the heathen do... your father knows the things you have need of before you ask Him." What He is saying is that the Father knows our needs and loves us, so we don't have to beg God or bargain with Him, we just need to ask. God loves His children and He desires greatly to bless us with every good thing (see Matt 7:7-11).

THE DISCIPLES' PRAYER

In Matt 6:9-13, Jesus taught His disciples to pray. It is often called "The Lord's Prayer" but it is perhaps better understood as the Disciples' prayer.

"OUR FATHER IN HEAVEN," (MATT 6:9)

When Jesus taught His disciples to pray, He told them to begin by addressing God as "Our Father in heaven" (Matt 6:9). The fatherhood of God is one of the main subjects of this sermon, the Sermon on the Mount, and its focus is on His compassion and care for His children. Jesus says, "What man is there among you who, if his son asks for bread, will give him a stone? (...) how much more will your Father who is in heaven give good things to those who ask Him!" (Matt 7:9, 11). Thus, when we pray to God, we pray to our Father who has all the resources we need and loves us with a perfect Father's love.

"HALLOWED BE YOUR NAME." (MATT 6:9)

Praising God is good for its own sake—He is worthy of our praise— but praising God in prayer helps give us a right perspective, too. Lifting up God's hallowed name as we pray to Him reminds us that the One to whom we pray is worthy of our faith and more than able to meet our needs. Having this right perspective puts our mind in the right position to honor Him by boldly coming to Him requesting His will to be done.

"YOUR KINGDOM COME. YOUR WILL BE DONE ON EARTH AS IT IS IN HEAVEN" (MATT 6:10)

"Your kingdom come" (Matt 6:10) refers to the kingdom that was promised over and over throughout the Old Testament. In that day, the Lord Jesus will rule with righteousness (Isa 32:1), the curse of futility will be lifted (Psalm 72:16; Rom 8:20-21), Israel and indeed the whole world will be at peace (Ezek 34:25), and Satan will no longer deceive the nations (Rev 20:3). It is at this time when the next petition, "Your will be done on earth as it is in heaven" (Matt 6:10), will be fully realized. Desiring God's perfect will, we should look with anticipation for His glorious kingdom and exclaim with John, "Come, Lord Jesus!" (Rev 22:20).

"GIVE US THIS DAY OUR DAILY BREAD." (MATT 6:11)

Jesus told His disciples, *after* praising God's hallowed name and praying for God's kingdom to come and His will to be done perfectly, ask God to "give us this day our daily bread" (Matt 6:11). When God gave manna to the wondering Israelites, He gave it one day at a time (two days' worth on the day before Sabbath so that they could rest instead of gathering). Likewise, Jesus calls us to depend on God daily for Him to meet our needs for that day. And, while God does not promise to meet all of our wants, God does promise to meet all of our needs as we trust in Him (Phil 4:19). He is our loving heavenly Father, so we can confidently leave our care in His hands.

"FORGIVE US OUR DEBTS, AS WE FORGIVE OUR DEBTORS" (MATT 6:12)

This verse illustrates that sometimes the work of prayer does not stop with the prayer alone. Forgiveness, restoration of strained or broken fellowship after sin, requires that we forgive those who have wronged us (Matt 6:15). As we forgive those who have wronged us, we are reminded of all that God has forgiven us, and when we are mindful of all that God has forgiven us, we are more easily able to forgive others. Forgiving others can be difficult, especially when someone has hurt us deeply. The ability to forgive is one more thing we can pray for, knowing that God will delight in giving us that ability.

"DO NOT LEAD US INTO TEMPTATION, BUT DELIVER US FROM THE EVIL ONE" (MATT 6:13)

We know that God does not Himself tempt anyone (Jas 1:13); nevertheless, Jesus was led by the Spirit out into the wilderness to be tempted by Satan (Matt 4:1). Thus, knowing the disciples' weakness, He instructs them to pray, "Do not lead us into temptation, But deliver us from the evil one" (Matt 6:13). This prayer expresses a humble reliance on God. It expresses a deep desire to avoid sin, a desire for holiness. Thus, a prayer that begins with giving glory to God and asking for His will to be done on earth, seeks His will for our lives individually as well. Prayer, Jesus teaches, seeks to align our will with the holy God, our loving heavenly Father.

"FOR YOURS IS THE KINGDOM AND THE POWER AND THE GLORY FOREVER. AMEN." (MATT 6:13)

Ending a prayer with praise of God and acknowledgment of His eternal kingdom, power, and glory brings us back around to love and worship for our incredible Father. In the beginning of the prayer, God's compassion and love is stressed, at the end, His majesty. This reminds us that prayer is an expression of the giving and receiving of love and leaves us with great confidence in God's ability and desire to answer our prayers. In this way, prayer builds our faith, leading to sanctification.

LIVING IT OUT

Jesus taught the disciples to pray for God's will to be done. As He approached the most difficult trial imaginable, He lived out His own teaching. On the night before His crucifixion, He became "exceedingly sorrowful" (Matt 26:38); so He prayed, "O My Father, if it is possible, let this cup pass from Me; *nevertheless, not as I will, but as You will*" (26:39, emphasis added). He was in such agony that "His sweat became like great drops of blood falling down to the ground" (Luke 22:44). But He submitted to God's will and prayed for it to be done and followed that prayer with obedience to God's will. Likewise, Jesus forgave those who trespassed against Him in the most amazing way. Even as He hung on the cross, and He was mocked, He said, "Father, forgive them, for they know not what they do" (Luke 23:34). Jesus *lived* the same prayer and obedience He calls us to.

PAUL'S PRAYERS

Paul's prayers are great examples for us, because they show us the deepest desires of a man who was fully given over to Christ. One example is his prayer as recorded in Phil 1:9-11. It reads:

> And this I pray, that your love may abound still more and more in knowledge and all discernment, that you may approve the things that are excellent, that you may be sincere and without offense till the day of Christ, being filled with the fruits of righteousness which are by Jesus Christ, to the glory and praise of God.

Many times, people have the desire, but simply don't have the knowledge and discernment to be able to love people in a way that is pleasing to God. First John 4:7-11 teaches us that love is perfectly expressed in bringing people into and cultivating a relationship with God. So Paul prays for their love to abound increasingly in knowledge and discernment and that they will "approve the things that are excellent."

Many believers look at things that God abhors with approval. This may be licentiousness on one hand, or oppressive and judgmental legalism on the other, or a host of other things. Paul turns to the Lord in prayer for these believers, as we should for all believers, that they may approve the things God approves, holiness, humility, faith, hope, and love. His prayer has an end goal that these believers would be presented "sincere and without offense" at the *Bema*. Desire for His brothers to be presented well on that Day dominated many of Paul's prayers. This is a beautiful expression of His love for the brethren. We can desire no better thing for our loved ones than to finish well and be pleasing to the Lord.

We should also follow Paul's example here and follow our prayers with action. Paul prays for the Philippians to abound in knowledge and discernment, and then he fills the rest of his letter full of the tools they will need to experience it. Even more so, when Jesus prayed His High Priestly Prayer in John 17:20-26, that we would be glorified together with Him, and that we would be one in Him, He laid down His life and conquered death in order to provide for our need as only He is able (more on Jesus' High Priestly Prayer in the next lesson).

When we pray for our brothers and sisters in the Lord, and the Lord has given us tools to aid them, we should use them for their help. For example, if a brother needs money for groceries and we pray for him, we should also buy him groceries if we are able (Jas 2:15-16; 1 John 3:17).

CONCLUSION

Prayer is a splendid privilege. Because we have the ear of the Almighty God, and He delights in blessing us through prayer, we never need to be paralyzed by fear of any circumstance or anxious about any outcome. Prayer rests on the work of Jesus Christ, brings glory to God, and results in a greater love relationship with our Father.

Prayer is also an awesome responsibility. As the great philosopher, Peter Parker's Uncle Ben once said, "With great power comes great responsibility." We have brothers and sisters in the Lord in need all over the world. They are struggling with sin, with deception, and with persecution, and God's full might is available to us in prayer. Pray for our brothers and sisters and watch God do amazing things!

PRACTICE

1) Read Jesus' High Priestly Prayer in John 17. What did you observe?

2) Read Paul's prayer for the Ephesian church in Eph 1:15-21. What did you observe?

3) Read Phil 4:6. Why is thanksgiving essential for the result promised?

4) Read Eph 6:10-20. What is Paul asking these brothers to pray for him? How does this relate to spiritual warfare as Paul has been discussing it?

5) Make a list of people who are working in ministry who you can pray for (please include me) and pray for these people regularly. Take note of how God answers these prayers.

DISCUSS

1) Discuss some times when you have noticed God abundantly answering your prayers.

2) Does prayer change God's will? Discuss.

3) How does prayer increase our faith?

4) What is important about praying corporately?

5) Discuss how you can have confidence in prayer when you are struggling spiritually.

In Christ

"There is probably no word of Scripture which more clearly defines the essential fact concerning the Christian than the phrase, *in Christ*; and as the Christian is the most important fact of all creation, there has never been a word uttered which was so far-reaching in its implication, or which is fraught with greater meaning to humanity than the phrase, *in Christ*. This phrase, with its equivalents, 'in Christ Jesus, in him, in the beloved, by him, through him, and with him,' appears in the grace teachings of the New Testament no less than 130 times. This most unusual emphasis upon one particular truth is arresting, and its import must not be slighted." *Lewis Sperry Chafer*[145]

LESSON OBJECTIVES

1. To show what it means that the believer is seated in the heavenly places in Christ

2. To show how this relates to the Christian life

---

[145] Chafer, *Systematic Theology*, Vol. 4, p. 98. Emphasis original.

UNITY WITH CHRIST

The believer's position in Christ is one of unity and fellowship. In Christ's High Priestly Prayer in John 17, Jesus stresses this unity:

> ...that they all may be one, as You, Father, are in Me, and I in You; that they also may be one in Us, that the world may believe that You sent Me. And the glory which You gave Me I have given them, that they may be one just as We are one: I in them, and You in Me; that they may be made perfect in one, and that the world may know that You have sent Me, and have loved them as You have loved Me. Father, I desire that they also whom You gave Me may be with Me where I am, that they may behold My glory which You have given Me; for You loved Me before the foundation of the world. O righteous Father! The world has not known You, but I have known You; and these have known that You sent Me. And I have declared to them Your name, and will declare it, that the love with which You loved Me may be in them, and I in them. (John 17:21-26)

This passage stresses not only our unity with one another, but our unity with Christ. He is in us as we are in Him.

Paul echoes this unity. But he goes beyond, showing that it is by virtue of our death and resurrection with Him that we are positioned in Him, and that we should live in a way that is consistent with that fact:

> If then you were raised with Christ, seek those things which are above, where Christ is, sitting at the right hand of God. Set your mind on things above, not on things on the earth. For you died, and your life is hidden with Christ in God. (Col 3:1-3)

Our mind should be focused on the things which are above, because where Christ is, we are also.

Watchman Nee has a book called *Sit, Walk, Stand* that is basically a short devotional commentary on Ephesians. There are a lot of gems in that book, but its greatest value to me was that it helped me to realize that Ephesians 1–3 is essentially a description of all that it means to us that God has "raised us up together, and made us sit together in the heavenly places in Christ Jesus," (Eph 2:6). These are three of the most theologically packed chapters in the Bible and they are not much different from a list of blessing after blessing that God has poured out on us. And all this is before Paul ever uses an imperative. The first one is found in 4:1, and even that points us back to the previous three chapters, calling us to live as if all of those things are true (because they are).

Ephesians 1:3 sets the tone: "Blessed be the God and Father of our Lord Jesus Christ, who has blessed us with every spiritual blessing in the heavenly places in Christ." It is a calling to bless God based on the fact that "every spiritual blessing" has already been given to us and that it is by virtue of our being placed "in the heavenly places in Christ." The list you made in Lesson 8 about the things God has done is a list of things that are true of us by virtue of our being in Christ.

Second Corinthians 5:17 is a classic passage which is said to teach that we are each (individually) new creatures in Christ. It reads: "Therefore, if anyone is in Christ, he is a new creation; old things have passed away; behold, all things have become new." However, in the Greek, the words "he is" do not appear. The verse is better translated: "Therefore, if anyone is in Christ, behold a new creation; old things have passed away; all things have become new."

In the context, Paul is discussing the fact that God has united all of humanity in the death of Christ: "if one died for all, then all died" (2 Cor 5:14). Before Christ, Paul joined the Jewish people in viewing themselves and others based upon physical lineage. Even their view of Christ had primarily to do with His Jewishness. But no longer: "Therefore, from now on, we regard no one according to the flesh. Even though we have known Christ according to the flesh, yet now we know Him thus no longer" (2 Cor 5:16). This verse sets up 2 Cor 5:17.

Thus, when taken in context, it becomes apparent that this is teaching not that the individual believer is himself a new creature, but that because if anyone is in Christ (and we are) there is a New Creation. The New Creation is the Church, the called out ones who are united with Christ by virtue of our death and resurrection with Him.[146]

God's purpose in the New Creation is revealed in Eph 1:9-10:

> ...having made known to us the mystery of His will, according to His good pleasure which He purposed in Himself, that in the dispensation of the fullness of the times He might gather together in one all things in Christ, both which are in heaven and which are on earth—in Him.

---

[146] For more information, see my article "In This Life Together," available at http://boldgrace.org/biblestudy/2cor5-14.html.

God's purpose for the ages is that He might gather all things together in Christ and that there would be nothing left in heaven or on earth outside of Him. This will be fully realized in His kingdom, but we experience this union now in the Church.

This is further illustrated in Paul's prayer for the Ephesians in which He prays for them to have a full understanding of their position in Christ:

> Therefore I also, after I heard of your faith in the Lord Jesus and your love for all the saints, do not cease to give thanks for you, making mention of you in my prayers: that the God of our Lord Jesus Christ, the Father of glory, may give to you the spirit of wisdom and revelation in the knowledge of Him, the eyes of your understanding being enlightened; that you may know what is the hope of His calling, what are the riches of the glory of His inheritance in the saints, and what is the exceeding greatness of His power toward us who believe, according to the working of His mighty power which He worked in Christ when He raised Him from the dead and seated Him at His right hand in the heavenly places, far above all principality and power and might and dominion, and every name that is named, not only in this age but also in that which is to come. And He put all things under His feet, and gave Him to be head over all things to the church, which is His body, the fullness of Him who fills all in all. (Eph 1:15-23)

Being seated in Christ, as members of His body, we are, "far above all principality and power and might and dominion." Because He is, and we are in Him, so are we.

Commenting on this passage, Dr. Lewis Sperry Chafer wrote:

> Growing out of this glorious relationship in Christ is a most natural responsibility to walk worthy of the calling; but the issues of a daily life and the character of the conduct which should enter into it, though important in their place, are lost and forgotten in the blaze of the eternal glory of that unchangeable grace which has brought the believer into the New Creation in Christ Jesus. To be in Christ is to be in the sphere of His own infinite Person, power and glory. He surrounds, He protects, He separates from all else and He indwells the one in Him. He also supplies in Himself all that the soul will ever need in time or eternity.[147]

---

[147] Chafer, *Systematic Theology*, p. 99.

In order to walk worthy of our call, we must first grab hold of and soak up the truth of our unity with Christ.

FACT, FAITH, AND EXPERIENCE

This brings us to the principle of *Fact, Faith, and Experience.* Because we are in Him, every spiritual blessing in the heavenly places—the love we need for others, the joy and peace we need to live in this life, the strength we need to endure trials, and every other spiritual thing we could ever need has already been given to us (Eph 1:3; 2 Pet 1:3). This is a fact. When we apply faith (believe that it is true), we experience those truths.

My former pastor and good friend, Dr. Dale Taliaferro, when teaching on this subject, asks the people he is teaching to close their eyes and imagine themselves at the top of a strong castle surrounded by a moat, looking down upon a group of enemies trying to attack them with spit balls that don't even make it across the moat. This is what it is like looking down from our place in Christ in the heavens at sin which is trying to assail us.

But when we try to handle our temptations and trials ourselves, the spit balls seem a lot more like mortar shells.

When my wife and I moved to Oregon from Texas to attend seminary, we needed to drive. It was around the turn of the New Year when we traveled and there was a blizzard throughout the Rockies, so we drove out to L.A. and then headed north. When we left Sacramento, they were requiring tire chains on I-5 and since we were from Texas, this concept was very new to me. Obviously we did not have chains to put on our tires. So, we had to head over to the coast and head North through the Redwood National Forest. As we wound through the mountains, the snow and sleet were coming down hard and with 200 foot trees on either side of us, it was as dark as night in the middle of the day. Our car was loaded down with everything we owned other than our books, which we mailed, so we needed to take it slow around the corners and up and down the mountains. An eighteen wheeler came up close behind us and impatiently urged us forward faster than I was comfortable going given the circumstances. By the time we reached Crescent City on the coast of California, I was completely exhausted, even though it had only been a few hours on the road. I think I fell asleep for the night at about six o'clock.

The following year, we flew to Texas. As we soared over the mountains at 35,000 feet, the plane was no more hindered by the mountains than it was by a blade of grass on the plains of Oklahoma. I remember looking through the window and thinking, "How beautiful is the handiwork of God!" What a different experience it was to be carried far above it all.

This illustrates the difference between trying to trudge through life on our own versus abiding above it all. This is why we have been seated in the heavenly places in Christ, and this is why Jesus can truly say, "My yoke is easy and My burden is light" (Matt 11:30). It's a light yoke and an easy burden because we don't carry it. If we don't live by faith, however, we might as well be winding around the mountain with an inch of sleet on the roads and a semi trying to run us off the road.

WHEN WE FAIL

When we sin, we experience broken fellowship with God. Our standing as justified saints and our eternal security does not change, but the fellowship we have with God is strained or interrupted. So, beyond justification, which occurs once and is permanent, we need forgiveness whenever we sin.

There's a beautiful verse in First John that is a great source of encouragement to me. I hope it will be to you as well. It's 1 John 1:9, and it reads, "If we confess our sins, He is faithful and just to forgive us our sins and to cleanse us from all unrighteousness."

Before I get into this verse, I want to point out the verses around it to provide important context. First John 1:8 says, "If we say that we have no sin, we deceive ourselves, and the truth is not in us." 1:10 reads, "If we say that we have not sinned, we make Him a liar, and His word is not in us." What John is saying is that pretending we have no sin is not an expression of truth, and saying we have not sinned is not an expression of His word.

So, John is laying out the principle first and bringing it back up after, that we all have sin in our lives. If this is true, and it is, then it only makes sense that we should confess our sins to God. He already knows everything.

The word "confess" comes from the Greek word *homologeō* which essentially means, "I say the same." So, to confess is to say the same things about our sins that God says. For example, I should agree with God that I have sinned (as 1:10 suggests). I should agree with Him that sin is destructive and wasteful. And I should agree with Him that I should not continue in it.

But there's another aspect of saying the same about our sins that we often miss: our sins are taken away by the blood of Christ. We are justified by faith, and we stand righteous before God, not by our own merit, but because of Christ. When we agree with God about our sins (when we confess), part of that is recognizing the value of the blood of Christ (though the other aspects mentioned above are necessary too).

This restoration of fellowship is illustrated beautifully in Isa 6:1-8:

> In the year that King Uzziah died, I saw the Lord sitting on a throne, high and lifted up, and the train of His robe filled the temple. Above it stood seraphim; each one had six wings: with two he covered his face, with two he covered his feet, and with two he flew. And one cried to another and said: "Holy, holy, holy is the LORD of hosts; the whole earth is full of His glory!" And the posts of the door were shaken by the voice of him who cried out, and the house was filled with smoke. So I said: "Woe is me, for I am undone! Because I am a man of unclean lips, and I dwell in the midst of a people of unclean lips; for my eyes have seen the King, the LORD of hosts." Then one of the seraphim flew to me, having in his hand a live coal which he had taken with the tongs from the altar. And he touched my mouth with it, and said: "Behold, this has touched your lips; your iniquity is taken away, and your sin purged." Also I heard the voice of the Lord, saying: "Whom shall I send, and who will go for Us?" Then I said, "Here am I! Send me."

Seeing God in all His awesomeness and glory terrified Isaiah. Not only is the Lord glorious and powerful, but He is perfectly holy. Isaiah understandably became so aware of his own sinfulness that he proclaimed "Woe is me, for I am undone [i.e., ruined, destroyed]!" Yet, the Lord cleanses his sin by sending the seraphim to touch his lips with a live coal. So, when the Lord asks "Whom shall I send...?" Isaiah is confident and volunteers excitedly. Faith in the Lord's cleansing made all the difference in the world.

Isaiah agreed with the Lord; he confessed his sin on both sides of the purging. Without God's purging, his sin would lead to his destruction and inability to be in God's presence. With God's purging, his guilt did not need to hinder him from fellowship or service. Forgiveness erases the distance in fellowship created by sinning.

But God also promises that when we confess our sins, He will "cleanse us from all unrighteousness." What this means is that God works the sin out of our lives over time as we live transparently before Him.

This is why confession is so important. It isn't some ritualistic woo-woo; it is bringing our thoughts and prayers into alignment with God's Word. And when we do this, we know that God is faithful (that means He always will), and just (that means He is right in what He does) to forgive us our sins (fix the broken fellowship) and cleanse us of all unrighteousness (clean up our thoughts and behaviors and bring them into alignment with His will).

Our part in this is really easy. We just have to agree with what God says about our sin. He knows everything and is always right and good, so it only makes sense to do that anyway.

Be honest with yourself and with Him and enjoy sweet fellowship with the Almighty God while you watch His cleansing work a transforming miracle in your life.

CONCLUSION

The believer has been called to a life that is far more holy and righteous than what was called for in the law, but by giving us Christ to indwell and empower us, God has supplied everything to make that not only possible but *realistic*. "[W]e are more than conquerors through Him who loved us." (Rom 8:37). When we come short, however, we must always remember that His grace is more than enough to cover our failures and restore us to fellowship with Him.

PRACTICE

1) What about being in Christ seems most significant to you?

2) If anyone who believes in Christ is part of the New Creation and distinctions based upon race, class, and gender have been done away in Christ (Gal 3:28; Col 3:11), what does this say about racism?

3) Do a word study on the phrase "in Christ." What did you learn? Did anything surprise you?

DISCUSS

1) The Father loves Christ with an infinite love. How does knowing that you are in Christ affect your understanding of the Father's love for you?

2) What are some ways in which the life we are called to is more holy and righteous than what the law required?

3) There is a common teaching today that says that fellowship with God can never be upset by sin. What does the Bible say about this view?

4) Have you ever tried to go through a trial on your own? What did you learn from that experience?

5) What should you do if you still feel guilty after you have confessed your sins and done all you can to heal any hurt relationships with others?

SECTION | 4

Life in the Body of Christ

SECTION GOALS

1. To demonstrate from Scripture how the believer who is walking in the Spirit relates to the Body of Christ
2. To promote a missional[148] viewpoint regarding the Universal Church and the local church
3. To demonstrate the importance of and how-to of endeavoring to keep the unity of the spirit
4. To give practical help regarding the difficulties of life in the local church

INTRODUCTION

The subject of Life in the Body of Christ still awaits a thoroughly Biblical treatment in Biblical literature. In America, Christianity is over-individualized. Personal holiness is seen as the end goal rather than as a necessary step toward the greater goal of edifying the Body and magnifying the glory of God in Christ.

The Christian life is not solely one of individual relationship with God. It is also one of corporate relationship with both the Body of Christ and with God.

As I shared with you in the introductions to Sections 2 and 3, the concepts of Free Grace and Life and Liberty both had a substantial impact on my life. Learning about Life in the Body, the subject of this section, impacted me every bit as much as the other two.

---

[148] Missional means being in relation to a mission.

Through learning about Free Grace and Life and Liberty, I discovered the folly both of trying to impress God and of judging others. For the first time, I began to rest in Christ more fully, to enjoy His life within me, and to have victory over sin (though, of course, I still do sin). Through learning about Life in the Body of Christ, I began to understand my purpose and my place in God's unimaginably majestic plan. I fell more deeply in love with my God, but I also began to see and share in Christ's love for His Body, the Church. My prayer for this section of this book is that through it you can discover God's love for His Church, see your brothers and sisters through Christ's eyes, and be spurred on to participate in God's mission.

RECOMMENDED BOOKS ON THE LIFE IN THE BODY

Title	Author	Audience
The Nature of the Church[148]	Earl Radmacher	Intermediate
Sit, Walk, Stand[149]	Watchman Nee	All

---

[149] Earl Radmacher, *The Nature of the Church* (Hayesville, NC: Schoettle Publishing Co., 1996).

[150] Watchman Nee, *Sit, Walk, Stand* (Bombay: Gospel Literature Service, 1957).

God's Mission, our Mission

"To me, who am less than the least of all the saints, this grace was given, that I should preach among the Gentiles the unsearchable riches of Christ, to make all see what is the fellowship of the mystery, which from the beginning of the ages has been hidden in God who created all things through Jesus Christ; to the intent that now the manifold wisdom of God might be made known by the church to the principalities and powers in the heavenly places, according to the eternal purpose which He accomplished in Christ Jesus our Lord, in whom we have boldness and access with confidence through faith in Him." *Ephesians 3:8-12*

LESSON OBJECTIVES

1. To demonstrate what Scripture says regarding God's plan for man
2. To show that God is a missional God
3. To illustrate that Scripture is tied together by God's mission
4. To introduce our place in God's mission

INTRODUCTION

God's plan for man is spectacular! It goes beyond our wildest dreams in scope and glory, and we are the beneficiaries of it, not because we deserve it, but because God is gracious.

Lucifer, also called Satan, that once majestic angel became enamored with his own beauty and became puffed up:

> How you are fallen from heaven,
> O Lucifer, son of the morning!
> How you are cut down to the ground,
> You who weakened the nations!
> For you have said in your heart:
> "I will ascend into heaven,
> I will exalt my throne above the stars of God;
> I will also sit on the mount of the congregation
> On the farthest sides of the north;
> I will ascend above the heights of the clouds,
> I will be like the Most High." (Isa 14:12-14)

By his exalting himself in pride, Satan raised the ultimate cosmic question, "Can a creature prosper independently of the Creator?" One third of the angels (Rev 12:4, 7-9) agreed with him that one could.

God's mission is to answer this question in such a definite and astonishing way that it will never again be asked.

In comparison to the angels, mankind is the weaker creature. We are created from dust, fallen from there, but God graciously restored us by unifying us with His Son. We will be made like Jesus (Rom 8:29; 1 John 3:2) and experience a glory to which our present sufferings cannot be compared (Rom 8:18). Through the grace of God in Jesus Christ, the lesser creature (man), purchased by Christ's blood, will be crowned with more glory and honor than the greater (angels).

> For He has not put the world to come, of which we speak, in subjection to angels. But one testified in a certain place, saying: "WHAT IS MAN THAT YOU ARE MINDFUL OF HIM, OR THE SON OF MAN THAT YOU TAKE CARE OF HIM? YOU HAVE MADE HIM A LITTLE LOWER THAN THE ANGELS; YOU HAVE CROWNED HIM WITH GLORY AND HONOR, AND SET HIM OVER THE WORKS OF YOUR HANDS. YOU HAVE PUT ALL THINGS IN SUBJECTION UNDER HIS FEET." For in

that He put all in subjection under him, He left nothing that is not put under him. But now we do not yet see all things put under him. But we see Jesus, who was made a little lower than the angels, for the suffering of death crowned with glory and honor, that He, by the grace of God, might taste death for everyone. For it was fitting for Him, for whom are all things and by whom are all things, in bringing many sons to glory, to make the captain of their salvation perfect through sufferings. For both He who sanctifies and those who are being sanctified are all of one [or, all one], for which reason He is not ashamed to call them brethren. (Heb 2:5-11)

Thus mankind is destined to rule over all of God's creation. In 1 Cor 6:3 Paul says that we will even rule over the angels!

In the end we will be the ultimate proof that God is wise and good, and that it is foolish to desire independence from His loving care. Paul said:

To me, who am less than the least of all the saints, this grace was given, that I should preach among the Gentiles the unsearchable riches of Christ, and to make all see what is the fellowship of the mystery, which from the beginning of the ages has been hidden in God who created all things through Jesus Christ; *to the intent that now the manifold wisdom of God might be made known by the church to the principalities and powers in the heavenly places*, according to the eternal purpose which He accomplished in Christ Jesus our Lord. (Eph 3:8-11, emphasis added)

God's mission is making this proof evident to all creatures everywhere. It was begun in the Garden of Eden and it will ultimately be fulfilled in Messiah's kingdom. Jody Dillow expands on this:

The final significance of man is the fulfillment of God's commandment in the Garden of Eden, "let them rule" [Gen 1:26]. A fifth column had been placed in the Satan's world, and the man and his wife, even though they were less than the angels, were commanded to take back that which the Satan had stolen. They were to live in dependence and obedience, in contrast to the Satan's disobedience and unbelief. The lesser creature who lived by these principles would one day obtain a higher position than the greater creature aspired to, thus rebuking pride.

The arduous flow of history reveals the operation of these principles, and one day in the messianic partnership with the

Second Man and the Last Adam, human destiny will finally be achieved, and God's grace will be gloriously manifested.[151]

When I refer to God's mission, this is what I mean. Our mission, on the other hand, is our part to play in His grander plan.

OUR PART IN GOD'S MISSION

The mission is God's, but He has chosen us to have a role to play. This role involves our whole lives, and every little thing can be eternally significant when done by faith and for the glory of the Lord. But the two main functions of our role in God's mission are evangelism[152] and discipleship.

God has designed the Body in such a way that we each play unique roles in these tasks that the Church is given. This means living out Christ's life in our unique roles to encourage others to come closer to God in a relationship of love, trust, and obedience to Him.

The Apostles understood God's mission and therefore they gave their lives in pursuit of it, knowing that "the sufferings of this present time are not worthy to be compared with the glory which shall be revealed in us" (Rom 8:18).

Like the Apostles, our involvement in the world and especially in the Body of Christ should not be a merely passive one.

GOD IS A MISSIONAL GOD

God is missional. God reveals this about Himself in the fact that creation exists. God has always experienced complete, fulfilling love relationships within the Godhead. He exists eternally in a perfect triune relationship. So we were created not merely to provide Him with someone to live in a fulfilling love relationship with Him. He already had this. We were also created as an expression of His missional character. He wants to reveal His glory in us.

---

[151] Dillow, *Final Destiny*, p. 963.

[152] Evangelism is the work of teaching the gospel to non-believers.

God also reveals Himself as missional by His very name, YHWH.[153] He is not merely "I AM" in the static sense that the English translation of His name can imply. Sigmund Mowinckel wrote about the Divine name:

> He is the God who "is," *haya*, in the fullest meaning of the word (...) But this "being" is not the abstract Greek *einai*, the mere existence *per se*. To the Hebrew "to be" does not just mean to exist—as all other beings and things do as well—but to be active, to express oneself in active being, "The God who acts." "I am what in creative activity I always and everywhere turn out to be," or "I am (the God) that really acts."[154]

In other words, God says that He is what He reveals Himself to be through His actions. We have an incomplete picture of this now. We see as in a mirror dimly (1 Cor 13:12). But when His kingdom is established upon the return of Christ, all will see the full truth of the name YHWH and bow before His glory.

GOD'S MISSION TIES ALL SCRIPTURE TOGETHER

Dr. Charles Ryrie correctly notes in his excellent book, *Dispensationlism*,[155] that the overall purpose of Scripture is God's glory. But, to understand how the Bible's big story arc unfolds, it may help to be more specific. The overarching theme of Scripture is the glory of God, shown in His kingdom program, in which He demonstrates the blessedness of dependence on Him and the folly of pride, by graciously pouring out love and glory on the lesser being, man. This theme begins in the Garden of Eden, runs through all 66 books of the Bible, and it is fully realized in the future pictured in the last three chapters of Revelation. Each dispensation, each major change in God's interaction with man, is a step toward that ultimate fulfillment.

---

[153] YHWH the Anglicized version of the tetragrammaton the four Hebrew letters of God's name (יהוה), often pronounced Yahweh or in English, Jehovah.

[154] Sigmund Mowinckel, "The Name of the God of Moses," *Hebrew Union College Annual* 32 (1961): p. 127 (transliteration of Greek and Hebrew mine).

[155] Charles Ryrie, *Dispensationalism Revised and Expanded* (Chicago: Moody Press, 2007).

THE GARDEN OF EDEN AND BEYOND

When God said "Let Us make man in Our image, according to Our likeness" (Gen 1:26), He was using terms that would be clear to Moses and his contemporaries. In Moses' day, kings would set up images of themselves all around territories they ruled, thus defining the area of their authority.

As Eugene Merrill states:

> In line with recent scholarship, it is argued here that the trans-lation of *besalmēnū* ("in our image") and *kidmūtēnū* ("according to our likeness") ought to be "as our image" and "according to our likeness" respectively. That is, man is not *in* the image of God, he *is* the image of God. The text speaks not of what man is like but of what he is to be and do. It is a functional statement and not one of essence. Just as images or statues represented deities and kings in the ancient Near East, so much so that they were virtually interchangeable, so man as the image of God was created to represent God Himself as the sovereign over all creation.[156]

Man, as the image of God, is God's declaration to the world, "I am King here. This is mine."

God said of this image, "let them have dominion over the fish of the sea, over the birds of the air, and over the cattle, over all the earth and over every creeping thing that creeps on the earth" (Gen 1:26). Then to this same image He said, "Be fruitful and multiply; fill the earth and subdue it; have dominion..." (1:28). God was declaring that man should rule as His proxy and that by man, evidence of God's rule would extend throughout the whole earth.

This dominion was interrupted when Satan deceived Eve and she and Adam took of the fruit of the Tree of the Knowledge of Good and Evil (Gen 3:1-7). Since this time, the Usurper, Satan, has ruled this world (2 Cor 4:4; 1 John 5:19) but he has already been defeated through the cross. Satan's rule will come to an end and be replaced forever by Messiah's Kingdom (1 Cor 15:20-28).

---

[156] Eugene A. Merrill, "A Theology of the Pentateuch," *A Biblical Theology of the Old Testament*, Roy B. Zuck, ed. (Chicago: Moody Press, 1991), p. 14.

DEATH DEFEATED

Man had utterly failed in carrying out God's mission. Rather than reigning in life, Adam and Eve found death. Rather than ruling as God's proxy, we abdicated and became slaves of Satan, willing captives, carrying out his desires (Eph 2:1-3). Our whole being was dead to God's will.

Death now ruled man, and man was helpless to do anything about it. So God, the Son, became a man to obtain victory for man and to release us from bondage:

> Inasmuch then as the children have partaken of flesh and blood, He Himself likewise shared in the same, that through death He might destroy him who had the power of death, that is, the devil, and release those who through fear of death were all their lifetime subject to bondage. (Heb 2:14-15)

And also:

> So when this corruptible has put on incorruption, and this mortal has put on immortality, then shall be brought to pass the saying that is written: "DEATH IS SWALLOWED UP IN VICTORY." "O DEATH, WHERE IS YOUR STING? O HADES, WHERE IS YOUR VICTORY?" The sting of death is sin, and the strength of sin is the law. But thanks be to God, who gives us the victory through our Lord Jesus Christ. (1 Cor 15:54-57)

Now, through simple faith in Christ, instead of death, we have everlasting life. Through Him, instead of slavery to the devil, we have a restored destiny of ruling over all of creation.

Death which once ruled us will be totally destroyed. "And God will wipe away every tear from their eyes; there shall be no more death, nor sorrow, nor crying. There shall be no more pain, for the former things have passed away" (Rev 21:4).

We now experience a seemingly never ending struggle, but we *will* live in inexpressible magnificence:

> "Come, I will show you the bride, the Lamb's wife." And he carried me away in the Spirit to a great and high mountain, and showed me the great city, the holy Jerusalem, descending out of heaven from God, having the glory of God. Her light was like a most precious stone, like a jasper stone, clear as crystal. Also she had a great and high wall with twelve gates, and twelve angels at the gates, and names written on them,

which are the names of the twelve tribes of the children of Israel: three gates on the east, three gates on the north, three gates on the south, and three gates on the west. Now the wall of the city had twelve foundations, and on them were the names of the twelve apostles of the Lamb. And he who talked with me had a gold reed to measure the city, its gates, and its wall. The city is laid out as a square; its length is as great as its breadth. And he measured the city with the reed: twelve thousand furlongs [About 1500 miles—2400 kilometers—the distance from New York City to Dallas, TX, or from London to Athens, Greece!]. Its length, breadth, and height are equal. Then he measured its wall: one hundred and forty-four cubits, according to the measure of a man, that is, of an angel. The construction of its wall was of jasper; and the city was pure gold, like clear glass. The foundations of the wall of the city were adorned with all kinds of precious stones: the first foundation was jasper, the second sapphire, the third chalcedony, the fourth emerald, the fifth sardonyx, the sixth sardius, the seventh chrysolite, the eighth beryl, the ninth topaz, the tenth chrysoprase, the eleventh jacinth, and the twelfth amethyst. The twelve gates were twelve pearls: each individual gate was of one pearl. And the street of the city was pure gold, like transparent glass. But I saw no temple in it, for the Lord God Almighty and the Lamb are its temple. The city had no need of the sun or of the moon to shine in it, for the glory of God illuminated it. The Lamb is its light. And the nations of those who are saved shall walk in its light, and the kings of the earth bring their glory and honor into it. Its gates shall not be shut at all by day (there shall be no night there). And they shall bring the glory and the honor of the nations into it. But there shall by no means enter it anything that defiles, or causes an abomination or a lie, but only those who are written in the Lamb's Book of Life. And he showed me a pure river of water of life, clear as crystal, proceeding from the throne of God and of the Lamb. In the middle of its street, and on either side of the river, was the tree of life, which bore twelve fruits, each tree yielding its fruit every month. The leaves of the tree were for the healing of the nations. And there shall be no more curse, but the throne of God and of the Lamb shall be in it, and His servants shall serve Him. They shall see His face, and His name shall be on their foreheads. There shall be no night there: They need no lamp nor light of the sun, for the Lord God gives them light. And they shall reign forever and ever. (Rev 21:9b–22:5)

This splendid victory for Christ and His bride is the culmination of God's mission.

CONCLUSION

God's mission is greater than we can truly understand, and His love for us has placed us at the center of it. We will be the perfect answer to the ultimate question. We have been given an opportunity of an eternity to work toward the establishing of a perfect world. This perfect world will not come until Christ's return, but even now we have the privilege of developing the servant leaders who will be essential parts of that kingdom then. Our weakness makes us perfectly suited to this work, so that it can be Christ's strength in us, instead of our own that answers the Adversary's question. As weaker creatures, yet recipients of abundant grace, we will rule over the greater creatures.

The more we participate in God's mission now, the more we will experience the fruit of our participation then—"you were faithful over a few things, I will make you ruler over many things" (Matt 25:21).

May we all hear, "Well done, good and faithful servant" (Matt 25:21).

PRACTICE

1) What is God's mission, as defined in this lesson?

2) Define God's mission in your own words.

3) What do you see as *your* part in God's mission?

4) How are you as an individual fulfilling "our part" in God's mission? How can you do better?

5) What does it mean to be the image of God?

DISCUSS

1) Those who seek God now still only see in a mirror dimly. There are those who do not seek Him at all and yet hate Him for whom they perceive Him to be. How will the fulfillment of God's mission impact this?

2) How is your church fulfilling "our part" in God's mission?

3) How can you help your church to be more effective in fulfilling "our part" in God's mission?

4) What about God's mission makes you excited to participate?

5) How can you overcome your fears about participating in God's mission?

Election and Mission

"This doctrine of divine election has fallen into disrepute because those who were so chosen and called (the 'elect') so often saw themselves as exclusive beneficiaries of God's choice, rather than trustees on behalf of the nations. But this disastrous misunderstanding, so manifest in the story of Israel and in the life of the church in all generations, cannot negate the fundamental truth of the doctrine of election. It is God who chooses, calls and sends" *Lesslie Newbigin*[157]

LESSON OBJECTIVES

1. To distinguish the Biblical doctrine of election with the popular ones

2. To show that in the Bible election is a call to mission

3. To encourage you to live out your election in Christ

INTRODUCTION[158]

The Biblical doctrine of election (Hebrew, *bachar*, Greek, *eklegomai*, *eklektos*, *eklogē*) is one of the most misunderstood doctrines in the Bible. Calvinists and Arminians have sought to understand it in different ways, but both miss its meaning because both seek to understand

---

[157] Lesslie Newbigin, *The Open Secret: An Introduction to the Theology of Mission*, Revised edition (Grand Rapids, MI: Wm. B. Eerdmans Publishing Company, 1995), p. 17-18.

[158] For more discussion on this topic, see Newbigin, *The Open Secret*, pages 68-72 and Bud Brown "Mission, Godliness and Reward in 2 Peter 1:5-11," *Journal of the Grace Evangelical Society* (Spring 2012).

it as dealing with exclusive personal privilege. The argument has never been settled between the contrasting views of Calvinists and Arminians because both sides have passages that are difficult to reconcile with their views.

The Calvinist sees election as God unconditionally choosing someone for salvation. If that were the case, why would Jesus be called "elect" (Isa 43:10; 49:1; 1 Pet 2:6)? Surely He deserves every blessing He could ever get.

The Arminian seems to struggle with the fact that it is God who does the choosing (John 15:16).

The question, "is it God who chooses particular men to be saved or is it individual men who make the choice for themselves?" actually has nothing to do with the Biblical doctrine of election.

The Bible presents election differently. God does not elect us to privilege *per se*, but to a task, and that task generally has to do with His mission to bless the whole world.

God reveals Himself as having a universal purpose (salvation available to all John 3:16; 2 Cor 5:14-15, 19; 1 Tim 2:3-6) and having particular people, places, and events chosen (elected) to share this purpose with everyone (more on this below). In other words, God's salvation is available to everyone, but He calls a particular people (and sometimes events and sometimes cities, etc.) to bear that message. Our election is not primarily about us. It is about being called to participate in God's mission. Our election is the answer to His question, "Whom shall I send, and who will go for Us?" (Isa 6:8).

Here are a couple of clear examples of the concept of being elected to participate in God's mission:

John 15:16

> You did not choose Me [Jesus], but I chose (Greek, *eklegomai*) you and appointed you that you should go and bear fruit, and that your fruit should remain, that whatever you ask the Father in My name He may give you.

Acts 15:7

> And when there had been much dispute, Peter rose up and said to them: "Men and brethren, you know that a good while ago God chose (*eklegomai*) among us, that by my mouth the Gentiles should hear the word of the gospel and believe."

THE ELECTION OF ABRAHAM

Biblically, the foundation of what it means to be elect is the calling of Abraham in Genesis 12:1-3, and the culmination of election is found in Jesus Christ. God's election of Israel bridges this gap.

As discussed in the previous lesson, prior to the call of Abraham, God had made the general call to all men to "[b]e fruitful and multiply" and "fill the earth" (Gen 1:28 and 9:7). Because of mankind's ultimate failure to do so, as seen at the Tower of Babel (Genesis 11), God instituted the principle of election. He would choose specific people to bear His blessing to the world.

Genesis 12:1-3 says:

> Now the LORD had said to Abram: "Get out of your country, From your family And from your father's house, To a land that I will show you. I will make you a great nation; I will bless you And make your name great; And you shall be a blessing. I will bless those who bless you, And I will curse him who curses you; And in you all the families of the earth shall be blessed."

The Hebrew word for *elect*, *bachar*, doesn't appear in that text, but it is applied to that event in Neh 9:7, "You are the LORD God, Who chose (*bachar*) Abram, And brought him out of Ur of the Chaldeans, And gave him the name Abraham."

There are three main aspects of this that become repeated themes in Scripture where election is concerned:

The first is *the call to go*: "Get out of your country..."

The second is *the command to be a blessing*. Here it is translated, "And you shall be a blessing" but it is perhaps better translated, "And be a blessing."

Third, *the blessing is to extend broadly*; "And in you all the families (nations) of the earth shall be blessed."

ISRAEL, THE ELECT

The Bible often calls Israel God's Elect (Isa 43:10, 20-21; 44:1; 45:4 and many other places). As Deut 4:5-8 shows, Israel was called to be a light to the world. By their obedience to the law, the world would see that God is good.

Throughout Isaiah, God connects the concept of election and Israel's call to be God's witness. Let's take a look at how these concepts are connected. Isaiah 43:10, 20-21; 44:1-2 and 8 taken together, say:

> "You are My witnesses," says the LORD, "And My servant whom I have chosen, That you may know and believe Me, And understand that I am He. Before Me there was no God formed, Nor shall there be after Me. (…)

> The beast of the field will honor Me, The jackals and the ostriches, Because I give waters in the wilderness And rivers in the desert, To give drink to My people, My chosen. This people I have formed for Myself; They shall declare My praise. (…)

> "Yet hear me now, O Jacob My servant, And Israel whom I have chosen. Thus says the LORD who made you And formed you from the womb, who will help you: 'Fear not, O Jacob My servant; And you, Jeshurun, whom I have chosen.'" (…)

> Do not fear, nor be afraid; Have I not told you from that time, and declared it? You are My witnesses. Is there a God besides Me? Indeed there is no other Rock; I know not one.

These are just some highlights from one extended passage, but the concept is found throughout Isaiah, Ezekiel, Jeremiah, and many other Biblical books. Election is the call to be God's witness.

The failure of Israel in this regard is best typified in one prophet, Jonah, and one group of people, the Pharisees.

Jonah was called to be God's witness to Nineveh, an Assyrian city (Jonah 1:1-2). Instead of following the Lord's command, he fled in the opposite direction (1:3). His reasoning for doing so is that if he were to preach to the Ninevites, they might repent and escape destruction (4:1-2).

Israel had become prideful about their election because they had seen it as an election to personal privilege instead of election to the task of sharing God with the world. They thought of themselves as elect in the sense of being the exclusive beneficiaries of God's love. Why then, Jonah thought, would he want to share God's love with a wicked nation like Assyria?

Likewise, the Pharisees typified this prideful view of election by perverting the law into something that excludes the love of and mission to other peoples (when the young lawyer was reminded of the greatest commandments, especially "Love your neighbor as yourself," his question was, "And who is my neighbor?" hoping to exclude as many as possible). One example is how the Pharisees instructed the Israelites to walk around Samaria to avoid the Samaritan "dogs" rather than going actively to them to minister to them. See John 8:33-59 for another good example.

JESUS, THE ELECT

Because of Israel's failure to be a light to the world, God elected another Servant, His Son Jesus Christ, to be that blessing to all.

Jesus speaks of His own election through the prophet Isaiah (49:1, 5-6):

> "Listen, O coastlands, to Me,
> And take heed, you peoples from afar!
> The LORD has called Me from the womb;
> From the matrix of My mother
> He has made mention of My name…
> And now the LORD says,
> Who formed Me from the womb to be His Servant,
> To bring Jacob back to Him,
> So that Israel is gathered to Him
> (For I shall be glorious in the eyes of the LORD, And My God
> shall be My strength),
> Indeed He says,
> 'It is too small a thing that You should be My Servant
> To raise up the tribes of Jacob,
> And to restore the preserved ones of Israel;
> I will also give You as a light to the Gentiles,
> That You should be My salvation to the ends of the earth.'"

Likewise, In Jesus' earthly ministry, He quoted Isaiah 61:1-2a in Luke 4:18-19 as something like a personal mission statement:

> "The Spirit of the Lord GOD is upon Me,
> Because the LORD has anointed Me
> To preach good tidings to the poor;
> He has sent Me to heal the brokenhearted,
> To proclaim liberty to the captives,
> And the opening of the prison to those who are bound;
> To proclaim the acceptable year of the LORD."

As God's Elect One, He was called to go to those who were overlooked. We see Jesus live this out in His earthly ministry. He went to the poor, the sick, the sinners, and even the Samaritans (John 4), proclaiming salvation in Him for all who would believe.

ELECT IN HIM

Jesus extended His election to His disciples: "So Jesus said to them again, 'Peace to you! As the Father has sent Me, I also send you,'" (John 20:21; see also Matt 28:18-20; Mark 1:17; John 15:16). He also extends this election beyond them to all who would believe in Him through their word (John 17:20-26; Acts 1:8).

Paul repeatedly says that he was "called to be an apostle" (and similar phrases). An apostle is one who is sent. He was called (elected) to go to the Gentiles, to get out of his home country and be a blessing to all the nations of the world.

Paul applies this same call to us (though for many it can be done in the mission field we have where we are). This is why Paul speaks as he does of our election in Eph 1:3-14. We were elected in Christ: "He chose us in Him" (1:4) to be "to the praise of His glory" (1:6, 12). All of us who are in Christ by faith are called to share the praise of His glory. But this is specifically in the application of His will found in 1:9-10:

> ...having made known to us the mystery of His will, according to His good pleasure which He purposed in Himself, that in the dispensation of the fullness of the times He might gather together in one all things in Christ, both which are in heaven and which are on earth—in Him.

This is the reason we are called—to begin the work of gathering all things together in Christ. This is what Paul means when he said in the next verse, "being predestined (Greek *proorizō*, that is, preappointed to the task) concerning the purpose[159] (mentioned in vv 9-10) of Him who works all things according to the counsel of His will" (1:11, edited from the NKJV). In other words, anyone and everyone who is in Christ through faith has been appointed to share in His purpose of being a blessing to all the nations. The doctrine has to do with our task, not our salvation.

---

[159] The word here is *prothesis* which is essentially "a thing placed before" and can be used for shewbread (Matt 12:4; Mark 2:26, etc.), as in something set on display, or it can be something that is figuratively set before one's eyes as a goal (Acts 27:13), as it is here. Here it is in reference to the goal God has for creation, that in the end He will gather all things together in Christ. See also its use in Eph 3:11.

God's Redemptive Purpose in Election

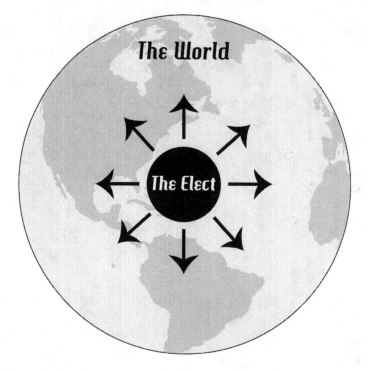

I hope that by this you can see the error of turning our election into one of exclusive privilege. The attitude of Jonah and the Pharisees is all too prevalent in the Church today, but if we can manage to see the purpose of our calling, we can begin to live it out.

---

[160] This is also the subject of Rom 8:28–11:33, but an exegesis of this passage is beyond the scope of this lesson.

A SUMMARY OF GOD'S REVEALED PROCESS IN ELECTION

God desires all the nations to experience His blessing, so He calls Abraham to carry that blessing (Gen 12:1-3; Neh 9:7). God desires the blessing to be continued by a child from Abraham and his wife Sarah, so this election goes to Isaac rather than Ishmael (Genesis 16:1–18:15; 21:1-7). God chooses Isaac's younger son, Jacob, to continue the mission, later naming him Israel (Gen 25:19-34; 27:1-29). Through Moses, Israel is given the explicit calling of being a blessing to the nations (Deut 4:6-8). Israel as a nation rejects this calling, so God elects Jesus to fulfill it (Isa 49:1, 5-6). Through His death and resurrection, He unites all Jews and Gentiles who believe in Him into one Body and we share in His election because we are in Him (John 15:16; 17:20-26; 20:21; Eph 1:3-14; 1 Pet 2:6-9).[159]

CONCLUSION

There is an amazing amount of blessing that comes with being in Christ. But that blessing is so vast that it is intended to overflow to all around us and to all with whom we have the privilege to share Christ.

We have all been chosen in Christ to carry out the purpose of gathering all things together in Him. So, like Abraham, like the Lord Jesus, and like Paul, let us leave our comfort zone and be a blessing to all the nations of the world.

PRACTICE

1) What are the aspects of election found in Abraham's call in Gen 12:1-3?

2) What does it mean that Israel is elect in Isa 43:20-21? (See Deut 4:6-8.)

3) What does it mean that Jesus is God's Elect One in 1 Pet 2:4-6?

4) How does Peter extend this election to the believers he is writing to in 1 Pet 2:7-10?

5) What does John 15:16 mean?

DISCUSS

1) What did Jonah not understand about his election? Do you see this same error today?

2) How does Isa 49:1-6 illustrate the doctrine of election?

3) How would you explain election to someone else?

4) How is Jesus the culmination of election?

5) What does it mean that we are "elect in Christ"?

Accepting the Reality of Post-Christendom

"For here we have no continuing city, but we seek the one to come." *Hebrews 13:14*

LESSON OBJECTIVES

1. To demonstrate that Western Culture has moved away from Christian values

2. To point out the opportunity that this brings for the spread of the gospel

3. To offer some practical steps toward effectively carrying out God's mission in post-Christendom

POST-CHRISTENDOM

BACKGROUND OF THE TERM

The Missional Church Movement has a lot of buzz words and that can sometimes be off-putting. But that movement has brought out some good and healthy discussion and some of these buzz words can help us better understand what is being communicated; and that can help us see truth and opportunity where we might not have seen it before.

One of those off-putting but helpful words is "post-Christendom." Here's the background of the term. The Roman Emperor Constantine (who ruled from AD 306-337) converted to Christianity and this led to things like the building of numerous impressive cathedrals, the appointment of Christians to places of governmental authority, and the requirement that people worship their god (or God) on Sunday.

Less than a century later, Augustine of Hippo became a proponent of Amillennialism, the belief that Christ's 1000 year reign should not be taken literally, but as allegorically fulfilled in the Church. This became the justification for the institutional church's amassing of political power. Under the authority of the Popes, the Catholic Church began to exert a great deal of control over the governments of Europe. Even after the power of the Catholic Church had waned, to a large degree, nation states were still considered "Christian."

Here are a few significant developments, and related problems, that came with the rise of Christendom:[161]

1) The assumption that all citizens were Christian by birth.

   • Not surprisingly, this largely did away with evangelism.

2) The definition of "orthodoxy" as the common belief shared by all, which was determined by powerful church leaders supported by the state.

   • This largely replaced the Bible with tradition. Even in Protestant churches during and after the Reformation, creeds and confessions constructed by the elite were often treated as if they were more authoritative than the Bible. Tradition continues to be a hindrance to Biblical exegesis,[162] but with the fall of Christendom, this problem is lessening because more and more people are not tied to any Christian tradition.

3) The construction of massive and ornate church buildings.

   • This tended to make people think of church as a place rather than a people. In addition, it helped lead to #4 below.

4) A strong distinction between clergy and laity, and the relegation of the laity to a largely passive role

   • The Apostle Paul said that God gave church leaders "for the equipping of the saints for the work of ministry" (Eph 4:12), and that God has given each of us spiritual gifts as He pleases so that

---

[161] For information about the rise of Christendom and its effects, see Brad Brisco & Lance Ford, *Missional Essentials: A Guide for Experiencing God's Mission in Your Life* (Kansas City, MO: The House Studio, 2012), p. 47.

[162] Exegesis is deriving the authors' intended meaning from the text.

"when every part does its share" the Body grows. This requires an active laity.

Prior to Constantine, Christians endured great suffering and persecution for their faith. We've all heard of Christians being fed to lions in the Colosseum, and of Nero's burning of Christians. These and other persecutions were common. But the Church enjoyed exponential growth, nonetheless, and the churches were filled with committed disciples.

Later, Christians enjoyed the comfort of the state's approval (as long as they followed the official teaching). But participation in church became organizational and ritualistic rather than an expression of personal faith and worship.

The term post-Christendom is intended to suggest that the nations which were once considered "Christian" are no longer based upon Christian values. There are many Christians in the United States, for example, but the culture has moved away from respecting Christian beliefs and values and the State is hostile to it rather than supportive.

Christian views are openly mocked by the government and media, and people are dismissed entirely and treated as unworthy of dialogue if they believe in a Creator God, if they attach an intrinsic value to human life, if they believe in Biblical inerrancy, or even if they believe in Biblical morality.

For example, New Jersey has recently enacted a law that would make it illegal to help anyone, even victims of sexual abuse, overcome unwanted same-sex attraction.[163] And currently the Freedom From Religion Foundation is seeking to get a physics professor fired from Ball State University for demonstrating evidence for Intelligent Design in an elective class.[164] In our public educational system, it doesn't matter what the empirical evidence demonstrates, if it doesn't promote an atheistic view of origins, talking about it isn't allowed.

Those who are in parts of the world that have never been predominately Christian often face similar circumstances, though often the persecution can be much more severe.

---

[163] http://newjersey.news12.com/multimedia/news-conference-held-on-conversion-therapy-1.5210296, Last accessed on June 12th, 2013.

[164] http://christiannews.net/2013/05/22/ball-state-university-science-professor-under-fire-for-questioning-evolution/. Last accessed on June 14th, 2013. See also Ben Stein's documentary *Expelled: No Intelligence Allowed* for further information on similar cases.

POST-CHRISTENDOM BRINGS GREAT OPPORTUNITY

The movement of a culture away from Christian values presents difficulty, but it also presents great opportunity.

PERSECUTION

It is true that being open about our faith can lead to persecution. Depending on where we live, what our families are like, and what we do for a living, that persecution can vary a great deal. In the United States, a Christian working in the private sector may experience ridicule or loss of opportunity. But in Nigeria and many other countries, Christians are being slaughtered by Islamic ruling elites.[165]

One of the places with the most intense persecution of Christians over the last thirty years is Sudan. The Voice of the Martyrs describes it this way:

> Persecution of the Church has been most intense since 1985. Deliberate attempts to eliminate a viable Christian presence are extreme and include bombing of Sunday church services; destruction of churches, hospitals, schools, mission bases and Christian villages; massacres and mutilation; and murder of pastors and leaders.[166]

Paul said, "Yes, and all who desire to live godly in Christ Jesus will suffer persecution" (2 Tim 3:12), and Jesus told His disciples:

> "If the world hates you, you know that it hated Me before it hated you. If you were of the world, the world would love its own. Yet because you are not of the world, but I chose you out of the world, therefore the world hates you" (John 15:18-19).

So it should come as no surprise to us that Christians experience this kind of persecution. If we follow in the Lord's footsteps, we will find ourselves experiencing various kinds of persecutions.

But the example of Sudan teaches us a great deal. Despite the heavy persecution, the number of Christians has increased from an estimated 1.6 million in 1980 to 11 million in 2011.[167] In the early Church, the

---

[165] http://www.persecution.net/nigeria.htm. Last accessed on June 14th, 2013.

[166] http://www.persecution.net/sudan.htm. Last accessed on June 14th, 2013.

[167] *Ibid.*

great persecution they suffered opened the way for the gospel. When Christians submitted quietly to being eaten by lions in front of 50,000 spectators, people took notice and the spread of the gospel flourished.

As Paul sat in prison for Christ, he wrote:

> But I want you to know, brethren, that the things which happened to me have actually turned out for the furtherance of the gospel, so that it has become evident to the whole palace guard, and to all the rest, that my chains are in Christ. (Phil 1:12-13)

But if we remain faithful in our suffering and persecutions, rejoicing in what the Lord is doing despite the circumstances, these hardships can become opportunities for the spread of the gospel.

Paul also said, "For I consider that the sufferings of this present time are not worthy to be compared with the glory which shall be revealed in us" (Rom 8:18). Knowing that the Lord will lavishly reward those who endure suffering for His sake helps to give us comfort in troubling times.

GOING TO CHURCH SERVICES IS NO LONGER EXPECTED

Decades ago, there was a societal expectation in the United States that everyone would be in a church service on Sundays. But because of the shift of our culture away from Christianity, that expectation has diminished. Many churches have countered this shift by tailoring their services to be appealing to unbelievers. But the Biblical example of church services is that they are intended for the equipping of believers for the work of ministry, not for appealing to unbelievers, and the rise of seeker sensitive churches has not resulted in the spread of the gospel. While some of these churches have become quite large, the number of Christians in the United States has been dwindling rather than growing, and much of their growth has come from people moving away from their own church homes to these larger churches. Some studies have concluded that 90% or more of church growth comes from other churches and from progeny rather than from evangelistic growth.[168]

But it has not all been negative. Many churches are recognizing that expensive advertising and seeker sensitive services are not the answer and

---

[168] See http://www.xenos.org/books/satan/churchdecline.htm, last accessed on June 15th, 2013, and http://www.god21project.org/zr-90-of-church-growth-is-due-to-transfer-growth-and-not-churches-striking-into-the-heart-of-our-enemys-territory.html. Last accessed on June 15th, 2013.

that real growth of the gospel must come from believers going out with the gospel rather than by attracting people to come in.

Unbelievers are not commanded to go to church services, but Scripture repeatedly instructs believers to go to unbelievers with the gospel (Matt 28:19; John 20:21; Acts 1:8; Rom 10:13-15). Paul wrote that growth of the Body comes when every part does its share (Eph 4:16). Faced with the truth that if we want to grow the Universal Church we must go and share the gospel, many believers are waking to their call to participate in the furtherance of the gospel.[169]

The Missional Church Movement is one way that some believers have responded to this need. Typically, a church that is part of this movement is small, meets in private homes or public places, and is focused on planting new churches. By design, these churches effectively get everyone involved in this process. These churches have enjoyed exponential growth and much of that growth comes from making new believers.

But other church structures can easily enjoy the same growth when every church member gets involved in sharing the gospel, making disciples, and supporting others who do so. Whatever your local church structure, real growth begins with the involvement of its members (Eph 4:11-16).

MISINFORMATION ABOUT CHRISTIANITY

There's a great deal of misinformation about Christianity that must be overcome. Westboro Baptist Church, a tiny church in Topeka, Kansas, garners enormous media attention by protesting funerals and preaching a message of hate. Though almost no one agrees with their beliefs or methods, they define for many what it is to be a Christian.

What's more is that Lordship Salvation teachers, Catholics, and others who confuse the gospel with works have helped to hide the message of grace. Most people's understanding of Christianity is that it teaches that if you don't shape up, you're going to hell, and if you're homosexual, forget it. They think that Jesus came into the world to condemn it, not to save it. All in all, the caricature of Christianity that the world has created is entirely graceless.

This does add some difficulty because mentioning you're a Christian can often cause people to clam up for fear of being judged.

---

[169] Everyone's role in this is different. See the following lesson for more discussion on this principle.

But it also opens up a door for the gospel because the message of Free Grace, that God loves the world and that anyone, no matter his past, can have eternal life given to him freely because of Christ's death and resurrection for him, is refreshing and welcome.

Share *grace* boldly. Because of the misinformation, people will be amazed that God loves them despite their wrongdoing, and that's a good foundation for fruitful evangelism.

RAMPANT UNRIGHTEOUSNESS

Unrighteousness is rampant all over the world. People live selfishly, in search of immediate gratification, and God is dishonored everywhere.

This is not new. Even in John's day, he could accurately write, "...the whole world lies under the sway of the wicked one" (1 John 5:19). But what is new to many who live in societies that have only recently become post-Christian is that these behaviors are much more out in the open than they were a few decades ago.

Many Christians have expressed surprise at the fact that speaking out for righteousness in government or society is met with so much scorn. This happens because unbelievers are trying to escape guilt without changing their behavior and they are either unaware of the Savior or have rejected Him. Self-justification is human nature. So, being outspoken about moral virtue is often met with vitriol.

While *righteous* (morally upright or virtuous) ideals are often ridiculed in these cultures, no one can dismiss *goodness* (action for the benefit of others) when it is lived out, especially when it is in such sharp contrast with the world around.

Peter wrote:

> For this is the will of God, that by doing good you may put to silence the ignorance of foolish men—as free, yet not using liberty as a cloak for vice, but as bondservants of God. (1 Pet 2:15-16)

The message that we Christians are free in Christ, yet because of Christ's love we live and act for the benefit of others, is a powerful one-two punch combo against the folly of the world.

For example, Pastor Lee Jong-rak in Korea, noting the widespread problem of women abandoning their children in his country, built a drop box onto the side of his house with a simple sign that says, "A place to leave babies." He has rescued six children so far that would have likely died.[170] This is a powerful witness. Even the director of the documentary about Pastor Lee Jong-rak's work became a Christian during filming.

Likewise, on May 5th, 2013, after an F5 tornado ripped through Moore, Oklahoma, killing twenty-four people, an NBC reporter said, "If you're waiting on the government to help, you'll be waiting a long time. The men at the Baptist church will have you taken care of tomorrow." This is honoring to Christ and effective at reaching people.

In short, standing up for righteous ideals, while important, is not very effective in post-Christendom. And if it is not seasoned with grace it can actually hinder the gospel. But by doing good we can draw genuine positive attention to Christ and His gospel that even our post-Christian society will understand and respond to positively.

CONCLUSION

We need to accept the reality that society has moved away from respecting and exalting Christian values and direct our efforts accordingly. Instead of trying to reform society, we should simply do good and point people to Christ. Instead of waiting for unbelievers to come to us to hear the gospel, we need to go to them. Instead of hiding Christ in us for fear of misunderstanding, we should share grace *boldly*. Instead of complaining about persecution when it comes, we should endure it joyfully, knowing that Christ rewards such endurance (Matt 5:11-12; Jas 1:12).

The effectiveness of our mission depends upon accepting the reality we see around us. This can be difficult to do because it requires that we let go of many pleasant things that our countries may have enjoyed. But it can open up many windows of opportunity if we accept it and live as the Bible calls us to, as mere sojourners here, as citizens of Heaven (Phil 3:20).

---

[170] Visit this site to read about the movie "The Drop Box" which chronicles Pastor Lee Jong-rak's work with his baby box: http://www.christianpost.com/news/the-drop-box-documentary-takes-home-grand-prize-at-christian-film-festival-91014/. Last accessed on June 14th, 2013.

PRACTICE

1) What does Acts 5:17-42 teach us about living in a culture that is hostile to Christ?

2) Richard Dawkins states that Christians should be mocked and ridiculed rather than engaged in conversation. What should you do if you are mocked while sharing Christ?

3) Are there any thoughts or actions in your life that hinder you in being an effective witness in a post-Christian society? How can you become more effective?

4) Before Constantine, no buildings were constructed exclusively for church functions. How might not having church buildings have changed the way people viewed church?

5) How did the blending of church and State impact the Church and society in the Middle Ages?

6) How does the lack of societal expectation to attend church services necessitate change in the way we participate in outreach?

DISCUSS

1) What problems can arise in evangelistic endeavors from treating our society as if it were supportive of Christianity?

2) What problems can arise in disciplemaking if we do not recognize that our society has moved away from Christianity?

3) Paul said in Phil 1:12 that his imprisonment had "actually turned out for the furtherance of the gospel." How might this have happened?

4) How can your church grow in a post-Christian culture?

5) How do we raise children in a post-Christian society?

6) How can politics be a hindrance to the gospel?

Spiritual Gifts

> "There ought to be no idle members, but rather opportunities for service for every person. These responsibilities ought to be accepted joyfully and carried out diligently and in orderliness for God's glory." *Earl Radmacher*[171]

LESSON OBJECTIVES

1. To show that God is seeking unity through diversity, not uniformity

2. To help the reader to see that God calls us all to be active in the body and that none of the members are to be exclusively passive receivers

3. To show how God has equipped each of us for the good of the whole

4. To demonstrate that the abuse of the gift of tongues goes against the principle above

INTRODUCTION

In a sermon entitled "The Essential Ingredient"[172] given at a GES National conference, Dr. Earl Radmacher told a story about how he went to a church service where a guest speaker butchered Scripture for the whole message. He couldn't wait to get out of there, but when the service was over, his wife, Ruth, was speaking with an elderly lady, so

---

[171] Radmacher, *The Nature of the Church*, p. 352.

[172] http://www.boldgrace.org/audio/radmacher-the-essential-ingredient.mp3. Last Accessed August 2nd, 2013.

he had to wait. He confessed that he was waiting impatiently during that time. But in that conversation, Ruth thanked this elderly lady for her faithfulness in praying for her, among other things. This dear sister told Mrs. Radmacher that she had been feeling like she had nothing to offer anymore. Her family and friends had all died and she needed help to get around. She told Ruth that her encouraging words had just given her an understanding of why God wanted her to stay here, so that she could pray for Ruth. Ruth had listened to her and thanked her. By doing so, she gave this woman encouragement and a reason to live.

Ruth hadn't gotten anything more out of the sermon than Dr. Radmacher did, but she was not there for what she could get out of it. She was there to give what she could to the Body, to love her brothers and sisters as Christ loved the Church.

The author of Hebrews wrote:

> And let us consider one another in order to stir up love and good works, not forsaking the assembling of ourselves together, as is the manner of some, but exhorting one another, and so much the more as you see the Day approaching. (Heb 10:24-25)

When people reject the principle of Heb 10:24-25 because they cannot find a church they are happy with or they do not get enough out of their time, they do so because they are forgetting their purpose in the Body. When we "get it," we know that we need to meet with the local church body regularly so that we can serve our brothers and sisters.

UNIQUE EQUIPPING—UNITY IN DIVERSITY

God has equipped each of us uniquely to be able to play an important role in God's masterpiece, the Church (Eph 2:10).[173] One of the things He has done to equip us is to give us each spiritual gifts. There are many gifts listed in the New Testament, including (definitions that may not be self-evident are given in parentheses):

- Discernment (the ability to gauge a situation or statement wisely)
- Exhortation (the ability to motivate people toward obedience to God)
- Faith (the ability to strengthen the faith of others by example)
- Giving

---

[173] See http://boldgrace.org/doctrine/gods-masterpiece-what-is-it.html

- Healing
- Hospitality
- Interpretation of Tongues (the ability to understand a tongue even when the interpreter doesn't know the language being spoken)
- Knowledge
- Leadership
- Miracles
- Prophecy (speaking forth God's truth)
- Teaching
- Tongues (the ability to speak a language that one does do not know)
- Serving
- Showing Mercy
- Administration
- Wisdom (the ability to give wise counsel)

The Bible also lists several offices as gifts to the Church, including apostles, evangelists, and pastor-teachers. These are not spiritual gifts, but are offices given for the equipping of the saints for the work of ministry.

Spiritual gifts, with the exception of tongues and miracles, are given for the edification of the Body of Christ and they are not intended (at least primarily) as blessings to the individual who has them. They are responsibilities to those who have them and are gifts to the larger Body. "But the manifestation of the Spirit is given to each one for the profit of all" (1 Cor 12:7).

Zane Hodges taught that each individual in the Body of Christ has only one spiritual gift.[174] There is some ambiguity on that issue, but one thing is certain—our spiritual gifts as individuals are intentionally limited.

There are great preachers (with exhortation or prophecy as their gift) who are poor teachers, and great teachers who are poor preachers. There are people who are excellent at hospitality but are poor at administration, and people who are excellent leaders who are poor at exhortation. Some excel at service with little knowledge, and some who are full of mercy have little discernment.

---

[174] Zane mentioned this during a Lord's Table meeting when I visited Victor Street Bible Chapel in 2002.

God made us this way so that we would need each other. There are two ways to promote unity: through uniformity (everyone is the same), or through diversity (everyone is different). God unifies us through diversity. Because one member has a gift that others don't, he is needed. Because he does not have the gifts that others have, he needs them as well.

Paul explains this in 1 Cor 12:14-26:

> For in fact the body is not one member but many. If the foot should say, "Because I am not a hand, I am not of the body," is it therefore not of the body? And if the ear should say, "Because I am not an eye, I am not of the body," is it therefore not of the body? If the whole body were an eye, where would be the hearing? If the whole were hearing, where would be the smelling? But now God has set the members, each one of them, in the body just as He pleased. And if they were all one member, where would the body be? But now indeed there are many members, yet one body. And the eye cannot say to the hand, "I have no need of you"; nor again the head to the feet, "I have no need of you." No, much rather, those members of the body which seem to be weaker are necessary. And those members of the body which we think to be less honorable, on these we bestow greater honor; and our unpresentable parts have greater modesty, but our presentable parts have no need. But God composed the body, having given greater honor to that part which lacks it, that there should be no schism in the body, but that the members should have the same care for one another. And if one member suffers, all the members suffer with it; or if one member is honored, all the members rejoice with it.

We have the Spirit in common, and that alone promotes our unity, but our differences further bind us together.

We do the body a disservice when we do not recognize our limitations. This is a difficult temptation sometimes for pastors and other church leaders. Often they are naturally gifted people with a strong spiritual gift in one area that fits with the job of pastor. But when they rely on their natural gifts instead of sticking with their spiritual gift(s), others are not given opportunity to express their spiritual gifts. In the end that brother suffers due to lack of activity in the Body and the Body suffers because it does not receive the benefit of his spiritual service.

In the end, the Body grows as every part does its share, not as a few members carry the whole load. This is explicitly stated by the Apostle Paul:

> And He Himself gave some to be apostles, some prophets, some evangelists, and some pastors and teachers, *for the equipping of the saints for the work of ministry*, for the edifying of the body of Christ, till we all come to the unity of the faith and of the knowledge of the Son of God, to a perfect man, to the measure of the stature of the fullness of Christ; that we should no longer be children, tossed to and fro and carried about with every wind of doctrine, by the trickery of men, in the cunning craftiness of deceitful plotting, but, speaking the truth in love, may grow up in all things into Him who is the head—Christ—from whom the whole body, *joined and knit together by what every joint supplies, according to the effective working by which every part does its share, causes growth of the body for the edifying of itself in love.* (Eph 4:11-16, emphasis added)

In short, church leaders are given by God to the local church to equip the saints so that every member of the Body can participate in its edification. This leads to the Body's growth.

THE BEST WAY TO FIND OUT YOUR SPIRITUAL GIFTS

Many times I am asked how a person can know his spiritual gifts. I don't believe that spiritual gift tests are helpful. But one thing I have seen effective over and over is that as people volunteer or just generally start being active in ministry, their spiritual gifts become apparent. If you aren't sure what your spiritual gift is, ask your church leadership what you can do to help the church and serve heartily in whatever opportunity they give you. If, after some time and effort, you find that you aren't gifted in that area, ask for a new task. When you find the right one, it will become obvious.

TONGUES

The gift of tongues is the only spiritual gift that was given a specific definition in the Bible. This definition is found in Acts 2:4-11, in which we see that the disciples were speaking languages that they themselves did not know.

First Corinthians 12–14 discusses this. In the beginning of this section, Paul says, "Now concerning spiritual gifts brethren..." (1 Cor 12:1), but the word *gifts* here is not in the original but is supplied by the translators. Paul literally says, "concerning spiritual things," a category that is more broad than spiritual gifts. Paul is rebuking the Corinthians for the way they were practicing something he calls "a tongue," but is distinct from the spiritual gift of tongues. This can be confusing to us who were not there in the Corinthian church to see what was happening, but when Paul talks about the spiritual gift of tongues, he uses the plural, and when he talks about this other practice, he uses the singular.

Tongues were given for a specific purpose. In 1 Cor 14:21, Paul quotes Isa 28:11-12 to express that purpose. "With men of other tongues and other lips I will speak to this people; and yet, for all that, they will not hear me." In the context of Isaiah, we see that it is a pronouncement of judgment upon the people of Israel to which the Israelites would not respond. Paul follows this up with, "Therefore tongues are for a sign, not to those who believe but to unbelievers..." (14:22). Tongues were given for a warning to unbelieving Israel, not for use in the church. In 13:8, Paul hints that tongues, unlike prophecies and knowledge, will cause themselves to cease at some point before Christ's return. Many believe (as do I) that this has already happened (most likely at AD 70).

Many people who speak in a tongue (as opposed to the spiritual gift of tongues) find it to be edifying and cathartic and Paul does not forbid it. However, he does show that speaking in a tongue in a church meeting is self-edification and against the principle of love. He would rather people speak prophecy (proclaiming God's Word) when they come together so that the whole church is edified. When those who speak in a tongue have come into our church meetings, I have asked them to do it at home in privacy if they so choose and to refrain from doing it in our church meetings. All spiritual things that are from God are in the control of the believer (1 Cor 14:32), so this is a reasonable request. If they are unable to control it, it isn't from God.

A member speaking in a tongue can still be the source of a serious problem, even if it is only done in privacy. This occurs when those who speak in a tongue boast about it and judge others for not doing so, or even if they just carry an arrogant spirit about it. Sometimes this judgment can be implicit with subtle suggestions that those who don't speak in a tongue are spiritually immature. This ignores the principle that spiritual gifts are given to the individual by the Holy Spirit's decision, not by the individual's efforts, and that it occurs when they are spiritually baptized into the Body, i.e. when they first believe (1 Cor 12:11, 13, 18). So boasting or judgment about tongues is to be forbidden and the one who does it should be rebuked in keeping with the principles of Titus 3:10 and Matt 18:15-17 (remembering that the purpose is not just going through the motions until you can remove them from fellowship, but seeking reconciliation).

Spiritual gifts are sometimes divided by Bible teachers into Body gifts and non-Body gifts. The division is based upon whether or not it should be expressed in church meetings. I believe tongues have ceased, but even if they have not, the gift of tongues is a non-Body gift. When it is abused and used within the church meetings, Paul says that the speaker does not edify the hearer (1 Cor 14:17), but that he only edifies himself (14:4). The exception would be if it is done one at a time with an interpreter :

> If anyone speaks in a tongue, let there be two or at the most three, each in turn, and let one interpret. But if there is no interpreter, let him keep silent in church, and let him speak to himself and to God. (1 Cor 14:27-28)

Even so, Paul also says, "in the church I would rather speak five words with my understanding, that I may teach others also, than ten thousand words in a tongue" (14:19).

This discussion on tongues surrounds this description of love in chapter 13:

> Though I speak with the tongues of men and of angels, but have not love, I have become sounding brass or a clanging cymbal. And though I have the gift of prophecy, and understand all mysteries and all knowledge, and though I have all faith, so that I could remove mountains, but have not love, I am nothing. And though I bestow all my goods to feed the poor, and though I give my body to be burned, but have not love, it profits me nothing. Love suffers long and is kind; love does not envy; love does not parade itself, is not puffed up; does not behave rudely, does not seek its own, is not provoked, thinks no evil; does not rejoice in iniquity, but rejoices in the truth; bears all things, believes all things, hopes all things, endures all things. Love never fails. (1 Cor 13:1-8a)

Every aspect of this love is humble and seeks the good of the beloved. This kind of love is what Jesus called us to in His great commandment, "A new commandment I give to you, that you love one another; as I have loved you, that you also love one another" (John 13:34). So, what we do in the church meetings should always be for the edification of others. You aren't there to be blessed; you are there to bless others. Of course, you will be blessed as well, but that's not the main purpose of your being there.

CONCLUSION

You were placed in the Body of Christ with unique gifting and that makes you important to the Body. Get involved in service in your local church and when you know your spiritual gift(s), use it with gusto. But always keep in mind that your gifting is intentionally limited, and don't seek to become a one-person show.

Lastly, keep in mind that your gift is a responsibility to you and a gift to the church. You are part of His masterpiece and your role in it is the edification of others.

PRACTICE

1) What is your spiritual gift(s)? If you don't know, how can you find out?

2) How does knowing that spiritual gifts are responsibilities to the individual and gifts to the Church change your understanding of the gift of faith?

3) Can someone without the spiritual gift of wisdom still be exceptionally wise in the Lord?

4) Read Rom 12:4-8. What does this teach about spiritual gifts?

5) Use your spiritual gift(s) to encourage someone.

DISCUSS

1) If someone has the gift of giving and his only major service to the Body is giving lavishly to help those in need and support others in ministry, is he doing his share (Eph 4:11-16)?

2) What ways can one person wearing many hats hinder the growth of the body?

3) Can a believer be living obediently without assembling regularly with the brethren? Why or why not?

4) How can the gift of mercy be effective in building up the body?

5) How can tongues be a problem in the body?

Liberty in the Church

"Therefore let us pursue the things which
make for peace and the things by which
one may edify another." *Romans 14:19*

LESSON OBJECTIVES

1. To show how to live in unity through Christian liberty
2. To help believers see the connection between liberty and mission

INTRODUCTION

Christian liberty can be a major source of contention, or it can be
a great unifier. Like anything, the difference is having the right
(Biblical) perspective.

The essence of Christian liberty is that Christians are free to do anything that is not against the principles of faith in Christ and love for the
brethren laid out in the law of Christ (see John 13:34; 14:1; Gal 6:1-2;
1 John 3:23). Many issues are covered by chapter and verse (in the Church
economy), where it can clearly be seen that those practices are against this
law, but everything else comes under the realm of Christian liberty.

ROMANS 14

In Romans 14, a classic passage on Christian liberty, Paul addresses two
different groups of believers, the *strong* [in faith] brothers and the *weak*
brothers, and his concern is unity between the two groups. The weak
brothers are primarily addressed in the first half of the chapter, while the
strong brothers are primarily addressed in the second half of the chapter.

Before I break down the passage, a quick chart explaining the different groups addressed and their respective responsibilities is below:

Group	Characteristics	Responsibility
Weak Brothers (vv 1-13)	Do not express Christian liberty	Not to judge or hinder the strong brother in his expression of liberty.
Strong Brothers (vv 14-23)	Do express Christian liberty	To express Christian liberty with sensitivity and love.

The text of the first section, Rom 14:1-13 is below:

> Receive one who is weak in the faith, but not to disputes over doubtful things [literally, *opinions*]. For one believes he may eat all things, but he who is weak eats only vegetables. Let not him who eats despise him who does not eat, and let not him who does not eat judge him who eats; for God has received him. Who are you to judge another's servant? To his own master he stands or falls. Indeed, he will be made to stand, for God is able to make him stand. One person esteems one day above another; another esteems every day alike. Let each be fully convinced in his own mind. He who observes the day, observes it to the Lord; and he who does not observe the day, to the Lord he does not observe it. He who eats, eats to the Lord, for he gives God thanks; and he who does not eat, to the Lord he does not eat, and gives God thanks. For none of us lives to himself, and no one dies to himself. For if we live, we live to the Lord; and if we die, we die to the Lord. Therefore, whether we live or die, we are the Lord's. For to this end Christ died and rose and lived again, that He might be Lord of both the dead and the living. But why do you judge your brother? Or why do you show contempt for your brother? For we shall all stand before the judgment seat of Christ. For it is written: "AS I LIVE, SAYS THE LORD, EVERY KNEE SHALL BOW TO ME, AND EVERY TONGUE SHALL CONFESS TO GOD." So then each of us shall give account of himself to God. Therefore let us not judge one another anymore, but rather resolve this, not to put a stumbling block or a cause to fall [lit., *hindrance*] in our brother's way.

The strong brother is defined as the brother who "eats all things," and "esteems every day alike." These may not seem like very big taboos to us today, but these were issues related to the Mosaic Law, so they were very taboo to those who had a Jewish background. Today's taboos in the Church seem to be things like alcohol, hugging, television and movies, but the list could be extended on and on. The admonitions in the passage are as follows:

To the strong brothers:

1. Receive (accept openly into the church fellowship) the weak brothers, but not so that they can fight about opinions.

2. Don't put a stumbling block in the weak brother's way. This means that the strong brother should not encourage the weak brothers to go against their conscience.

To the weak brothers:

1. Don't judge the strong brother for expressing his Christian liberty. He has the right to do so and God will uphold him in the temptations that come with such expression.

2. Keep your personal convictions to yourself. They are for you alone and not for anyone else.

3. Don't hinder the strong brother's expression of Christian liberty.

The principle of Christ as the Judge of the brethren overrides it all. We are accountable to Him alone, so judging one another is usurping His role.

All areas of Christian liberty that are typically in question have to do with things that involve temptation. Is it sin to be a drunk? Of course it is, because drunkenness dulls and dissipates life, and can lead to doing stupid and harmful things. Does that mean that alcohol itself is a sin? Of course not. Jesus drank wine (real wine, the idea that he was drinking grape juice or water with a little wine mixed in is unfounded; see Matt 11:19), and provided 120-180 gallons of it for a wedding party (John 2:1-11). We need to understand that no matter what the thing is, Jesus is bigger than that thing and the temptations that may come with it.

The second section of the chapter focuses on the strong brother.

Romans 14:14-23:

> I know and am convinced by the Lord Jesus that there is nothing unclean of itself; but to him who considers anything to be unclean, to him it is unclean. Yet if your brother is grieved because of your food, you are no longer walking in love. Do not destroy with your food the one for whom Christ died. Therefore do not let your good be spoken of as evil; for the

kingdom of God is not eating and drinking, but righteousness and peace and joy in the Holy Spirit. For he who serves Christ in these things is acceptable to God and approved by men. Therefore let us pursue the things which make for peace and the things by which one may edify another. Do not destroy the work of God for the sake of food. All things indeed are pure, but it is evil for the man who eats with offense. It is good neither to eat meat nor drink wine nor do anything by which your brother stumbles or is offended [literally, *trips or is stumbled*] or is made weak. Do you have faith? Have it to yourself before God. Happy is he who does not condemn himself in what [H]e approves. But he who doubts is condemned if he eats, because he does not eat from faith; for whatever is not from faith is sin.

This passage begins with an encouragement to the strong brothers that indeed they are free in Christ. Nothing is unclean of itself. However, the strong brother needs to understand that the weak brothers are right to restrict their own liberty. Something that is perfectly acceptable to you may not be okay for another. The difference is the conscience. If your conscience condemns you in a certain practice, you should avoid that practice because you cannot live in faith if you are acting against your conscience.

Because of this, the strong brother needs to deal gently with the weak brothers so that they are not ostracized or pushed into acting against their conscience. This is what Paul means by verse 21, literally, "It is good neither to eat meat nor drink wine nor do anything by which your brother trips or is stumbled or is made weak." The weak brother being offended is not the issue (Paul has just said that they have no right to be offended by the strong brother's expression of liberty).[175] The issue is their stumbling, defined in the context as their going against their own conscience.

How does this work out practically? If you are a strong brother, never pressure others to partake in your liberties against their conscience. Above all, walk in love. If you love your brother, you will help him pursue Christ and will never seek to harm him, especially over something trivial like food or alcohol.

This leads us to the unifying principle of Christian liberty. If weak brothers keep their personal convictions to themselves and live without

---

[175] See the unpublished dissertation of Dr. B. Dale Taliaferro, *The Pauline Concept of Stumbling in Romans 14:1-15:6 and 1 Corinthians 8:1-11:1*. Available at www.boldgrace.org/pdfs/taliaferro.pdf

judgment, and the strong brothers accept the weak brothers and treat them lovingly, there is unity in that diversity. How could there possibly be disputes over issues of liberty if everyone accepts each other and is loving toward one another? In my experience, teaching these principles clearly in the church leads to the unity that would be expected. People of all ages and backgrounds can fellowship in love when these sources of contention are removed.

Legalism always breeds division, and grace unifies. Peter's removal from fellowship with the gentiles in Antioch (Gal 2:11-13) is a great example of such division. Yet throughout Galatians, as Paul defends grace, he speaks of the unity of the brethren in liberty (see especially, Gal 3:27-28; 5:13-14).

LIBERTY, UNITY, AND MISSION

As I cover in the next lesson, John 13–17 reveals that Jesus' priority is our love for one another. His priority should be ours as well. But we haven't often kept that priority. One problem is that legalism, of which we have way too much, destroys love and unity, especially when expressed in community.

Paul tells us about an example of this in Gal 2:11-16.

> Now when Peter had come to Antioch, I withstood him to his face, because he was to be blamed; for before certain men came from James, he would eat with the Gentiles; but when they came, he withdrew and separated himself, fearing those who were of the circumcision. And the rest of the Jews also played the hypocrite with him, so that even Barnabas was carried away with their hypocrisy. But when I saw that they were not straightforward about the truth of the gospel, I said to Peter before them all, "If you, being a Jew, live in the manner of Gentiles and not as the Jews, why do you compel Gentiles to live as Jews? We who are Jews by nature, and not sinners of the Gentiles, knowing that a man is not justified by the works of the law but by faith in Jesus Christ, even we have believed in Christ Jesus, that we might be justified by faith in Christ and not by the works of the law; for by the works of the law no flesh shall be justified."

What was happening here is that Peter had been enjoying regular fellowship with Gentile (non-Jewish) Christians. He would eat with them, celebrating the Lord's Supper. I am sure that this was a huge encouragement to these Christians, to be accepted on equal footing with an apostle, enjoying each other's company. I would love to sit with Peter and hear His stories about Jesus that we don't get to read about in the Gospels. But when some people came in and said something like, "Peter, what are you doing at this catfish fry? Don't you know it's forbidden in the Law?" Peter succumbed to the pressure and withdrew from these Gentile brothers and sisters.

This is just one example of why Paul calls the law "the enmity" and the 'middle wall of separation" between Jews and Gentiles (Eph 2:14-15). (Thank you, Jesus, for breaking that wall down and abolishing that enmity.) But legalism doesn't just separate Jews and Gentiles; it divides along lines of race generally, age, economic class, gender, and position in the local church.

It tends to start with the mistaken idea that God wants unity in the Church to be based upon uniformity, rather than diversity. But this isn't God's way. As I discussed in the previous lesson, God's way is illustrated in the body metaphor that is often used to describe the Church. Just as the body has many different members with different functions, so is the Body of Christ. This has to do primarily with spiritual gifts, but there are many things that make us each uniquely suited to fulfill a certain role in the Body. You and I don't do the same things, and that's exactly God's design. I can't do everything that needs to be done or reach everyone who needs to be reached, and neither can you. But together, we are much more capable.

We're supposed to be different so that we need each other.

Paul wrote:

> For though I am free from all men, I have made myself a servant to all, that I might win the more; and to the Jews I became as a Jew, that I might win Jews; to those who are under the law, as under the law, that I might win those who are under the law; to those who are without law, as without law (not being without law toward God, but under law toward Christ [literally, lawful with respect to Christ]), that I might win those who are without law; to the weak I became as weak, that I might win the weak. I have become all things to all men, that I might by all means save some. (1 Cor 9:19-22)

This demonstrates that Paul used his liberty in Christ to adapt to those whom he could not reach if he didn't do so. To the extent that we are able, we should do the same.

But someone who drives a Harley and has a long beard and tattoo sleeves can reach with the gospel of Christ people who may not give me the time of day. And that person I can't reach needs the love of Christ just as much as everyone else. So, instead of judging the brother who looks or lives differently from me, I thank God for him. And I thank God for the differences between us.

Judgment of each brother and sister in Christ is Christ's job, not ours (Rom 14:10-12). It is our job to thank the Lord for our brothers and sisters in Christ and to love them and help them to be as effective a sojourner in this world as they can be. In doing this, we multiply our own ministries.

PRACTICE

1) What does "...Indeed he will be made to stand, for God is able to make him stand" in Rom 14:4 mean?

2) How does the doctrine of the Judgment Seat of Christ help promote Christian liberty in community?

3) How does Christian liberty help unify the body?

4) Why does Paul call the law "the enmity" in Eph 2:15? How does this reconcile with his statement that the law is "holy and just and good" (Rom 7:12)?

5) How does the strong brother live in liberty and be sensitive to the weak brother?

DISCUSS

1) How is Christian liberty, "...let each be fully convinced in his own mind" (Rom 14:5), different from moral relativism (the idea that there are not moral absolutes)?

2) In what ways do Christians often try to enforce uniformity where diversity would be more effective for mission?

3) How does Rom 13:8-10 relate to the doctrine of Christian liberty?

4) Imagine that you are a leader in a church and two people ask you to help them work through a dispute. One says that she wants only hymns sung in the church and thinks that contemporary worship songs sound too much like secular music. The other prefers the contemporary worship songs, and he thinks that hymns are often corny. Discuss how to counsel them in this dispute. If possible, choose actors to play the different roles in this counseling session.

5) What are some ways that Christian liberty can help us be more effective in carrying out God's mission?

Striving for Unity

"Behold, how good and how pleasant it is
For brethren to dwell together in unity!"
Psalm 133:1

LESSON OBJECTIVES

1. To establish the priority that God places on unity in the Body

2. To demonstrate that holiness and striving for unity are inseparable

3. To give practical helps to the reader on how to strive for unity

INTRODUCTION-GOD'S PRIORITY ON UNITY

There are many times in Scripture when God reveals His priorities, but there are a few times when His priorities are most clearly seen.

JESUS

Perhaps the most powerful expression of God's priorities is seen in the Upper Room Discourse in John (chapters 13–17). This discourse occurs on the night before Jesus went to the cross and was His final message to them before His death and resurrection. The Gospel of John's literary structure mirrors the temple. The Holy Place and the Holy of Holies are pictured by chapters 13–16 and 17 respectively. From 13:31 on, only Jesus and the eleven faithful disciples are present. The only recorded prayer of our Lord that is more than a couple of lines occurs in chapter 17 and it fills the whole chapter. 17:20-26 is the only time in Scripture in which we see what Jesus prays specifically for us. This chapter is a peek into the Holy of Holies where Jesus, as our High Priest, communes with the Father.

So, it is evident that this moment has special significance for Jesus and His faithful disciples, and it is not surprising that we find some of the most intimate moments of Scripture here.

It is here that Jesus gives His new commandment, "A new commandment I give to you, that you love one another; as I have loved you, that you also love one another" (John 13:34). He said then, "By this all will know that you are My disciples, if you have love for one another" (13:35).

Only a few paragraphs later, Jesus says, "He who has My commandments and keeps them, it is he who loves Me. And he who loves Me will be loved by My Father, and I will love him *and manifest Myself to him*" (14:21, emphasis added).

The commandments in context are to love one another as He has loved us and to believe in Him (14:1). If we want the Lord to manifest Himself (to reveal Himself, show Himself) to us, we must obey the command to love one another. This also results in an additional portion of love from the Father.

This means that if we refuse to love the brethren, we greatly hinder our ability both to know and understand God, and we hinder our fellowship with Him.

When Jesus prayed for us in 17:20-26, He specifically prayed that we would be one with Him and each other just as He and the Father are one (vv 21-22), and that through our unity the world would know that He was sent by the Father (v 23). Besides this, His only request for us is that we would see His glory. This demonstrates that perhaps His greatest desire for us in this world is that we would obey His command to "love one another; as [He has] loved [us]."

One theme in this sermon is that our witness is dependent on our love for our brothers in Christ (13:35; 17:23). It is easy, when faced with ridicule by those with opposing views, to respond with a sharp quip or an avalanche of all the reasons they are wrong. But when we do so, we are falling into the Enemy's trap. As Dr. Earl Radmacher said, "Satan wants to do everything he can to keep me from giving the greatest apologetic for Jesus Christ. And that [apologetic] is how I treat my brother."[176]

When it comes to the reputation we seek in support of our witness, our gentleness toward others should stand out: "Let your *gentleness* be known to all men. The Lord is at hand" (Phil 4:5, emphasis added). Too much introspection is not good, but we should take inventory when we see such

---

[176] Earl Radmacher, "The Essential Ingredient" available at http://www.boldgrace.org/audio/radmacher-the-essential-ingredient.mp3. Last accessed, August 2nd, 2013.

exhortations, consider what might stand out to others in our lives, and compare that with our calling.

PAUL'S LETTERS

Most of Paul's letters to churches were written to address certain issues or questions they had. Philippians and Ephesians are the only exceptions. Philippians was written as a thank you for their support of His mission (Phil 4:10-19). Ephesians, however, doesn't seem to be occasioned by anything in particular. What we see instead is Paul writing about his top priorities.

In Ephesians 1–3, Paul beautifully lays out many of the great blessings and purposes God has for us in Christ. It is not so much a defense of grace, as Romans 3–4 is, but rather a story of its significance. By grace we are in Christ and we share in all of the blessings God intends for His Son. God's motivation: "that in the ages to come He might show the exceeding riches of His grace in His kindness toward us in Christ Jesus" (Eph 2:7).

The first command in Ephesians doesn't come until after three rich chapters cataloging the value of our calling. It occurs in 4:1 where he calls us "to walk worthy of the calling with which [we] were called."

This consists in our humbling ourselves, lovingly bearing with one another, and endeavoring to maintain unity in the Sprit. The whole passage warrants quoting:

> I, therefore, the prisoner of the Lord, beseech you to walk worthy of the calling with which you were called, with all lowliness and gentleness, with longsuffering, bearing with one another in love, endeavoring to keep the unity of the Spirit in the bond of peace. There is one body and one Spirit, just as you were called in one hope of your calling; one Lord, one faith, one baptism; one God and Father of all, who is above all, and through all, and in you all. (Eph 4:1-6)

To walk worthy of our calling is to recognize the value of what God has done by uniting us in Christ and to therefore strive for the maintenance of that unity in Him. In other words, *godliness and striving for unity are inseparable.*

PAUL'S GOSPEL AND UNITY

Because Christ died for the whole world, taking the law and sins out of the way (Col 2:14; John 1:29), anyone can have a right relationship with God through faith. This puts us all on the same level.

This is why when Paul talks about Christ's death in relationship to our freedom from the law he then also talks about our unity in Christ. Galatians 3:26-28 looks back on 3:13-25. So, when Paul says:

> For you are all sons of God through faith in Christ Jesus. For as many of you as were baptized into Christ [note: this is spiritual baptism, not water baptism] have put on Christ. There is neither Jew nor Greek, there is neither slave nor free, there is neither male nor female; for you are all one in Christ Jesus. (Gal 3:26-28)

It is because:

> Christ has redeemed us from the curse of the law, having become a curse for us (...) the law was our tutor to bring us to Christ, that we might be justified by faith. But after faith has come, we are no longer under a tutor (3:13, 24-25)

See also Eph 2:13-16, Col 2:11-23 and 3:11, and many other places in Paul's writings. Love for the Gospel is love for the unity of brothers. This is illustrated in that when Paul publicly rebuked Peter for having removed Himself from fellowship with Gentile believers (Gal 2:11-18), Paul said Peter and those who "played the hypocrite with him" were "not straightforward about the truth of the gospel."

DIVISION IS SERIOUS DISOBEDIENCE

There are not many clear examples in Paul's letters of instructions on specific kinds of people to remove from fellowship. One of those types of people is a divisive person. Paul told Titus that after a first and second admonition, he should reject a divisive man (Titus 3:10). What this means is that he should be excluded from the fellowship. Paul does not even call for the rejection of those who are fornicating with pagan temple prostitutes (1 Cor 6:15-20), or getting drunk at the Lord's Supper (1 Cor 11:21-22), which we all recognize are serious problems.

Another clear example we have of excommunication is a man who was sleeping with his father's wife. The instructions on dealing with a divisive brother and this brother are essentially the same, and this should tell us a great deal about the seriousness of causing division.

Eight of the seventeen works of the flesh (hatred, contentions, jealousies, outbursts of wrath, selfish ambitions, dissensions, heresies, envy) listed by Paul in Gal 5:20-21 deal with various things that promote divisiveness. And Paul treated the divisiveness of the Corinthians as proof that they were carnal Christians (1 Cor 3:1-4).

Having correct doctrine is important. But it is love that is the fulfillment of the law (Rom 13:10); so if we have the truth and do not love one another, we are not honoring Christ with that truth.

RECOGNIZING THE TRUE ENEMY

When Paul discussed spiritual warfare, he made it clear that "we do not wrestle against flesh and blood, but against principalities, against powers, against the rulers of the darkness of this age, against spiritual hosts of wickedness in the heavenly places" (Eph 6:12). In other words, our enemy is not the person who attacks us or who disagrees with us, not really. This is true even when we are right and he is wrong. Our true enemies are the wicked angelic forces that have led to that person's error.

Paul was in prison when he wrote this, but he was not looking for personal vengeance. In fact, he was glad for the opportunity his chains presented for the furtherance of the gospel, even reaching some of Caesar's household (Phil 1:12-14; 4:22; Philippians was written concurrently with Ephesians). If Paul had not been clear that those who imprisoned him were not his enemies, how might this have affected his mission to them?

COMMUNICATION AND HUMILITY

Paul told Timothy,

> But avoid foolish and ignorant disputes, knowing that they generate strife. And a servant of the Lord must not quarrel but be gentle to all, able to teach, patient, in humility correcting those who are in opposition, if God perhaps will grant them repentance, so that they may know the truth, and that they may come to their senses and escape the snare of the devil, having been taken captive by him to do his will. (2 Tim 2:23-26)

In today's social media infused culture, there are plenty of opportunities to get into foolish and ignorant disputes, but we are called to avoid fighting.

What this does not mean is that we cease our concern or our outreach to those who are opposed to the truth. We should use all of our resources to persuade them. This includes our training in Scripture, but it also includes our demonstration of the fruit of the spirit.

A truthful word spoken without love is not often received. And even if it is received, what kind of example have we set? But a truthful word spoken with gentleness and love has much more power for breaking down strongholds. Speak the truth in love (Eph 4:15).

When I counsel couples, I often talk about communication. In right perspective, the point of communication is to be understood. When couples keep this in mind it radically changes the way they disagree. Instead of seeking to win an argument, we should seek to be understood. If we are understood and our perspective is well founded, we have made a big stride toward persuading our loved one, and we have made an even bigger stride toward reconciliation. This applies to all of our interactions with others.

Don't argue with men; persuade them of the truth. Don't curse those who oppose you; pray for them.

We cannot always maintain peace with everyone. But, "If it is possible, as much as depends on you, live peaceably with all men" (Rom 12:18). Much of the time doing so has more to do with humbling ourselves than anything else. We are not the judge of men; Christ is.

We must humble ourselves to realize what we do and do not control. We cannot control people's beliefs beyond seeking to persuade them of the truth. We cannot control how others speak of us or of Christ. We can control *how* we disagree *when* we disagree, and we can control how we treat those with whom we disagree. And we can do good to all (Gal 6:10), even to those with whom we disagree.

We must also humble ourselves to listen to those who oppose our beliefs. We must seek to understand their point and why they believe it. When we do so, we might learn something that we did not know (none of us have every aspect of our theology right), or at least we will be better prepared to persuade them because we will be speaking to their understanding instead of speaking against someone else's views.

GRACE AND TRUTH

Jesus Christ is "full of grace and truth" (John 1:14). He is the full embodiment of both. Often, teachers and others view grace and truth as opposite ends of the spectrum and say they must be kept in balance with one another. This is not strictly accurate.

Grace and truth are dependent upon one another. If our so-called truth is graceless, it omits an essential aspect of the truth. For example, many treat truth as if it equals condemnation, but the truth is that Christ has died and grace is offered freely to all. It would be a half-truth to say to someone who sins, "That action is harmful to yourself and others and is dishonoring to God." But if it is coupled with a reassurance of grace, it is a whole truth.

Likewise, if our grace is not expressed in truth, it is counterfeit grace. If someone says to a brother who is sinning, "Don't worry about it; God has justified you," that is not grace; it is licentiousness. Grace does not treat sin lightly; it condemns it fully but counts it nailed to the cross. But if someone were to say to a sinning brother, "That action is harmful to yourself and others and is dishonoring to God. Thank Him that He has justified you and given you strength to overcome that sin," grace would be fully manifested in that statement.

Grace without truth is no grace at all, and truth without grace is a lie.

CONCLUSION

When someone wrongs us, our place is to forgive him (Col 3:13). Vengeance is the Lord's (Deut 32:35; Rom 12:19).

We must also humble ourselves to become the servants of others. Serving others is one way to do our part in promoting unity. When Christ gave the command "love one another; as I have loved you" (John 13:34), He had just washed the feet of the disciples (including Judas Iscariot). While He had the right to be served, He became the servant and demonstrated the love He had for them. He demonstrated this love even more powerfully when He took on the sins of the world and died for us, which He would do on the following day. His death for all was the ultimate example of unification (2 Cor 5:14-18; Eph 2:11-22).

The concept of striving for unity is often treated as if we have to make a choice between the truth and unity. While many have sacrificed truth for the sake of unity, this is not necessary by any means and this dichotomy is set up to avoid doing what we are commanded to do. Having the truth, we have the choice to obey the Lord or not. We can love our brothers by humbling ourselves, teaching patiently and gently, and striving for unity, or not. We can obey the Lord by loving our enemies and seeking to live peaceably with all men, or not.

Let us choose to obey the Lord in this together, so that we can draw the world's attention to Christ instead of our squabbles.

PRACTICE

1) Read 1 Cor 3:1-4. Some say that this does not mean these people were generally carnal, but that it was just one area of their lives. This does not match what we see of these brothers throughout the rest of the epistle. But even if it were accurate, is it appropriate to look at divisiveness as an isolated issue, unrelated to their general spiritual walk? Why or why not?

2) Read Eph 6:10-20. Who is our enemy and how do we do battle with Him?

3) Read Col 3:12-13 and 2 Tim 2:23-26. How does humility promote unity?

4) Read Matt 5:3-12. What are peacemakers (in v 9) and what does it mean that they will be called sons of God? (Hint: See vv 3 and 12 for the appropriate context)

5) Read John 13:34 and 14:21. Does striving for unity result in knowing Christ more intimately? Why or why not?

DISCUSS

1) Do truth and grace need to be held in balance, or are they complementary?

2) Why do you suppose so many treat truth and grace as if they are in conflict?

3) Can someone be godly and divisive? Why or why not?

4) Is divisiveness a practical denial of the gospel? Why or why not?

5) The gospel unifies the races, social and economic classes, and genders (Gal 3:28; Col 3:11), yet most churches are divided on lines of race, wealth, age, and other worldly factors. How can your church or group help correct this?

The Kingdom

SECTION GOALS

1. To demonstrate that a literal kingdom is a sure promise from God
2. To show how the Bible describes the kingdom
3. To help foster the student's hope for the kingdom

INTRODUCTION

Jesus Christ is coming back, and He along with His overcomers will rule the nations in the only truly righteous government the world will ever know. This is a coming reality for which we are to wait eagerly and to labor diligently in anticipation.

The kingdom is one of those doctrines that sat in me for several years before it took hold of me. I could see how important the kingdom was for understanding the Bible, and I knew what a motivating force it was for Paul and the other Apostles, but it did not drive me until later. I am thankful to Curtis Tucker for his excellent book *Majestic Destiny*[177] which helped me to get a tiny peek into just how breathtaking the kingdom will be. Since that time, Jesus' statement in Matt 6:33, "But seek first the kingdom of God and His righteousness, and all these things shall be added to you," has become for me much more than just something to remember to do.

I am the kind of person who can become weighed down by the state of the world and the struggle of all the churches. It gets to me that there are over a billion people who don't have clean drinking water, or that there are an estimated 27 million people living in slavery, many of whom are young girls in the sex trade, or that human life is treated as cheap and valueless throughout the world in many cases, or that the Church at large

---

[177] Curtis Tucker, *Majestic Destiny* (Redmond, OR: Last Chapter Publishing, 2011).

doesn't seem to understand grace. When the truth of the kingdom finally took hold of me, I found that it was much easier for me to cast these kinds of cares on Jesus.

My prayer for this section is that it would help you to have a peek into what's ahead for us and that it would take hold of you as well.

RECOMMENDED BOOKS ON THE KINGDOM

Title	Author	Audience
Majestic Destiny	Curtis Tucker	All
Final Destiny[177]	Joseph Dillow	Advanced
The Greatness of the Kingdom[178]	Alva J. McClain	Intermediate
Various Commentaries and Books	Robert Govett (beware of his position that believers can miss the rapture. This is biblically inaccurate).	Advanced
Firstborn Sons: Their Rights and Risks[179]	G.H. Lang (also believes in a partial rapture)	Intermediate
The Outer Darkness[180]	Marty Cauley	Advanced
The Redeemer's Return[181]	Arthur Pink (later works by him not recommended)	All

---

[178] Joseph Dillow, *Final Destiny: The Future Reign of the Servant Kings* (Monument, CO: Paniym Group Inc., 2012).

[179] Alva J. McClain, *The Greatness of the Kingdom* (Winona Lake: BMH Books, 1974).

[180] G.H. Lang, *Firstborn Sons: Their Rights and Risks* (Hayesville, NC: Schoettle Publishing Co., 1980).

[181] Marty A. Cauley, *The Outer Darkness: Its Interpretations and Implications*, 2 Vols. (Sylva, NC: Misthological Press, 2012).

[182] A.W. Pink, *The Redeemer's Return* (Place Unknown: Bible Truth Depot, 1918).

The Covenants

"I led you up from Egypt and brought
you to the land of which I swore to your
fathers; and I said, 'I will never break
My covenant with you.'" *Judges 2:1b*

LESSON OBJECTIVE

1. To help the reader understand the Biblical covenants as they
   relate to the kingdom

INTRODUCTION

A covenant between God and man is essentially a contract. God
promises to perform certain actions. In some of the Biblical covenants, man has a part to play in these contracts as well, though God's
part in the covenant is not always conditioned upon man's upholding
his end of the contract.

By giving the Bible an understandable structure, the covenants help
us to see the big picture and understand how God interacts with man in
bringing about His ultimate plan for the world. Additionally, the covenants help us to see God's faithfulness.

There are many covenants between God and man in the Bible. Several
of these covenants play a major role in the advancement of God's kingdom program. These are the *Abrahamic* (Gen 15:18-21), the *Mosaic*
(Exodus 19–Deuteronomy 34), the *Davidic* (2 Sam 7:8-17), and the *New*
(Jer 31:31-34).

ABRAHAMIC COVENANT

Many people confuse the calling of Abraham and the promises—that God would make him a great nation (Gen 12:1-3) and that his seed shall be a blessing to the nations (22:18)—with the Abrahamic Covenant. These are indeed promises that God made to Abraham, but they are not, strictly speaking, the Abrahamic Covenant. The Church partakes in the calling of and promises to Abraham in Gen 12:1-3 (Gal 3:14), but the covenants are made with Israel, not the Church (Rom 9:4). We learn as the story of Genesis plays out, the Abrahamic covenant did not include all of his children, but those born of his son Isaac and his grandson Jacob (whom God later named Israel).

The Abrahamic Covenant is a promise of land to Abraham's descendants. The forming of this covenant is found in Gen 15:7-21:

> Then He said to him, "I am the LORD, who brought you out of Ur of the Chaldeans, to give you this land to inherit it."
>
> And he said, "Lord God, how shall I know that I will inherit it?"
>
> So He said to him, "Bring Me a three-year-old heifer, a three-year-old female goat, a three-year-old ram, a turtledove, and a young pigeon." Then he brought all these to Him and cut them in two, down the middle, and placed each piece opposite the other; but he did not cut the birds in two. And when the vultures came down on the carcasses, Abram drove them away.
>
> Now when the sun was going down, a deep sleep fell upon Abram; and behold, horror and great darkness fell upon him. Then He said to Abram: "Know certainly that your descendants will be strangers in a land that is not theirs, and will serve them, and they will afflict them four hundred years. And also the nation whom they serve I will judge; afterward they shall come out with great possessions. Now as for you, you shall go to your fathers in peace; you shall be buried at a good old age. But in the fourth generation they shall return here, for the iniquity of the Amorites is not yet complete."
>
> And it came to pass, when the sun went down and it was dark, that behold, there appeared a smoking oven and a burning

torch that passed between those pieces. On the same day the LORD made a covenant with Abram, saying:

"To your descendants I have given this land, from the river of Egypt to the great river, the River Euphrates—the Kenites, the Kenezzites, the Kadmonites, the Hittites, the Perizzites, the Rephaim, the Amorites, the Canaanites, the Girgashites, and the Jebusites."

The symbol of this kind of covenant, in which animals are cut in two and the parties of the covenant pass between the pieces, may sound strange. What it means is that the parties of the covenant are saying, "If I don't keep my end of the covenant, let what happened to these animals happen to me." The unusual thing about this particular covenant is that only God passed between the split carcasses, where normally both parties would pass through. In effect, God was saying, "This covenant only depends upon me, not on you at all."

Another thing to note about this covenant is that the land is described with geographical data. The land mentioned here extends from inside Egypt through Iraq, from the Arabian Peninsula well into Turkey. Israel has never possessed all of this land, so this covenant's fulfillment is still future.

MOSAIC COVENANT

The Mosaic Covenant is a promise for blessing for keeping the Mosaic Law and cursing for failure to keep it. The law held over six hundred commandments that codified and controlled every aspect of life. The Ten Commandments were given soon after the Lord delivered the children of Israel from slavery in Egypt. The law included both positive, "do," and negative, "do not," commands along with punishments for failure to keep them. Breaking some of the commandments could be forgiven through animal sacrifices performed by priests at the Temple in Jerusalem, but others resulted in the death or exile of the offender.

Deuteronomy 27:11–28:68 outlines the national blessings and curses for Israel based upon their keeping or failing to keep the law. If the nation as a whole would walk in the ways outlined in the Mosaic Covenant, it would be able to remain in the Promised Land, be safe from adversaries, and enjoy prosperity. If they as a nation failed to keep the law, they would be scattered or carried away into captivity by other nations.

The Mosaic Covenant was entirely breakable, and indeed it was broken, but this does not affect the fulfillment of the other covenants.

DAVIDIC COVENANT

In the Davidic Covenant, given in 2 Sam 7:8-17, God promised David that his Son (we know now to be Jesus) would rule on his throne over the house of Israel forever.

The Davidic Covenant is unconditional, and failure of the people to keep the Mosaic Covenant in no way jeopardized the sure fulfillment of the Davidic Covenant. This is discussed at length in the next lesson.

NEW COVENANT

The New Covenant is outlined in Jer 31:31-34, which reads:

> Behold, the days are coming, says the LORD, when I will make a new covenant with the house of Israel and with the house of Judah—not according to the covenant that I made with their fathers in the day that I took them by the hand to lead them out of the land of Egypt, My covenant which they broke, though I was a husband to them, says the LORD. But this is the covenant that I will make with the house of Israel after those days, says the LORD: I will put My law in their minds, and write it on their hearts; and I will be their God, and they shall be My people. No more shall every man teach his neighbor, and every man his brother, saying, "Know the LORD," for they all shall know Me, from the least of them to the greatest of them, says the LORD. For I will forgive their iniquity, and their sin I will remember no more.

The New Covenant is a great point of disagreement among scholars. Amongst Dispensationalists, there are three major views regarding whether or not the Church is currently under the New Covenant.

One view is that there are two separate New Covenants, one for Israel and one for the Church, the second being revealed in Heb 13:20.

Another view is that while the Old Testament limits the New Covenant to Israel, the New Testament reveals that the Church is indeed under the New Covenant (see 2 Cor 3:6; Heb 8:8-13; 10:16-17).

The third view is that the New Covenant is for Israel and will be in effect during the kingdom, but because Jesus has paid for the New Covenant once for all (Matt 26:28, Heb 7:22), the Church also experiences the forgiveness of sins that was promised to Israel under the New Covenant. All three views have their difficulties.

The view that there are two New Covenants, one for the Church, and one for Israel which is still future has been held by many great Dispensational scholars, including Lewis Sperry Chafer. In his *Systematic Theology*, he wrote:

> God has made unconditional covenants with His earthly people [that is, Israel]. He will yet make a new covenant with them when they enter their kingdom. That new covenant will govern their conduct and will supersede the Mosaic covenant of the Law (cf. Jer. 31:31-33; Deut. 30:8). This new covenant for Israel will be in four parts, but these four features are the present blessings of the Church. This heavenly people [the Church] are sheltered under a new covenant made in His blood. It is individual in its application and everlasting. It guarantees ever divine grace upon those who believe in Christ as Savior.[183]

The problem with this view is that it takes passages that use identical language to Israel's New Covenant and applies it to the Church. No passage in Scripture clearly says that there are two New Covenants.[184]

The second view, that the Church is currently under the New Covenant, is also held by many excellent Dispensational scholars. Nevertheless, several concerns arise in response to this view:

1) The New Covenant is explicitly said to be for Israel in the Old Testament (Jer 31:31).

2) Under the New Covenant, the law will be put in the minds of the recipients, and written on their hearts, but the Church has nothing to do with the law (Rom 6:14; Eph 2:11-16). Instead, we have a Person, Jesus Christ, in our hearts (2 Cor 3:3).

3) Under the New Covenant it is said that "No more shall every man teach his neighbor, and every man his brother, saying, 'Know the LORD,' for they all shall know Me, from the least of

---

183 Chafer, *Systematic Theology*, Vol. IV, p. 49.

184 For further study on this view, see Charles C. Ryrie, *The Basis of the Premillennial Faith* (Neptune, NJ: Loizeaux Brothers, 1953), pp. 115–25; and John F. Walvoord, *The Millennial Kingdom* (Grand Rapids: Zondervan, 1959), pp. 208–20.

them to the greatest of them…" (Jer 31:34). This is certainly not the case today. The *vast majority* of people today do not know the Lord, and even within the Church, most do not know the Lord in the intimate sense spoken of in this passage.

4)   It is not until the return of Christ that we will no longer need teachers (1 Cor 13:8-12; Eph 4:11-16).[185]

The last view, that the New Covenant is not for the Church but for Israel alone, is also not without its difficulty, but it may be preferable to the other views. The difficulties lie in the passages in the New Testament in which the New Covenant is mentioned (see especially Second Corinthians 3; Hebrews 8; 10:16-17; 12:24). However, none of these passages explicitly say that the New Covenant is in effect today. Certainly, the Mosaic Covenant was done away when the New Covenant was purchased (which occurred when Christ died, Luke 22:20). This seems to be the point that is being made by the Author of Hebrews. Also, the reference to the New Covenant in 2 Cor 3:6 is simply that we are made sufficient as ministers of the New Covenant. If we rule with Christ in His kingdom we will be ministers of the New Covenant as Christ's co-rulers. It does not seem unusual for Paul to say that God has prepared us for that future by giving us His Spirit, as he does in 2 Cor 3:6. Finally, Heb 7:22 says, "Jesus has become a surety of a better covenant." A surety is a guarantee of something to come. Why would Jesus be a surety of something that is already here? Clearly, the Church also enjoys forgiveness of sins, but for us this is not a function of the New Covenant. It is a function of the value of the blood of Christ.[186]

The significance of the last view, and perhaps the main reason I believe it to be correct, is that it gives us a picture of God's love for Israel and shows how He is going to accomplish the fulfillment of the previous covenants. While the Abrahamic and Davidic Covenants are unbreakable, nevertheless, God repeatedly says that he will not fulfill them in a disobedient nation. The New Covenant takes the question of the obedience of Israel, and places the burden of making it happen on God alone. *He* will

---

[185]   For more information regarding this view, see Andy Wood's article at this address: http://www. spiritandtruth.org/teaching/documents/articles/12/12.htm?x=x (Last accessed, Feb. 8th, 2013) and Zane Hodges's treatment here: http://www.faithalone.org/journal/2006ii/05%20Hodges-Justification.pdf (Last accessed, Feb. 8th, 2013)

[186]   For further study on this perspective, see Christopher Cone's article here: http://www.bbc. edu/council/documents/Christopher_Cone_Hermeneutical_Ramifications_of_Applying_the_New_Covenant_to_the_Church.pdf (Last accessed, Feb 9th, 2013). See also William R. Newell, *Hebrews: Verse by Verse* (Chicago, Moody, 1947).

write the law on their hearts. *He* will make the people know Him. *He* will restore them to right relationship with Him. And by doing so, He makes it so that all of the blessings of the Abrahamic and Davidic Covenants can be realized for the nation He loves, the children of Israel.

The simple chart below outlines the covenants.

Covenant/ Reference	Blessing/Cursing	Breakable?
Abrahamic (Gen 15:18-21)	Land	No
Mosaic (Exodus 19– Deuteronomy 34)	Dwelling in the land and physical blessing/ Being scattered and physical danger	Yes
Davidic (2 Sam 7:8-17)	David's Son will rule in His kingdom for the ages	No
New (Jer 31:31-34)	Law written on hearts, everyone will know the Lord, forgiveness of sins	No

CONCLUSION

The covenants help us see the big picture of the Bible. We see that God moves from covenant to covenant, developing over time the process by which He will give His kingdom blessing to the world. Ultimately, His faithfulness will be demonstrated through the New Covenant, the means by which He will fulfill His promises in the previous covenants.

PRACTICE

1) Describe the Abrahamic, Mosaic, Davidic, and New Covenants in your own words.

2) What past, present, and future aspects do you see regarding Paul's statement about the New Covenant in 1 Cor 11:23-26?

DISCUSS

1) Is the New Covenant in effect today? Why or why not?

2) What is the significance of the Abrahamic Covenant?

3) How are the Abrahamic, Davidic, and New Covenants related?

4) How is the Mosaic Covenant separate from the Abrahamic, Davidic, and New?

5) How is the Abrahamic Covenant (Gen 15:18-21) different from his election in Gen 12:1-3?

The Kingdom Promised and Confirmed

"Once I have sworn by My holiness;
I will not lie to David:
His seed shall endure forever,
And his throne as the sun before Me;
It shall be established forever like the moon,
Even like the faithful witness in the sky"
Selah. Psalm 89:35-37

LESSON OBJECTIVES

1. To show that God promised a literal kingdom to Israel
2. To show that the promise was confirmed in such a way that it is impossible for it not to be fulfilled as promised

INTRODUCTION

There are several views about the kingdom. By far the most common is the view, of which there are many variants, that the kingdom will not be literally fulfilled, that Christ will not rule from a literal throne in literal Jerusalem, but that Christ now rules in the hearts of believers. This is a non-literal approach to kingdom prophecies and promises.

All who adopt consistent literal interpretation throughout the Bible agree that Christ is not currently seated on His throne, but that He will return to earth in the future to take His seat on His throne in Jerusalem. This view is called Dispensational Premillennialism.

THE KINGDOM PROMISED

That God intends man to rule over creation as His proxy is clearly seen from the beginning, when God said, "Let Us make man in Our image, according to Our likeness, let them have dominion over the fish of the sea, over the birds of the air, and over every creeping thing that creeps on the earth" (Gen 1:26). When man sinned, Satan usurped this role, but God immediately promised that the Seed of the woman would crush the serpent's head (Gen 3:15). This prefigures Christ's work to restore man's place of rule.

After promising to make of Abraham a great nation and that through him all the world would be blessed, God established the nation Israel as His chosen nation. Israel's first great king (second king overall) was David, a man after God's own heart. David wanted to build God a house to replace the tabernacle. Though God would not allow David to build the temple because he had fought many wars, in response to this demonstration of love, God promised David that his Son would rule on his throne forever. The full text is below:

> Now therefore, thus shall you say to My servant David, "Thus says the LORD of hosts: 'I took you from the sheepfold, from following the sheep, to be ruler over My people, over Israel. And I have been with you wherever you have gone, and have cut off all your enemies from before you, and have made you a great name, like the name of the great men who are on the earth. Moreover I will appoint a place for My people Israel, and will plant them, that they may dwell in a place of their own and move no more; nor shall the sons of wickedness oppress them anymore, as previously, since the time that I commanded judges to be over My people Israel, and have caused you to rest from all your enemies.' Also the LORD tells you that He will make you a house. 'When your days are fulfilled and you rest with your fathers, I will set up your seed after you, who will come from your body, and I will establish his kingdom. He shall build a house for My name, and I will establish the throne of his kingdom forever. I will be his Father, and he shall be My son. If he commits iniquity, I will chasten him with the rod of men and with the blows of the sons of men. But My mercy shall not depart from him, as I took it from Saul, whom I removed from before you. And your house and your kingdom shall be established forever before you. Your throne shall be established forever.'" According to all these words and

according to all this vision, so Nathan spoke to David. (2 Sam 7:8-17)

Charles Feinberg skillfully explains this passage:

> First of all, David, whose desire had been that the Lord might have a fitting place in which to dwell in the midst of Israel, is told that the Lord will appoint a place for His people Israel where they will be established and where they will be at peace from all their enemies who have afflicted them. The settlement in the promised land is to be permanent. The second provision of the covenant is a Davidic house or dynasty. David's seed will be set up after his death and the Lord will establish his kingdom. The primary application, of course, is to Solomon who will be used to set up that house, the throne of which God will establish forever. The second provision includes the throne and the kingdom which are necessarily linked with the dynasty. Another feature of the promise is chastisement upon the Davidic house for disobedience. Although a paternal relationship is to exist between the seed of David and God, they will receive chastening from the rod of men and from the stripes of the children of men. That this cannot possibly refer to the Lord Jesus is evident from the clause "if he commit iniquity." This chastisement was carried out in the division of the Solomonic kingdom and the Assyrian and Babylonian captivities.
>
> Still another point of interest in the promise is the assurance that sin in the Davidic line will not abrogate or disannul the covenant. The final provision of the oath, and indeed it runs throughout the passage, is that all its features, except the chastisement, are to be eternal.[187]

Clearly the original author would have understood the Davidic Covenant to be a promise of a literal kingdom, in a literal place, with a literal king, sitting on a literal throne. On this, all interpreters agree. The difference between views regarding this promise is that some say it was nullified due to Israel's repeated disobedience, especially in the rejection and crucifixion of the Messiah.

---

[187] Charles Feinberg, *Premillennialism or Amillennialism?* (Wheaton, IL: Von Kampen Press, Inc., 1954) pp. 37-8.

But God's promises are based on His own faithfulness, not the faithfulness of men. As Paul says, "...the gifts and the calling of God are irrevocable." (Rom 11:29)

JESUS IS NOT CURRENTLY ON DAVID'S THRONE

This promise has not yet been fulfilled because Jesus is not currently seated on His throne, David's throne. Christ is in Heaven, but the thrones of the house of David are not in heaven, they are in Jerusalem:

> Jerusalem is built
> As a city that is compact together,
> Where the tribes go up,
> The tribes of the LORD,
> To the Testimony of Israel,
> To give thanks to the name of the LORD.
> For thrones are set there for judgment,
> The thrones of the house of David. (Psalm 122:3-5)

Christ is currently seated at the right hand of the Father on the Father's throne (Heb 1:3). Some say that the throne Jesus is on now, the Father's throne, is the same as His own throne. But on the contrary, Jesus said, "To him who overcomes I will grant to sit with Me on My throne, as I also overcame and sat down with My Father on His throne" (Rev 3:21). These two thrones are distinguished here by the Lord Himself, so when theologians say these thrones are one and the same, they are contradicting the Lord Jesus.

But what is He doing there on the Father's throne? Hebrews 10:12-13 says, "But this Man, after He had offered one sacrifice for sins forever, sat down at the right hand of God, from that time waiting till His enemies are made His footstool." This shows us what the Lord is doing on the Father's throne in reference to His kingdom. Right now He is waiting. He is waiting at the right hand of the Father until the Father makes His enemies His footstool (which will occur in the Tribulation). Once this is accomplished, and not before, He will take His seat on His throne and begin His reign as the rightful King of the universe.

Jesus said, "When the Son of Man comes in His glory, and all the holy angels with Him, *then* He will sit on the throne of His glory" (Matt 25:31, emphasis added). Clearly Jesus has not yet come in His glory with all the holy angels. So, His sitting on the throne of His glory is also still future.

THE PROMISE CONFIRMED

Though the promise of the kingdom has not yet been fulfilled, we can be sure it will be. It would be enough for God to make a promise. He is God. He always tells the truth. But God, knowing our weakness, confirmed His promise over and over. There are many passages that confirm that the promise of the kingdom is sure, no matter what, but two passages stand out in particular.

Psalm 89:20-37 reads:

> "I have found My servant David; with My holy oil I have anointed him, with whom My hand shall be established; also My arm shall strengthen him. The enemy shall not outwit him, nor the son of wickedness afflict him. I will beat down his foes before his face, and plague those who hate him. But My faithfulness and My mercy shall be with him, and in My name his horn shall be exalted. Also I will set his hand over the sea, and his right hand over the rivers. He shall cry to Me, 'You are my Father, My God, and the rock of my salvation.' Also I will make him My firstborn, the highest of the kings of the earth. My mercy I will keep for him forever, and *My covenant shall stand firm with him.* His seed also I will make to endure forever, and his throne as the days of heaven. *"If his sons forsake My law And do not walk in My judgments,* if they break My statutes and do not keep My commandments, then I will punish their transgression with the rod, and their iniquity with stripes. *Nevertheless My lovingkindness I will not utterly take from him, nor allow My faithfulness to fail. My covenant I will not break, nor alter the word that has gone out of My lips. Once I have sworn by My holiness; I will not lie to David: his seed shall endure forever, and his throne as the sun before Me; it shall be established forever like the moon, even like the faithful witness in the sky."* Selah. (emphasis added)

This passage directly addresses the claims that some make that God will not fulfill His promise to David because of Israel's disobedience. If Israel is disobedient, His covenant still stands firm. God swore by His own holiness, not Israel's.

Jeremiah 33:19-22:

> And the word of the LORD came to Jeremiah, saying, "Thus says the LORD: 'If you can break My covenant with the day and My covenant with the night, so that there will not be

day and night in their season, then My covenant may also be broken with David My servant, so that he shall not have a son to reign on his throne, and with the Levites, the priests, My ministers. As the host of heaven cannot be numbered, nor the sand of the sea measured, so will I multiply the descendants of David My servant and the Levites who minister to Me.'"

As long as there are night and day, God's covenant with David remains.

There are a great number of confirmations of this promise throughout Scripture. In fact, any time the Bible says again that Israel will be restored and that the kingdom is coming, God is, in effect, confirming His promise to David. Here are just a few of the more significant confirmations in Scripture: Ezekiel 37; Daniel 2; 7; 9; Hosea 1; 3:4-5, Obad 17-21; Micah 4:6-8; Matt 25:31; Luke 1:32-33; Rom 11:26-36; Revelation 20–22. These promises come before and after the incredible wickedness we saw in Israel under rulers like Ahab and Manasseh, and both before and after the rejection and crucifixion of Messiah.

Israel's wickedness at times was staggering. Israel (the Northern Kingdom) had abandoned the true God and worshipped monstrous idols. They worshipped them with witchcraft and sexual perversion but it was much worse than that. (Warning: If you have a particularly soft heart, you may want to skip to the next paragraph.) They would create hollow bronze idols, burn wood in them until they became red hot and lay their infant children on the red hot bronze to burn to death. They would play drums loudly to drown out the screams. This sacrifice was supposed to bring rain.

God sent many prophets to Israel to warn them to turn from their ways. Some were killed. All were persecuted. None were heeded.

This continued for over 200 years when God released his restraint on Assyria which then conquered Israel, took them away into captivity, split up the family units they didn't kill, and forced them into slavery.

Judah (the Southern Kingdom) disobeyed similarly, though not as extremely, and suffered a similar fate at the hands of the Babylonians, though not as severe.

Then, when Christ came and offered Israel the kingdom that was promised, that beautiful kingdom where Israel would be exalted and God honored in the whole of creation, they crucified Him. When the choice was given to spare either Jesus or the murderer, Barabbas, they chose to save Barabbas (Mark 15:6-15).

But despite all of this, God's promise stands firm. It stands firm even though Israel has been unfaithful beyond imagining because it isn't based upon their faithfulness, it is based upon God's faithfulness. Sometimes as humans we make promises that, because of unforeseen circumstances, we can't keep. But God knew all of this when He made His promise. He knows the end from the beginning. He promised it nonetheless. We can know for certain that He will bring it to pass.

CONCLUSION

God promised David that his son would sit on his throne over the house of Israel forever. Though Christ is not currently seated on David's throne, God's promise stands firm. Christ will return with all of His holy angels with Him and will take His seat on His throne.

Praise God! He is faithful!

PRACTICE

1) Read Matt 25:31. When will Jesus take His throne?

2) How does knowing that God remains faithful to Israel, despite their disobedience and rejection of Christ, impact your view of God?

3) Read 2 Cor 4:3-4; Eph 6:12; and 1 John 5:19. Who rules in this age? How does this answer the idea that Christ is ruling in His kingdom now through the Church?

4) Where are the thrones of the house of David?

5) Based on Rev 3:21 and Heb 8:1, upon what throne is Jesus seated now? Is this David's throne?

DISCUSS

1) Those who believe that Israel has disobeyed too much for God to fulfill His promises to them also often believe that the promise of eternal life can be lost, or that if we do not persevere, we prove we were never saved to begin with. Do you see a connection between these doctrines? How does the sureness of God's promises to Israel confirm His promises to us?

2) Read Rom 11:25-36. How are the phrases "all Israel will be saved" and "the gifts and the calling of God are irrevocable" related? What is the context?

3) Since the fifth century, the majority of Christians have believed that God is done with Israel and that the promises made to David will not be fulfilled literally. How do you think this has affected the Church?

4) Is it fair to say that anti-Semitism has been held up in some ways by the belief that God is done with Israel and that He will not fulfill His promises to them? Why or why not?

5) If the kingdom is still in the future, how do we join Paul in "preaching the kingdom of God" (Acts 28:31)?

The Kingdom Described

"The Establishment of the Mediatorial Kingdom on earth will bring about sweeping and radical changes in every department of human activity; so far reaching that Isaiah speaks of its arena as 'a new earth' (65:17). Every need of humanity will be anticipated and provided for: 'Before they call,' God says, 'I will answer' (Isa. 65:24). The King and His kingdom will come down upon the world 'like rain upon the mown grass,' healing the arid and devastated areas of human life (Ps. 72:6). Under His divine government there will be made a 'feast of fat things,' and the beneficiaries will be 'all people' (Isa. 25:6). Working through the chosen nation, God will 'fill the face of the world with fruit' (Isa. 27:6). There will be an 'abundance of salvation' (literally, 'salvations'), so that no legitimate aspect of human life will be left without the regal saving activity (Isa. 33:6, ASV)." *Alva J. McClain*[188]

LESSON OBJECTIVE

1. To give the student a Biblical idea of what the kingdom will be like

---

[188] McClain, *The Greatness of the kingdom*, p. 217. For a fuller treatment of the subject of this lesson, see Chapter XVIII: The Blessings of the Prophetic Kingdom.

THE PEOPLE WILL LIVE RIGHTEOUSLY

THE CHURCH'S RIGHTEOUSNESS

During the Millennium, the first one thousand years of the kingdom, which will occur on this earth, sin will not be completely eradicated in the world, but the world and its system will be ruled by Christ and His saints, and will be characterized by righteousness. Romans 14:17 says, "For the kingdom of God is...righteousness and peace and joy in the Holy Spirit."

After the thousand years have ended, sin will be eradicated, and therefore, all of the pain it brings will be gone, too: "And God will wipe away every tear from their eyes; there shall be no more death, nor sorrow, nor crying. There shall be no more pain, for the former things have passed away" (Rev 21:4).

But at the Rapture, prior to the beginning of the kingdom, in the twinkling of an eye, the Church will be made like Christ and we will be incapable of sinning: "Beloved, now we are children of God; and it has not yet been revealed what we shall be, but we know that when He is revealed, we shall be like Him, for we shall see Him as He is" (1 John 3:2). As the Apostle Paul puts it, we will be raised [resurrected] in power:

> So also is the resurrection of the dead. The body is sown in corruption, it is raised in incorruption. It is sown in dishonor, it is raised in glory. It is sown in weakness, it is raised in power. It is sown a natural body, it is raised a spiritual body... (1 Cor 15:42-44)

We will no longer suffer through the sin and disappointment we deal with today. See also Rom 8:29; 1 Cor 13:9-13; 2 Cor 3:18.

ISRAEL'S RIGHTEOUSNESS

God has constantly struggled with His chosen nation to lead them in His righteous ways. In Hosea, God calls the prophet Hosea to marry a prostitute to illustrate His own heartbreak brought on by Israel's wicked ways (Hos 1:2). Stiff-necked and rebellious are some of the more common adjectives used to describe Israel in the Bible. As the first Christian martyr, Stephen, said of Israel:

> "You stiff-necked and uncircumcised in heart and ears! You always resist the Holy Spirit; as your fathers did, so do you. Which of the prophets did your fathers not persecute? And they killed those who foretold the coming of the Just One, of whom you now have become the betrayers and murderers, who have received the law by the direction of angels and have not kept it." (Acts 7:51-53)

Israel's history is full of resistance to God's will. But it won't always be that way. In addition to the Church's righteousness in the kingdom, Israel will at last live righteously and glorify God as well.

Jeremiah 31:31-34

> Behold, the days are coming, says the Lord, when I will make a new covenant with the house of Israel and with the house of Judah—not according to the covenant that I made with their fathers in the day that I took them by the hand to lead them out of the land of Egypt, My covenant which they broke, though I was a husband to them, says the Lord. But this is the covenant that I will make with the house of Israel after those days, says the Lord: *I will put My law in their minds, and write it on their hearts*; and I will be their God, and they shall be My people. No more shall every man teach his neighbor, and every man his brother, saying, 'Know the Lord,' *for they all shall know Me, from the least of them to the greatest of them*, says the Lord. For I will forgive their iniquity, and their sin I will remember no more. (Emphasis added.)

Ezekiel 37:24-25

> David My servant shall be king over them, and they shall all have one shepherd; they shall also walk in My judgments and observe My statutes, and do them. Then they shall dwell in the land that I have given to Jacob My servant, where your fathers dwelt; and they shall dwell there, they, their children, and their children's children, forever; and My servant David shall be their prince forever.

Zephaniah 3:11-13:

> In that day you shall not be shamed for any of your deeds
> In which you transgress against Me;
> For then I will take away from your midst

Those who rejoice in your pride,
And you shall no longer be haughty
In My holy mountain.
I will leave in your midst
A meek and humble people,
And they shall trust in the name of the LORD.
The remnant of Israel shall do no unrighteousness
And speak no lies,
Nor shall a deceitful tongue be found in their mouth;
For they shall feed their flocks and lie down,
And no one shall make them afraid."

God's Word does not return void (Isa 55:11). He has set out to call His beloved nation, Israel, to walk in His ways and to carry His blessing to the world, and they will when Christ returns to restore Israel and take His throne.

THE CURSE OF FUTILITY LIFTED

When Adam sinned, he brought in not only death but various curses. One of those curses is called *the curse of futility*. In Gen 3:17-19, God said:

"Because you have heeded the voice of your wife, and have eaten from the tree of which I commanded you, saying, 'You shall not eat of it':

"Cursed is the ground for your sake;
In toil you shall eat of it
All the days of your life.
Both thorns and thistles it shall bring forth for you,
And you shall eat the herb of the field.
In the sweat of your face you shall eat bread
Till you return to the ground,
For out of it you were taken;
For dust you are,
And to dust you shall return."

Because of this curse, people struggle all their lives to provide for themselves and their families.

In the southwestern portion of the Great Plains in the late 1920s, rain was abundant and the ground was producing plentiful harvests. The farmers, thinking that this would last forever, pushed the ground too hard. They did not rotate their crops, but grew only wheat because it was the most profitable. Then the curse of futility hit—*hard*. The result is what we call The Dust Bowl. The rain stopped and for a full decade the area experienced desert-like conditions. Huge storms of sand and dust raged through regularly. When the larger dust storms would come through, it was said that it was so dark you could not see your own hand in front of your face. Virtually all livestock died and barely any wheat could be harvested. Many people, mostly children, died in these storms.

The Dust Bowl is just one clear example of this curse and our inability to do anything about it, but places all over the world experience food shortages all the time. Even modern science, which has created genetically modified foods in hopes of greater production, results in our food being less healthy. There's no good way to circumvent this curse.

When Christ returns, this curse of futility will be lifted.

Romans 8:20-21

> For the creation was subjected to futility, not willingly, but because of Him who subjected it in hope; because the creation itself also will be delivered from the bondage of corruption into the glorious liberty of the children of God.

Psalm 72:16

> There will be an abundance of grain in the earth, on the top of the mountains; its fruit shall wave like Lebanon; and those of the city shall flourish like grass of the earth.

Amos 9:13

> "Behold, the days are coming," says the LORD,
> "When the plowman shall overtake the reaper,
> And the treader of grapes him who sows seed;
> The mountains shall drip with sweet wine,
> And the hills shall flow with it.

No one will starve in the kingdom. Everyone will enjoy abundant fruit from their labors.

TRUE PEACE IN THE WORLD

Wars and other violence have ravished the world since Cain murdered his brother Abel. In the twentieth century, as weapons improved, hundreds of millions of people were killed in wars. Once the Lord takes His throne, He will rule the world in peace.

Isaiah 2:2-4

> Now it shall come to pass in the latter days
> That the mountain of the Lord's house
> Shall be established on the top of the mountains,
> And shall be exalted above the hills;
> And all nations shall flow to it.
> Many people shall come and say,
> "Come, and let us go up to the mountain of the Lord,
> To the house of the God of Jacob;
> He will teach us His ways,
> And we shall walk in His paths."
> For out of Zion shall go forth the law,
> And the word of the Lord from Jerusalem.
> He shall judge between the nations,
> And rebuke many people;
> *They shall beat their swords into plowshares,*
> *And their spears into pruning hooks;*
> *Nation shall not lift up sword against nation,*
> *Neither shall they learn war anymore.* (Emphasis added.)

Isaiah 9:6-7

> For unto us a Child is born,
> Unto us a Son is given;
> And the government will be upon His shoulder.
> And His name will be called
> Wonderful, Counselor, Mighty God,
> Everlasting Father, Prince of Peace.
>
> Of the increase of His government and peace
> There will be no end,
> Upon the throne of David and over His kingdom,
> To order it and establish it with judgment and justice
> From that time forward, even forever.
> The zeal of the Lord of hosts will perform this.

Zechariah 9:9-10

> "Rejoice greatly, O daughter of Zion!
> Shout, O daughter of Jerusalem!
> Behold, your King is coming to you;
> He is just and having salvation,
> Lowly and riding on a donkey,
> A colt, the foal of a donkey.

I will cut off the chariot from Ephraim
And the horse from Jerusalem;
The battle bow shall be cut off.
He shall speak peace to the nations;
His dominion shall be 'from sea to sea,
And from the River to the ends of the earth."

Jesus will establish a peace that will last a thousand years. There will be one short battle after Satan is released to deceive the nations at the end of the thousand years (Rev 20:7-10). Then there will never be war or death again.

THE WORLD WILL BE FULL OF THE KNOWLEDGE OF THE LORD

The whole world seems to be astonishingly confused about who God is and what His promises are. When Satan's world displays his evil schemes, God is blasphemed by those who don't know any better. People see God as ungracious, unloving, unmerciful, and unwilling or unable to help them—everything He isn't.

But when Christ returns, the full, undimmed glory of His Person will be seen by all, and the world will be full of the knowledge of Him.

Isaiah 11:9

They shall not hurt nor destroy in all My holy mountain,
For the earth shall be full of the knowledge of the LORD
As the waters cover the sea.

Jeremiah 31:34

No more shall every man teach his neighbor, and every man his brother, saying, 'Know the LORD,' for they all shall know Me, from the least of them to the greatest of them, says the LORD. For I will forgive their iniquity, and their sin I will remember no more.

Bible teachers will be out of a job, because Christ Himself will have completed their work (but don't worry, there will be plenty of other things for us to do in His service).

SAFETY FROM DANGERS

Every parent knows the dangers of this world in ways that he or she could not have known before caring for a child. The street is dangerous. Strangers are dangerous. Water is dangerous. Pointy corners on furniture are dangerous. Wild animals are dangerous. Germs are dangerous. New parents cover their entire houses with padding and child-safety locks because they have now become aware of just how dangerous this world can be, especially for little ones.

But the Lord will provide complete safety from dangers when He returns.

Isaiah 11:6-8

> The wolf also shall dwell with the lamb,
> The leopard shall lie down with the young goat,
> The calf and the young lion and the fatling together;
> And a little child shall lead them.
> The cow and the bear shall graze;
> Their young ones shall lie down together;
> And the lion shall eat straw like the ox.
> The nursing child shall play by the cobra's hole,
> And the weaned child shall put his hand in the viper's den.

The moms of the world will never have slept so well.

SATAN BOUND

This world system is full of deception. Truth that is readily observable and apparent is ridiculed. Those who accept God's truth are thought to be stupid or backwards. This is the work of Satan in his world system (2 Cor 4:4; 1 John 5:19).

But when Christ returns, He will shut up Satan into the bottomless pit so that he can't deceive the nations any longer.

Revelation 20:1-3

> Then I saw an angel coming down from heaven, having the key to the bottomless pit and a great chain in his hand. He laid hold of the dragon, that serpent of old, who is the Devil and Satan, and bound him for a thousand years; and he cast him into the bottomless pit, and shut him up, and set a seal on him,

so that he should deceive the nations no more till the thousand years were finished...

The lies of selfishness and violence and pride will be exposed, and the world will be freed from Satan's terrible grip.

LONGEVITY AND HEALTH TO ALL

"Life is short" has become a cliché because it's true. Eighty or ninety years is just a blink.

The Church will be in immortal bodies in the kingdom (1 Cor 15:42), but even the natural man (those who survive the Tribulation and enter into the kingdom at its start and their progeny) will live amazingly long and healthy lives.

Isaiah 33:24a

And the inhabitant will not say, "I am sick."

Isaiah 35:5-6

Then the eyes of the blind shall be opened,
And the ears of the deaf shall be unstopped.
Then the lame shall leap like a deer,
And the tongue of the dumb sing.
For waters shall burst forth in the wilderness,
And streams in the desert.

Isaiah 65:20

No more shall an infant from there live but a few days,
Nor an old man who has not fulfilled his days;
For the child shall die one hundred years old,
But the sinner being one hundred years old shall be accursed.

If someone dies at one hundred years old, we will say, "Oh, he was just a baby."

NO MORE OPPRESSION

For many, this world can offer no justice. Slave traders prey on the weak and corrupt governments look the other way. Governments killed more than one hundred and twenty million of their own citizens in the twentieth century and the genocides continue. Millions of children are aborted or thrown out to the elements. Despite the grave need, the UN is seeking to make "Baby Boxes"—safe places to leave unwanted children to be adopted—illegal worldwide. In many countries, women are treated as property, as little more than cattle. Mutilation of female genitalia is enforced in many Muslim countries. Christians are imprisoned, slain, and heavily oppressed by their governments in many countries.

Christ will establish a true, worldwide righteous government when He returns.

Isaiah 11:4-5

> But with righteousness He shall judge the poor,
> And decide with equity for the meek of the earth;
> He shall strike the earth with the rod of His mouth,
> And with the breath of His lips He shall slay the wicked.
> Righteousness shall be the belt of His loins,
> And faithfulness the belt of His waist.

Isaiah 65:21-22

> They shall build houses and inhabit them;
> They shall plant vineyards and eat their fruit.
> They shall not build and another inhabit;
> They shall not plant and another eat;
> For as the days of a tree, so shall be the days of My people,
> And My elect shall long enjoy the work of their hands.

Christ is the one true answer to the injustice in the world. And when Satan is cast out of his usurped place ruling this world, Christ will set right all of the injustices His children have experienced.

CONCLUSION

Christ's kingdom will be the ultimate example of righteousness, peace, and prosperity. As we watch or read the news and get a peek into the depth of corruption that has overtaken this world, let us look forward to His return with eager anticipation.

PRACTICE

1) The believer's hope is for the return of Christ, the redemption of our bodies (which are still indwelt by sin) and the possibility of ruling with Christ in the kingdom. Everything else is already ours and is not something we are yet to hope for. How does this change your perspective of Col 1:21-27?

2) How can we obey Christ's call to "seek first the kingdom" (Matt 6:33)? Does having a picture of what the kingdom will be like help? Why or why not?

3) Read Zech 2:6-13. What does this tell you about Israel's place in the kingdom?

4) Read Joel 2:21-27. How does the coming kingdom demonstrate God's love for Israel?

5) Read 1 John 3:2 and 2 Cor 3:18. What does this teach us about growth in Christ now and about our life when we see Christ as He is in His kingdom?

DISCUSS

1) What do you long for most in the kingdom?

2) The average income in the world is $850 per year; sickness and starvation run rampant, and over one billion people are without clean water to drink. How does that change your perspective about the kingdom?

3) Based on what you have learned, how will the question of "why is there evil in the world?" be answered by God?

4) Is it appropriate to try to establish the kingdom on earth before Christ's return? Why or why not?

5) How are the kingdom and Israel's election related?

The Kingdom—Inheritance and Ruling

"To him who overcomes I will grant to sit with Me on My throne, as I also overcame and sat down with My Father on His throne." Revelation 3:21

LESSON OBJECTIVES

1. To offer a brief review of the topic of the Judgment Seat of Christ

2. To help the reader understand the Biblical concepts of inheriting and ruling in the kingdom

INTRODUCTION

Justification before God and eternal life are free gifts, given to all who simply believe in Jesus Christ, and those gifts, once given, cannot ever be lost. As we discuss the Judgment Seat of Christ and reward according to works, we need to keep a couple of things in mind:

1. All of this is on top of our secure eternal destiny with God on the New Earth, where there will be no tears, no sin, no sickness, no death, and where we will all experience an eternity of overwhelming joy. There is no eternal punishment for the believer (John 5:24) and even if we receive no rewards at all, eternal happiness awaits us. Rewards should be a positive motivator but should not be a source of anxiety.

2. Only Jesus can live a life that is pleasing to God, and it is only as we "place no confidence in the flesh" and live out the "power of His resurrection" (Philippians 3) that we can have hope of

reward. All works that are self-directed and self-empowered are wood, hay, and stubble and will be burned up (1 Cor 3:9-15). It is "Christ in [us]" that gives us "the hope of glory" (Col 1:27).

First Corinthians 3:9-15 makes it clear that the Judgment Seat of Christ is a judgment based upon works that does not affect our salvation:

> For we are God's fellow workers; you are God's field, you are God's building. According to the grace of God which was given to me, as a wise master builder I have laid the foundation, and another builds on it. But let each one take heed how he builds on it. For no other foundation can anyone lay than that which is laid, which is Jesus Christ. Now if anyone builds on this foundation with gold, silver, precious stones, wood, hay, straw, each one's work will become clear; for the Day will declare it, because it will be revealed by fire; and the fire will test each one's work, of what sort it is. If anyone's work which he has built on it endures, he will receive a reward. If anyone's work is burned, he will suffer loss; but he himself will be saved, yet so as through fire.

On nearly every page of the New Testament, including all of Paul's letters other than Philemon, the topic of the Judgment Seat of Christ appears (that means it's a big deal). The one book of any substantial length that has very few references to the Judgment Seat of Christ is the Gospel of John. This is because John was written to tell unbelievers how to receive the free gift of eternal life, a different topic entirely.

The Judgment Seat of Christ is where the hope of the Christian will become the present possession of the Christian and where the one who lives faithfully will be given a share in Christ's kingdom rule. Because every New Testament book other than John was written to believers, the hope of the believer is understandably an ever present encouragement.

INHERITING THE KINGDOM

The Bible emphasizes the prospect of *inheriting* the kingdom. To enter the kingdom and to inherit it are not the same thing (though, see below). Common sense tells us this. I can certainly enter a home that I do not own (by invitation), but it is quite a different thing to be given that home. To inherit means to be given ownership.

Some Free Grace scholars who believe that entering the kingdom is a reward hold that all who enter the kingdom also inherit the kingdom.

This is based upon two observations. First, all who entered into the land with Joshua received an inheritance and this generation is a type of the believer entering the kingdom. Second, inheriting eternal life (a synonym for inheriting the kingdom) is equated with entering the kingdom in the Rich Young Ruler passages (Compare Mark 10:17 and 24, for example.).

All believers have an inheritance in one sense. We are "heirs of God" (Rom 8:17). Paul also says:

> *In Him also we have obtained an inheritance*, being predestined according to the purpose of Him who works all things according to the counsel of His will, that we who first trusted in Christ should be to the praise of His glory. (Eph 1:11-12, emphasis added)

This passage makes it clear that there is an inheritance in Christ that we have already obtained.

In 1 Cor 3:21-23, Paul puts it this way:

> Therefore let no one boast in men. For *all things are yours*: whether Paul or Apollos or Cephas, or the world or life or death, or things present or things to come—*all are yours*. And you are Christ's, and Christ is God's. (Emphasis added.)

In one sense, all the world, things present and things to come, are ours. We are the heirs of the God of the universe, and all that is His is ours. What a glorious inheritance indeed!

But there is yet another inheritance that is conditional. In the Ancient Near East, the firstborn son would receive a double portion in the inheritance, but this was conditioned on his representing the family well. If this son was not a good representative for the family, he would lose his firstborn rights when the inheritances were given out.

Romans 8:17 discusses these two aspects of our inheritance. Below is my literal translation:

> ...and if children, then heirs—on the one hand, heirs of God, and on the other, co-heirs with Christ if indeed we co-suffer [with Him], that we may also be co-glorified [with Him].

All believers are heirs of God, simply by virtue of being God's children. But those who co-suffer with the Firstborn Son, Jesus Christ, receive a firstborn's reward. The Firstborn Son's inheritance, as it is pictured in these contexts, is the kingdom He will rule when He returns.

God promises that all those who pursue Jesus, living by faith and overcoming the world will inherit the kingdom (not just for 1000 years, but forever). The one who does not overcome will not inherit the kingdom. The following passages speak of it in these terms:

Matthew 19:29:

> And everyone who has left houses or brothers or sisters or father or mother or wife or children or lands, for My name's sake, shall receive a hundredfold, and inherit eternal life.

Note, in Matthew's writings, inheriting eternal life means inheriting the kingdom.

Hebrews 6:11-12:

> And we desire that each one of you show the same diligence to the full assurance of hope until the end, that you do not become sluggish, but imitate those who through faith and patience inherit the promises.

First Peter 3:8-9:

> Finally, all of you be of one mind, having compassion for one another; love as brothers, be tenderhearted, be courteous; not returning evil for evil or reviling for reviling, but on the contrary blessing, knowing that you were called to this, that you may inherit a blessing.

Revelation 21:7:

> "He who overcomes shall inherit all things, and I will be his God and he shall be My son."

See also Matt 5:5; 19:29; 25:34; 1 Cor 6:9-10; Gal 5:19-21.

RULING IN THE KINGDOM

It is unclear whether or not all those who *inherit* also *rule* with Christ in the kingdom, but we do know that ruling with Him is a promise He makes to those who overcome. This is part of what we learn in the Parable of the Talents, "Well done, good and faithful servant; you were faithful over a few things, I will make you ruler over many things. Enter into the joy of your lord" (Matt 25:21) and the Parable of the Minas, "Well done, good servant; because you were faithful in a very little, have authority over ten cities" (Luke 19:17), but it is also stated in plain-literal language elsewhere:

Revelation 2:26-27

> And he who overcomes, and keeps My works until the end, to him I will give power over the nations—'HE SHALL RULE THEM WITH A ROD OF IRON; THEY SHALL BE DASHED TO PIECES LIKE THE POTTER'S VESSELS'—as I also have received from My Father;

Revelation 3:21

> To him who overcomes I will grant to sit with Me on My throne, as I also overcame and sat down with My Father on His throne.

Revelation 20:4-6

> And I saw thrones, and they sat on them, and judgment was committed to them. Then I saw the souls of those who had been beheaded for their witness to Jesus and for the word of God, who had not worshiped the beast or his image, and had not received his mark on their foreheads or on their hands. And they lived and reigned with Christ for a thousand years. But the rest of the dead did not live again until the thousand years were finished. This is the first resurrection. Blessed and holy is he who has part in the first resurrection. Over such the second death has no power, but they shall be priests of God and of Christ, and shall reign with Him a thousand years.

Who are the ones who overcome? Christ stated plainly that He has overcome the world (John 16:33), and as we walk by faith, letting Him replace us, His victory over the world becomes ours in experience. If that's how we live our lives, we can have a strong hope of ruling with Christ when He returns.

CROWNS AND RULING

Several passages in the New Testament speak of obtaining a crown as a reward for faithful service now. For example:

First Corinthians 9:24-27

> Do you not know that those who run in a race all run, but one receives the prize? Run in such a way that you may obtain it. And everyone who competes for the prize is temperate in all things. Now they do it to obtain a perishable crown, but we for an *imperishable crown*. Therefore I run thus: not with

uncertainty. Thus I fight: not as one who beats the air. But I discipline my body and bring it into subjection, lest, when I have preached to others, I myself should become disqualified. (Emphasis added.)

James 1:12

Blessed is the man who endures temptation; for when he has been approved, he will receive the crown of life which the Lord has promised to those who love Him.

Revelation 2:10

...Be faithful until death, and I will give you the crown of life.

Crowns are worn by kings. They represent rule and triumph. Those who overcome in this life will be given crowns along with the authority they are given.[189]

THE LAST WILL BE FIRST

The ones who will rule with Christ, will do so in service to creation. They will be given great authority as Christ's co-rulers, but they will be humble servants of all.

It is not surprising, then, that there are many passages that teach that humbling ourselves to be the servant of all, putting all others before ourselves now is the path to being great in the kingdom: "If anyone desires to be first, he shall be last of all and servant of all" (Mark 9:35, see also, Matt 19:30; 20:20-26; 23:11-12; Luke 14:11). The path to reigning with Christ is the low road.

Practically, this means that we should not seek the praise of men. We should not worry if our personal rights are violated (the Lord will make it right). We should go out of our way to help others even when it hurts, and not be afraid to let go of control of situations. Those who follow Christ's

---

[189] The 24 elders are seen casting their crowns at the feet of Jesus in Rev 4:9-11. This passage has been used to say that the crowns that the faithful saints will receive will be given up, and that they will not be worn by the overcomers. However, this is unlikely. Crowns represent rule, and the Bible clearly indicates that overcoming believers will rule with Christ forever. There are two possible ways to understand this passage. The first is that this refers to a process of worship that is repeated "Whenever the living creatures give glory and honor and thanks to Him who sits on the throne..." (Rev 4:9). The second is that the 24 elders are not humans at all, but angels. These angels are seen casting their crowns at Jesus' feet, declaring that their rule has come to an end and it is time for Jesus to take His kingdom. This is consistent with the concepts established in Hebrews 1–2, Ephesians 3, and elsewhere. Angels are currently ruling the world, but this will not be the case when Christ returns.

example in these things will share in His great inheritance as firstborn sons in His kingdom.

SO WHAT IS THE END GOAL?

The end goal of all of this isn't solely that we will be exalted, but that God's grace will be magnified through lifting us up. Ephesians 1–3 teaches that God's plan for the ages was to answer Satan's charge. He chose independence, seeking to be like God on his own. God answered this charge by choosing the lower being, man, to be His focus. He made us out of dirt and then we fell from there. Yet God has made us His very dwelling place, His heirs. Some will even be joint-heirs with Christ, sharing in His rule over the perfect kingdom. God will say to Lucifer, "Yes you were beautiful, but look at what glory is had by even these little ones who depended on Me. Look what ruin your independence has brought you." What an answer! Forever the question will be settled about whether it is better to trust in the Lord or to seek independence.

Those who rule with Christ as the King's Bride will be the fullest examples of the wisdom and power of God's grace.

PRACTICE

1) What has to happen before we inherit anything from our parents? How does this impact your understanding of kingdom inheritance?

2) In your own words, describe the difference between being heirs of God and being co-heirs with Christ.

3) What does it mean that it is "Christ in us" that gives us "the hope of glory" (Col 1:27)?

4) What is glory, as it relates to the kingdom?

5) How does humility impact kingdom inheritance?

DISCUSS

1) Is seeking kingdom reward selfish? Why or why not? (Hint: see Heb 12:1-2)

2) Will a legalistic believer who works hard to persevere in good works be rewarded for that work at the *Bema?* Why or why not?

3) How is the glory of God impacted by your answer to the previous question?

4) In what ways does the prospect of kingdom inheritance motivate you?

5) What kind of rulers will the overcomers be?

6) How can your group motivate others about kingdom inheritance and ruling with Christ?

Entering the Kingdom

> And when they had preached the gospel
> to that city and made many disciples, they
> returned to Lystra, Iconium, and Antioch,
> strengthening the souls of the disciples,
> exhorting them to continue in the faith, and
> saying, "We must through many tribulations
> enter the kingdom of God." *Acts 14:21-22*

LESSON OBJECTIVES

1. To present the various Free Grace views regarding entering the kingdom
2. To offer some objections to and potential solutions for each view

INTRODUCTION

Free Grace believers differ on whether or not entering the kingdom is a free gift or a reward, and on what entering the kingdom means. There is room for disagreement on this point. I hope to present the three main contemporary views impartially. While I will point out what view I hold, my hope is that students will work with their groups to determine which view best represents what Scripture teaches.

The differences in this view tend to be related to how each person handles the following passages:

- The Sermon on the Mount (Matt 5–7)
- Jesus' Exchange with the rich young ruler (Matt 19:16-30; Mark 10:17-25; Luke 18:18-25)
- Matt 18:3
- John 3:3, 5

VIEW #1: ALL BELIEVERS ENTER THE KINGDOM

This view is the most common among Free Grace believers who are involved in Grace Evangelical Society and Free Grace Alliance. This view was held by the late Zane Hodges and Art Farstad and is held by GES Executive Director Bob Wilkin, John Niemelä, and many other excellent Free Grace writers and teachers to whom I owe an unpayable debt. I am thankful for the input of my dear friend Bob Wilkin in helping me make sure this view is well represented.

Those who hold this view believe that references to the kingdom in the Bible do not refer to the Millennium, but to the kingdom of Christ as a whole, Daniel's Fifth Kingdom (Daniel 2), starting with the Millennium (Rev 20:1-6) and continuing on forever on the New Earth (Revelation 21–22). They also believe that all believers will enter the kingdom at the start of the Millennium.

In this view, John 3:3, 5 and Matt 18:3 are taken to explicitly state that entrance into the kingdom is by grace through faith. These passages are below:

John 3:3, 5

> Jesus answered and said to him, "Most assuredly, I say to you, unless one is born again, he cannot see the kingdom of God." (…) Jesus answered, "Most assuredly, I say to you, unless one is born of water and the Spirit, he cannot enter the kingdom of God."

Matthew 18:3

> "…Assuredly, I say to you, unless you are converted and become as little children, you will by no means enter the kingdom of heaven."

JOHN 3:3, 5

Regarding John 3, some have argued that being "born of water" equals water baptism,[190] but this is unlikely.[191] Being "born of water" likely means physical birth. In this case, the only condition for kingdom entrance

---

[190] For one such view from a Free Grace perspective, see Robert Govett, *Govett on John* (Hayesville, NC: Schoettle Publishing Co, 2010), pp. 77-88.

[191] Zane C. Hodges, "Water and Spirit—John 3:5," *Bibliotheca Sacra* 135 (July-Sept, 1978): pp. 206-20.

(other than physical birth) mentioned is being born again, which is by faith alone (John 3:1-16).

MATTHEW 18:3

In Matt 18:3, those who hold this view equate being converted and becoming as little children with trusting in Christ, rather than self, for everlasting life.

FIRST THESSALONIANS 5:9-10

Those who hold this view also point out that 1 Thess 5:9-10 says:

> For God did not appoint us to wrath, but to obtain salvation through our Lord Jesus Christ, who died for us, that whether we wake or sleep [that is, whether we are watchful or not, see v 5-8], we should live together with Him.

The context in this passage is the Rapture, but the argument is made that someone who misses the millennium cannot be said to "live together with Him."

THE SERMON ON THE MOUNT IN MATTHEW 5–7

The difficulty is that there are some passages that give the impression that entering the kingdom is by works. Those who hold to this view generally take those passages to be pre-evangelistic, that is, preparing people to believe the message of life when it is shared with them at a later time.

For example, Matt 5:20 states, "For I say to you, that unless your righteousness exceeds the righteousness of the scribes and Pharisees, you will by no means enter the kingdom of heaven." Those who hold to this view take this to mean that we must attain to a perfect righteousness to enter the kingdom, and because this is impossible, we must have Christ's righteousness imputed to us (i.e., we must be justified).

Zane Hodges wrote about this passage:

> If the kingdom honors the Law down to its smallest requirement, then it follows that no ordinary righteousness can be adequate for entrance into that kingdom. In fact, that is what Jesus affirms when he says in Matt 5:20, "For I say to you, that unless your righteousness exceeds the righteousness of the

scribes and Pharisees, you will by no means enter the kingdom of heaven."

The scribes and Pharisees were at that time the arbiters of the Law in its strictest form. They insisted on its strict observance and they were punctilious in observing it. To all appearances they were paragons of righteousness in Israel. (Jesus had not yet begun to excoriate them for their hypocrisy.)

Jesus affirms even their righteousness is inadequate for entrance into the super-strict realm of His future kingdom. The ordinary hearer of the Sermon on the Mount might well despair when he heard this statement.

And that was just the point. If His audience thought in terms of a works-righteousness obtained by keeping the Law, their case was hopeless. That hopelessness, in fact, was precisely what the Law was designed to produce in people. Paul makes this clear to us in Rom 3:20 when he writes: "Therefore by the deeds of the law no flesh will be justified in His sight, for by the law is the knowledge of sin."[192]

While in this context Jesus does not mention believing in Him to receive justification, the Bible clearly teaches this elsewhere. Zane here, like many others who hold this view, believe that Jesus is preparing people to receive this truth by pointing out the impossible standard of the law.

Similar explanations are given regarding the rich young ruler whom Jesus told to obey the commandments and sell everything he has, give it to the poor, and follow Jesus in order to enter the kingdom (Luke 18:18-24).

Regarding Matt 7:21, "Not everyone who says to Me, 'Lord, Lord,' shall enter the kingdom of heaven, but he who does the will of My Father in heaven"—those who hold this view see John 6:29 and 39 as a cross reference. There Jesus says, "This is the work of God, that you believe in Him whom He sent" and, "This is the will of the Father who sent Me, that of all He has given Me I should lose nothing, but should raise it up at the last day." Thus, doing the will of the Father in Matt 7:21 is equated with believing in Jesus. In other words, the one who believes in Jesus has done the will of the Father.

---

[192] Zane Hodges, "Law and Grace in the Millennial Kingdom" *Journal of the Grace Evangelical Society* (Spring 2007): p. 36.

Those who hold this view note that passages discussing a rich entrance into the kingdom, such as 2 Pet 1:10-11, refer to a reward consisting of more than mere entrance into the kingdom.

VIEW #2: ENTERING THE KINGDOM IS A REWARD

This view states that entering the millennial kingdom is a reward for faithful service, not a free gift. In this view, someone could have everlasting life and be eternally secure and still fail to enter the kingdom.

This is the view I hold. It is also held by Curtis Tucker, author of *Majestic Destiny*, and Dale Taliaferro, author of *Living Through Crises* and *Judas and Divine Grace*. In the era of systematized Dispensationalism (beginning with John Nelson Darby around 1828), this view was first widely accepted through the teaching of Robert Govett, Pastor of Surrey Chapel, Norwich (which had a building accommodating 1500) from 1854-1901. His work influenced his successor there, D.M. Panton, along with Jesse Penn-Lewis (who was one of his congregants) and Watchman Nee.

For the sake of clarity, I want to point out again that those who hold this view see entrance into the millennial kingdom as the issue, not eternal destiny generally. All who believe in Jesus have everlasting life and will be with God forever.

THE SERMON ON THE MOUNT

Those who hold this view tend to reject the idea that Jesus did pre-evangelism,[193] especially in the Sermon on the Mount. It is widely accepted that Matthew is not an evangelistic or a pre-evangelistic book in general. It was written to Jewish believers to help them understand why the kingdom was not present if Messiah had already come. In addition to this, while there were multitudes present, Jesus was addressing His disciples in the Sermon on the Mount. This is why He was seated when He addressed them (Matt 5:1-2), rather than standing to address the multitudes. To those He is addressing, He calls God their Father sixteen times in these three chapters, and says that they are "the salt of the earth" and "the light

---

[193] Even those who hold to the first view often themselves reject the practice of pre-evangelism, pointing out that in the only evangelistic book in Scripture, the Gospel of John, Jesus did not do pre-evangelism.

of the world" (5:14-15). This cannot be true of unbelievers. Jesus says, "unless your righteousness exceeds the righteousness of the scribes and Pharisees, you will by no means enter the kingdom of heaven" (Matt 5:20) only five verses later. No indication is given that He has changed audiences.

Those who hold this view also point out that the contexts of John 6 and Matthew 7 are very different. Someone who had only Matthew or who heard only Jesus' sermon in Matthew 5–7 would not conclude that doing the will of the Father was believing in Jesus, but that it was following the spiritual and practical teaching that Jesus had just covered. This seems to be confirmed by verse 24, "Therefore [referring back to 7:21-23], whoever hears these sayings of Mine, and does them, I will liken him to a wise man who built his house on the rock." Free Grace believers uniformly accept that 7:24-27 is a rewards passage. If verses 21-23 are an entirely separate topic from verses 24-27, the "therefore" would seem out of place.

MATTHEW 18:3

Those who hold this view also point out that in Matt 18:3, the condition for entering the kingdom is to be converted and to become like little children. Being converted means to be turned, is associated with turning from sin in other passages, and may not mean simply believing in Jesus. Furthermore, Jesus was addressing His disciples, not unbelievers, and was answering the question, "Who then is the greatest in the kingdom of heaven?" (Matt 18:1). This is clearly a rewards concept.

THE RICH YOUNG RULER

This view's proponents also point out that the phrases "inherit eternal life" and "have treasure in heaven," which are rewards concepts throughout Scripture, seem in the passages describing Jesus' interaction with the rich young ruler to be parallels to entering the kingdom. In addition, Mark tells us that "Jesus, looking at him [the rich young ruler], loved him..." (Mark 10:21) before telling him the only thing he lacked for entering the kingdom was to sell all his goods, give the money to the poor, take up his cross, and follow Him. If this man's issue was needing to believe in Jesus to receive eternal life, it seems like Jesus' love for him would be better expressed by telling him to believe in Him to receive eternal life. But if entering the kingdom is a reward, and this young man was seeking this reward, Jesus' response makes more sense. Those who hold this view believe that the rich young ruler was already a believer in Jesus before coming to Him and that Jesus' declaration that the young man only lacked one thing can be taken at face value.

JOHN 3:3, 5

In John 3:3, 5, Jesus did not say that all who are born again enter the kingdom, but that "...unless one is born again, he cannot see the king-dom of God." Those who hold this view do not believe that someone who does not believe in Jesus can enter the kingdom, but that believing is not enough by itself. This passage does not contradict this view.

WHAT HAPPENS TO BELIEVERS WHO MISS THE MILLENNIUM?

There are many views regarding what happens to believers who miss the Millennium. My view is that believers who fail to enter the kingdom will still be on earth during the Millennium, though they will be among the nations. Isaiah 60 pictures a great highway built into Jerusalem where the nations will continually bring their wealth into the kingdom. This suggests that at this point, there are nations outside of Messiah's king-dom but that they will be vassals to it. This fits the fact that Israel was promised a specific tract of land which they are still waiting to receive in the Abrahamic Covenant (Gen 15:18-21). Why was a specific land prom-ised if the kingdom would encompass the whole earth at the beginning? Isaiah 9:7 presents His kingdom as ever expanding, so it will eventually encompass the whole world and likely beyond.[194]

I like to say that believers who are not faithful at this time might find themselves living in Detroit (apologies to those living there now) during the Millennium. In my view, this is failing to enter the kingdom. On a practical level, those who hold View #1 (the view that all believers enter the kingdom) would also say a believer from today could find himself living in Detroit if he is not faithful, though, in their view, Detroit is in the kingdom. The difference is how to understand the various passages, rather than one of radically different perspectives about the experience of unfaithful believers. This may answer the objection mentioned above

---

[194] It is possible that only overcomers of Jewish origin will be able to inherit the land promised to Abraham. This would explain the lack of discussion of entering the kingdom in Paul's epistles which were written to Gentile Christians.

concerning 1 Thess 5:9-10, that a believer who fails to enter the kingdom cannot rightly be said to "live together with Him." If a believer can be in Detroit during the Millennium in View #1 and still be said to "live together with Him," he can also be there in View #2 and be said to "live together with Him," even if Detroit is not part of the kingdom at that time. The proximity to Jesus is the same in both views.

VIEW #3: ENTERING THE KINGDOM OFTEN MEANS TO EXPERIENCE KINGDOM LIFE NOW, OR TO BE GREAT IN THE KINGDOM

A third view is that the phrase "enter the kingdom" often means "to experience kingdom life now" and that other times it focuses on being great in the kingdom when Christ returns.

This view is more recent, but it is likely to gain some traction. It was first promoted in Jody Dillow's book, *Final Destiny*, a recent expansion of his earlier work, *The Reign of the Servant Kings*. When he wrote *The Reign of the Servant Kings*, he held to the first view. Many thanks to my friend Jody Dillow for his help in making sure that this view is represented fairly and accurately.

This view is rather complex and I cannot do it justice here with so limited space. Necessarily, I will need to simplify the discussion. Dillow has done a great deal of careful consideration of all passages related to this view, and while I do not agree with this view, it should be respectfully considered. I recommend the reader pick up *Final Destiny* to study this view in more detail. It can be purchased at jodydillow.com or at faithalone.org. It is an invaluable book in many respects.

Those who hold this view agree with the second view that works are in play with regards to many passages discussing entering the kingdom. But they also agree with the first view that all believers physically enter Messiah's kingdom at the start of the Millennium.

Jody Dillow points out that Matt 5:19-20 proposes a difficulty. The passage reads:

> "Whoever therefore breaks one of the least of these commandments, and teaches men so, shall be called least in the kingdom of heaven; but whoever does and teaches them, he shall be called great in the kingdom of heaven. For I say to you, that unless your righteousness exceeds the righteousness of the

scribes and Pharisees, you will by no means enter the kingdom of heaven."

Jody makes the point that the first person mentioned in this passage seems to be less righteous than the scribes and Pharisees, but he is nevertheless physically in the kingdom.[195]

The proposed solution to this problem lies in the meaning of the phrase "enter the kingdom." In Greek, eiserchomai, usually translated "enter," can mean "experience." So, when Jesus says, "unless your righteousness exceeds the righteousness of the scribes and Pharisees, you will by no means enter the kingdom of heaven," He is understood to mean, "unless your righteousness exceeds the righteousness of the scribes and Pharisees, you will by no means experience the kingdom of heaven now."

Dillow wrote:

> The Gr[eek] word, *eiserchomai*, can mean "to move into a space" in which case it would signify physical entrance into the realm of the millennial reign. However, what is often not appreciated, this word, unlike its English counterpart, often means "to experience" or "to enter into an event or state, to come to enjoy something." For example, "to enter life crippled" (Mark 9:43) is best understood "to experience life crippled." Or when the Lord says, "Pray that you may not enter into temptation," He means, "Pray that you will not be tempted" (Matthew 26:41; Luke 22:40).[196]

This is a valid point, as *eiserchomai* can indeed carry the meaning of "to experience."

One question is whether or not the kingdom can be experienced in any sense now. Those like Jody Dillow who believe that the Church partakes in the New Covenant today clearly would say yes, it can. Others would put every aspect of the kingdom and its experience in the future.

---

[195] Those who hold to the second view believe that the scribes and Pharisees were less righteous than the first example because they essentially taught disobedience to all of Jesus' commandments by making them external rather than from the heart. Zane Hodges pointed out that Jesus had not yet begun to discredit the teaching of the Pharisees, but it seems that this is one of the functions of the Sermon itself (See Matt 5:27-28; 6:1-5, 16-18, for example.).

[196] *Ibid.*, p. 254.

I want to be careful to point out that Jody is *not* saying that the kingdom is "already but not yet."[197] He says plainly:

> Dispensationalists have correctly noted that the fact that cer-
> tain aspects of the future millennial kingdom are being experi-
> enced today in no way justifies the teaching that the kingdom
> reign of David's Greater Son has been inaugurated and we are
> in it now.[198]

This view also recognizes that the concept of experiencing the kingdom
now does not apply to all passages related to entering the kingdom by
works. When appropriate, those passages are understood as being about
having a rich experience in the future millennial kingdom. One such
example is 2 Pet 1:11.

VARIOUS OTHER VIEWS AND DISTINCTIONS

It was common in the early days of View #2 to take passages using the
Greek word *gehenna* to mean that unfaithful believers will suffer torment
in a fiery place during the Millennium. This view is very unlikely. For one
thing, it is extremely odd to suggest that Jesus would spare the unfaithful
believer of the horrors of the Tribulation (1 Thess 5:9-10) and yet to send
them to fiery torment for 1000 years.[199] See Jody Dillow's book *Final
Destiny* for an excellent treatment of the topic of *gehenna*.

The phrase "enter the kingdom" can also mean, "enter the kingship."
This could be a solution to the differences between views 1 and 2 in
many passages. Because of the context, it fits very well in Matt 18:3 and
the passages about the rich young ruler. It seems forced in some passages,
however. See especially Matt 7:21-23.

There are many other variations among these views.

---

[197] The phrase "already but not yet," when it relates to the kingdom, refers to the non-dispensational view that the Kingdom is in some sense already here. In this view, Christ is presently
ruling on His throne, but His rule will be fully consummated upon His return. Jody's view,
by contrast, is that while the kingdom is completely still future, we, having the life of the King
within us, can live with kingdom power and righteousness now.

[198] *Ibid.*, 250.

[199] Those who hold this view also see the Rapture as a reward.

CONCLUSION

There are many views regarding passages related to entering the kingdom and it is good for us to hash these views out together. Discuss these viewpoints in your group with openness, speaking the truth in love, and see if your group can come to a point of agreement on this issue. Whatever one does with these passages, though, we should rejoice in our unity in sharing a clear message of eternal life given to us freely in Christ through faith alone, and we should look forward to Christ's kingdom with joyful anticipation.

PRACTICE

1) What is significant about the word "therefore" in Matt 7:24?

2) What is "the gospel of the kingdom" in Matt 4:23 (see also v 17) and how does it relate to the Sermon on the Mount?

3) How do you understand Matt 18:1-3? Defend your answer.

4) How do you understand Acts 14:22? Defend your answer.

5) Read Rev 19:4-10, noting the context. What is the wedding celebration here? Is it appropriate to use this to help us understand Matt 22:1-14?

DISCUSS

1) Which view about entering the kingdom do you believe best represents Scripture?

2) How do you answer the objections of the other views?

3) What impact does your view have practically?

4) How would accepting the view that entering the kingdom is a reward impact your understanding of Matt 7:13-14?

5) Are there any other doctrines that are impacted by your view on entering the kingdom?

Kingdom Hope

Therefore I say to you, do not worry about your life, what you will eat or what you will drink; nor about your body, what you will put on. Is not life more than food and the body more than clothing? Look at the birds of the air, for they neither sow nor reap nor gather into barns; yet your heavenly Father feeds them. Are you not of more value than they? Which of you by worrying can add one cubit to his stature? So why do you worry about clothing? Consider the lilies of the field, how they grow: they neither toil nor spin; and yet I say to you that even Solomon in all his glory was not arrayed like one of these. Now if God so clothes the grass of the field, which today is, and tomorrow is thrown into the oven, will He not much more clothe you, O you of little faith? Therefore do not worry, saying, 'What shall we eat?' or 'What shall we drink?' or 'What shall we wear?' For after all these things the Gentiles seek. For your heavenly Father knows that you need all these things. But seek first the kingdom of God and His righteousness, and all these things shall be added to you. *Matthew 6:25-33*

LESSON OBJECTIVES

1. To help the student to share in the early Christians' kingdom hope

2. To show how each aspect of *The Guts of Grace* relates to the reader's rewards

INTRODUCTION

In the closing section of Paul's final letter, Second Timothy, written shortly before he was beheaded for his hope in Christ, Paul had this to say:

> For I am already being poured out as a drink offering, and the time of my departure is at hand. I have fought the good fight, I have finished the race, I have kept the faith. Finally, there is laid up for me the crown of righteousness, which the Lord, the righteous Judge, will give to me on that Day, and not to me only but also to all who have loved His appearing. (2 Tim 4:6-8)

As he wrote this, he was imprisoned, alone, and awaiting death, yet his last words are full of hope and relief. Having run the race to the end, he knows the crown of righteousness is awaiting him.

NOT WORTHY TO BE COMPARED

It is important to understand that crowns represent rule. Those who receive crowns will *rule* with Christ in His glorious kingdom. This is why Paul was so hopeful as he went to his death. He knew that he had completed his course that the Lord had set out for him to run. And he knew that "the sufferings of this present time are not worthy to be compared with the glory which shall be revealed in us" (Rom 8:18). And did Paul ever suffer! Second Corinthians 11:23-28 chronicles a portion of the trials and pains he had gone through:

> Are they ministers of Christ?—I speak as a fool—I am more: in labors more abundant, in stripes above measure, in prisons more frequently, in deaths often. From the Jews five times I received forty stripes minus one. Three times I was beaten with rods; once I was stoned; three times I was shipwrecked; a night

and a day I have been in the deep; in journeys often, in perils of waters, in perils of robbers, in perils of my own country-men, in perils of the Gentiles, in perils in the city, in perils in the wilderness, in perils in the sea, in perils among false breth-ren; in weariness and toil, in sleeplessness often, in hunger and thirst, in fastings often, in cold and nakedness—besides the other things, what comes upon me daily: my deep concern for all the churches.

I can barely read that without weeping for my dear friend Paul. Yet, even these trials, Paul says, "are not worthy to be compared" with the joys he has waiting for him, and the same will be true for us when we endure various trials, enjoying the perseverance that can be produced by them and knowing that our Beloved awaits us with a reward beyond our imagining. That is why we are to "count it all joy when [we] fall into various trials" (Jas 1:2).

God has many motivators for His children. And while we should all recognize that the kingdom is very important to God, to Jesus, and to all of the apostles, it is possible that a believer could pursue righteous-ness and joy and peace in God without ever even knowing that kingdom rewards will be given out. While we are encouraged to "...hold fast the confession of our hope without wavering" (Heb 10:23), we should not assume that God will not reward believers who live by faith but do not have kingdom rewards as a motivation.

But what powerful hope it is for those who see that everything we experience now is temporary and if we handle these things well, keeping focused on the Lord, it will result in an exceeding weight of glory then. "For our light affliction, which is but for a moment, is working for us a far more exceeding and eternal weight of glory, while we do not look at the things which are seen, but at the things which are not seen. For the things which are seen are temporary, but the things which are not seen are eternal." (2 Cor 4:17-18).

Many times, while I've had the privilege to be around young believers hearing kingdom truths for the first time, I have heard things like, "This is amazing, I have to tell everyone," and "How can anything else really matter? It's all so temporary." These are normal reactions to kingdom truths. And in reality, one hundred quadrillion years from now, as we are still (and will forever be) enjoying the blessing of a reward we were given for faithfully enduring a trial that may have lasted for a few short moments (or even our whole mortal lives), which do you think will be important to us then? Sometimes I can hardly remember tough times I've gone through only a few short years ago.

Jesus encouraged everyone who came to Him looking for answers to simply drop everything and follow Him without reserve and without regret. The promise is made that in doing so, God will provide for our needs (Matt 6:25-34), and that we will have reward waiting in Heaven for us to receive in His kingdom.

In Rom 8:23-25, Paul says:

> ...we also who have the firstfruits of the Spirit, even we ourselves groan within ourselves, eagerly waiting for the adoption, the redemption of our body. For we were saved in this hope, but hope that is seen is not hope; for why does one still hope for what he sees? But if we hope for what we do not see, we eagerly wait for it with perseverance.

There are many passages that teach us to walk by faith, and each has a different focus. Some teach us to live believing we are dead to sin and alive to God or that we are to avoid legalism at all costs, knowing we are saved into liberty, or that law living and flesh living go hand-in-hand (Rom 6:1-14; 7:1-5; Gal 2:20; 5:1-21; Col 2:6; Heb 10:38). But one passage in particular teaches us to walk by faith, being unconcerned with the prospect of death, knowing that Jesus will reward faithfulness. This passage is found in 2 Cor 5:1-10:

> For we know that if our earthly house, this tent, is destroyed, we have a building from God, a house not made with hands, eternal in the heavens. For in this we groan, earnestly desiring to be clothed with our habitation which is from heaven, if indeed, having been clothed, we shall not be found naked. For we who are in this tent groan, being burdened, not because we want to be unclothed, but further clothed, that mortality may be swallowed up by life. Now He who has prepared us for this very thing is God, who also has given us the Spirit as a guarantee. So we are always confident, knowing that while we are at home in the body we are absent from the Lord. For we walk by faith, not by sight. We are confident, yes, well pleased rather to be absent from the body and to be present with the Lord. Therefore we make it our aim, whether present or absent, to be well pleasing to Him. For we must all appear before the judgment seat of Christ, that each one may receive the things

done in the body, according to what he has done, whether good or bad.

This gives us a powerful perspective. If we can truly see that everything that happens in this mortal life is for the purpose of preparing us for His kingdom and eternal blessing, the struggles of life don't seem so bad. In fact, with the right perspective, the difficult times can be a source of great joy.

"Rejoice and be exceedingly glad," Jesus says, when we are reviled and persecuted for Jesus' sake (Matt 5:11-12). Exceedingly. Let that sink in a bit. Are you exceedingly glad when people speak badly about you and harm you for Jesus' sake? You have plenty of reason to be. You will be rewarded with an eternally significant weight of glory and God will be glorified in you.

In Eph 5:22-33, we see that Jesus has purchased for Himself a bride, and He is preparing her for ruling with Him as His consort. He gave Himself for her and always works with and within her to cleanse and perfect her "that He might present her to Himself a glorious church, not having spot or wrinkle or any such thing, but that she should be holy and without blemish." In His kingdom, Jesus and His bride will rule side by side over the perfect world we all long for. Just as Jesus wants to give His bride everything that is His, we want Him to be pleased with her and to look on her with great joy.

FIVE SMOOTH STONES, ONE GOAL

When David, a young shepherd boy, went to face the giant Goliath (and his four brothers who may have sought revenge), he took with him five smooth stones, carefully chosen from the brook (1 Sam 17:40). Likewise, each of these five sections in *The Guts of Grace* is carefully chosen to prepare you with the essential tools and courage to face challenges far bigger than yourself, to overcome, and to stand confidently before our Savior, the Righteous Judge.

HANDLING SCRIPTURE WELL

James told his readers, "My brethren, let not many of you become teachers, knowing that we shall receive a stricter judgment" (Jas 3:1). A teacher's judgment is stricter because we are accountable for handling Scripture well and for living it out as an example to others.

Paul wrote to Timothy, "Be diligent to present yourself approved to God, a worker who does not need to be ashamed, rightly dividing the word of truth" (2 Tim 2:15). The idea of being ashamed or unashamed at the *Bema* is a common theme in Scripture (Mark 8:38; Luke 9:26; 2 Tim 1:12; 1 John 2:28; Rev 3:18).

Paul took this very seriously when it came to his handling of Scripture, as we saw in his charge to Timothy and in his statement to the Corinthians about his own ministry:

> But we have renounced the hidden things of shame, not walking in craftiness nor handling the word of God deceitfully, but by manifestation of the truth commending ourselves to every man's conscience in the sight of God. (2 Cor 4:2)

By contrast, following Paul's charge to Timothy in 2 Tim 2:16-18, he wrote of Hymaneus and Philetus:

> But shun profane and idle babblings, for they will increase to more ungodliness. And their message will spread like cancer. Hymenaeus and Philetus are of this sort, who have strayed concerning the truth, saying that the resurrection is already past; and they overthrow the faith of some.

A teacher's judgment is stricter because a false message "will spread like cancer" with the result that it can "overthrow the faith of some." In Acts 15:24 we see that a false message of legalism has the effect of "unsettling" the souls of its hearers.

But if we follow Paul's example of not "handling the word of God deceitfully," and we follow his instruction to "[b]e diligent to present yourself approved to God, a worker who does not need to be ashamed, rightly dividing the word of truth," we have no reason to fear. The hermeneutical tools laid out in Section 1 are enough to prepare you to handle God's Word correctly and confidently and look forward to the kingdom with joyful anticipation.

GRACE

Paul wrote Philippians as a thank you letter to a church in Philippi which supported his ministry. In the opening and closing of the book, Paul reminds the Philippians that their partnership with him in proclaiming the message of free grace, results in long-term ongoing building of kingdom rewards to their account. Looking at Phil 1:3-7 and 4:15-17 together helps us to see this picture:

Philippians 1:3-7

> I thank my God upon every remembrance of you, always in every prayer of mine making request for you all with joy, for your fellowship [literally, partnership] in the gospel from the first day until now, being confident of this very thing, that He who has begun a good work in you will complete it until the day of Jesus Christ; just as it is right for me to think this of you all, because I have you in my heart, inasmuch as both in my chains and in the defense and confirmation of the gospel, you all are partakers [partners] with me of grace.

Philippians 4:15-17

> Now you Philippians know also that in the beginning of the gospel, when I departed from Macedonia, no church shared [partnered] with me concerning giving and receiving but you only. For even in Thessalonica you sent aid once and again for my necessities. Not that I seek the gift, but I seek the fruit that abounds to your account.

Though many take Phil 1:6 "…He who has begun a good work in you will complete it until the day of Jesus Christ" to be a promise that God will complete the sanctification process in every believer, that isn't in keeping with the words of the verse or the context. The completion of the work goes until the day of Jesus Christ [which is a reference to the *Bema* and the kingdom], not until the end of their lives; and the good work which God had begun was their partnership in the gospel (i.e., their financial support of Paul's ministry of sharing the gospel), not their personal sanctification.

God is still completing this good work in that millions of people are still being encouraged by the letter it inspired. Paul rejoiced in the fruit that abounds to their account in the day of Jesus Christ, and what fruit it must be!

This verse should be a huge encouragement to all of us. When we hold fast to grace and work to share it, whether by our personally going out to share or by our ministry of support to those who do, the ripple effect continues to build fruit to our accounts and to all those who helped us. Our holding fast to and sharing the free grace of the Lord Jesus will be an eternal blessing to us at the Judgment Seat.

WALKING IN THE SPIRIT, IN LIBERTY

When the Colossians were being invaded by wolves in sheep's clothing who were teaching them to observe legalistic rules, Paul wrote to them:

> So let no one judge you in food or in drink, or regarding a festival or a new moon or sabbaths, which are a shadow of things to come, but the substance is of Christ. *Let no one cheat you of your reward,* taking delight in false humility and worship of angels, intruding into those things which he has not seen, vainly puffed up by his fleshly mind, and not holding fast to the Head, from whom all the body, nourished and knit together by joints and ligaments, grows with the increase that is from God.

> Therefore, if you died with Christ from the basic principles of the world, why, as though living in the world, do you subject yourselves to regulations—"Do not touch, do not taste, do not handle," which all concern things which perish with the using—according to the commandments and doctrines of men? These things indeed have an appearance of wisdom in self-imposed religion, false humility, and neglect of the body, but are of no value against the indulgence of the flesh. (Col 2:16-23, emphasis added)

Legalism has no power over the flesh, and we must walk in the Spirit—in freedom (2 Cor 3:17)—to conquer it (Rom 6:14; Gal 5:16). Paul told these brothers and sisters that if they let these people deceive them they would be powerless against sin and those wolves would have cheated them of their reward.

On the other hand, Christ "has become for us wisdom from God—and righteousness and sanctification and redemption—that, as it is written, 'He who glories, let him glory in the Lord'" (1 Cor 1:30-31). If we walk in the Spirit, letting Christ live out His life in us, we are more than capable. "But we have this treasure in earthen vessels, that the excellence of the power may be of God and not of us" (2 Cor 4:7). When we let that treasure be seen, we not only get to enjoy His love, joy, and peace now, we have the added benefit of receiving a "full reward" (2 John 8) then.

TAKING UP OUR MISSION IN THE BODY

In 1 Cor 3:9-15, Paul gives a telling description of the *Bema*. It reads:

> For we are God's fellow workers; you are God's field, you are God's building. According to the grace of God which was given to me, as a wise master builder I have laid the foundation, and another builds on it. But let each one take heed how he builds on it. For no other foundation can anyone lay than that which is laid, which is Jesus Christ. Now if anyone builds on this foundation with gold, silver, precious stones, wood, hay, straw, each one's work will become clear; for the Day will declare it, because it will be revealed by fire; and the fire will test each one's work, of what sort it is. If anyone's work which he has built on it endures, he will receive a reward. If anyone's work is burned, he will suffer loss; but he himself will be saved, yet so as through fire.

In talking to the Corinthian church, he says "you are God's building," and then he goes on to explain how each of us will be rewarded based upon how we build onto that building, the Church. This is our place in God's mission today. Growth of the Body happens "when every part does its share" (Eph 4:16). Christ will reward His saints based upon how they build onto His Church.

We are God's elect in Jesus Christ. This election is a call to action. While the tasks we have now are in reality "a few things," if we are faithful with them, He will make us "ruler over many things." (Matt 25:21)

HOLDING FAST TO OUR KINGDOM HOPE

In Col 1:21-23, Paul connects holding fast to our kingdom hope with being presented blameless at the *Bema*:

> And you, who once were alienated and enemies in your mind by wicked works, yet now He has reconciled in the body of His flesh through death, to present you holy, and blameless, and above reproach in His sight—if indeed you continue in the faith, grounded and steadfast, and are not moved away from the hope of the gospel which you heard, which was preached to every creature under heaven, of which I, Paul, became a minister.

The "hope of the gospel" pertains to what we have not yet received, and looks forward to our experience as co-heirs with Christ. But being presented "holy, and blameless, and above reproach in His sight" is conditioned upon our remaining steadfast in both faith and our kingdom hope. When we truly understand the glories that are to come in His kingdom, and God's desire for us to rule with Christ, this gives us a powerful motivation to press forward through trials and temptation.

Paul was talking about this motivation when he wrote:

> Do you not know that those who run in a race all run, but one receives the prize? Run in such a way that you may obtain it. And everyone who competes for the prize is temperate in all things. Now they do it to obtain a perishable crown, but we for an imperishable crown. Therefore I run thus: not with uncertainty. Thus I fight: not as one who beats the air. But I discipline my body and bring it into subjection, lest, when I have preached to others, I myself should become disqualified. (1 Cor 9:24-27)

Paul's desire to obtain the prize—an imperishable crown—led him to discipline his own body and bring it into subjection. In the context, he was talking about setting aside his own desires, adjusting his life for maximum effectiveness in reaching diverse peoples, and even forgoing financial benefit from his work in the gospel so that he could be all things to all men. We know that in this endeavor, he even went without food when necessary (2 Cor 11:27; Phil 4:12). But whatever trials came, he considered them light and not worthy of comparing to the glory that would result from them. Paul's kingdom hope gave him perseverance to endure these trials with joy.

CONCLUSION

Dear brothers and sisters, we are all ordinary saints, yet God has called us to extraordinary ministry and to an even greater and everlasting future. If we "hold fast the confession of our hope without wavering" (Heb 10:23), we will forever serve and rule over all of creation at our Savior's side, sharing His peace, justice, and love with His ever-expanding kingdom. Let us set aside every hindrance and press forward together with our eyes firmly set on the things above (Col 3:1-2).

PRACTICE

1) What are rewards primarily given out for?

2) Are there some other things in Scripture that you are aware of that Christ will reward?

3) List five things that you are excited about when it comes to the kingdom.

4) How does holding fast to our kingdom hope impact our future experience in the kingdom?

5) How does knowing that work done in the Church can continue to bear fruit until the return of Christ impact your understanding of the value of your work?

DISCUSS

1) Discuss the meaning and value of Matt 6:33.

2) Why does God spend so much time on the kingdom in Scripture?

3) The early Christians who went to their deaths in the Colosseum and elsewhere were known to take great comfort in the resurrection. How does understanding the hope of the kingdom help you to understand their peace?

4) Many times in Scripture when rewards are discussed, it is in the context of trials. Why?

5) Do you have any reservations or hang-ups that prevent you from being properly motivated by kingdom rewards? What are they and how can you overcome them?

Glossary

Below is a glossary of theological terms used in *The Guts of Grace* which may not be familiar to all, or which are often misunderstood.

Allegorizing - inventing an allegorical interpretation for a non-allegorical passage, usually to explain a passage that is difficult for the interpreter

Allegory - art or literature that is to be interpreted to reveal a figurative meaning, an extended metaphor

Amillennialism - the teaching that the thousand years in Revelation 20 represents a figurative age, most often seen as the church age

Analogy of Scripture - the principle that because all Scripture is in harmony, "Scripture interprets Scripture"

Anthropomorphism - ascription of human characteristics to God

Antithetic parallelism - literary structure in which corresponding lines express a contrasting but related idea

Antitype - a historic event or person that fulfills a corresponding type

Assurance of salvation - a regenerate person's confidence in his own salvation

Baptismal regeneration - the false teaching that water baptism is required for regeneration

Book structure - the framework of a book of the Bible

Chiasm - a literary structure which includes a reversal of clauses for emphasis

Church, local - an assembly of believers

Church, Universal - the collective group of all believers from the Church Age. These believers are spiritually united with Christ and with each other.

Concordance - a book that includes a list of English words as they appear in the Bible

Dispensationalism - a premillennial school of thought, derived from literal-grammatical-historical hermeneutics, which keeps Israel distinct from the Church, and maintains a doxological view of history

Dispensation - a distinct economy through which God relates to man

Doctrine - theological teaching on a subject

Doxology - 1. an expression of praise to God 2. the doctrine of God's glory

Dramatic irony - a situation in which the audience understands an unusual circumstance that the people within the situation do not understand

Dynamic equivalence - a translation philosophy in which the translators' understanding of the text prioritizes the reader's comfort over a strict adherence to the original words and grammar

Eisegesis - a poor approach to Bible study that seeks to impose the interpreter's meaning into the text rather than taking the authors' intended meaning out of the text

Election - 1. Biblically, God's choosing of people, places, and things to carry out His work 2. in Calvinism, the idea that God has chosen in advance whom He will save and whom He will condemn

Eternal life - the life of God, which exists eternally, but begins for Christians in the moment they put their faith in Christ. Eternal life cannot be lost and never ends

Eternal salvation - 1. (Christian slang) Usually in reference to the reception of eternal life (regeneration) 2. (Heb 5:9) eternal salvation as a term only occurs once in the Bible, in Heb 5:9, where it is in reference to eschatological promise that believers who persevere in obedience will rule with Christ forever

Eternal security - the doctrine that eternal life cannot be lost

Evangelism - the work of teaching the gospel to non-believers

Evangelistic - adj. pertaining to the work of teaching the gospel to non-believers (evangelism)

Everlasting life - spiritual life that begins for Christians in the moment they put their faith in Christ. Everlasting life cannot be lost and never ends

Exegesis - deriving the authors' intended meaning from the text

Free Grace - a soteriology that teaches that salvation is granted through faith alone regardless of works

Gentile - any non-Israelite person

Glory - high honor and magnificence

Literal-historical-grammatical interpretation - a hermeneutic approach that seeks the plain meaning of the original authors

Health, wealth, and prosperity gospel - the false teaching that Christians will definitely be blessed with material things if they exhibit faith

Hermeneutics - the art and science of interpretation

Hyperbole - an exaggeration intended to emphasize

Illegitimate identity transfer - an interpretive error in which a definition of a word in one context is incorrectly read into another context

Illegitimate totality transfer - an interpretive error in which the entire context of a particular usage of a word or phrase is transferred into that word or phrase's meaning elsewhere

Illocutionary force - the intention behind a word or phrase

Inclusio - a phrase that occurs twice within a book that indicates the start and end of a section

Interpret - To interpret is to ascribe a meaning to a text, either correctly or incorrectly.

Interpreter - the person who derives a meaning from a text

Israel - the nation consisting of descendants of Jacob, the son of Isaac, the son of Abraham

Jew - a member of the nation of Israel, or more specifically, the tribe of Judah

Jewish - an adjective meaning of the nation of Israel

Judah - 1. The tribe of Judah, one of the twelve tribes of Israel 2. The Southern Kingdom of Israel after the kingdom was split into two

Judaizing - the forcing of Jewish culture and Jewish religious laws onto Gentiles

Justified - to be declared right or just

Koine Greek - the language of the Greek world from 300 B.C.-300 A.D. The New Testament and Septuagint were written in Koine Greek

Lexicon - a word list that includes words and their meanings as they are used throughout literature

Literal interpretation - a hermeneutical approach that seeks the plain meaning of the original authors

Literal translation - an approach of translating to a new language that seeks to maintain the voice of the original language as much as is reasonable

Literary structure - the framework of a piece of literature

Litotes - a literary device in which less is said than what is meant

Lordship Salvation - a theological error that redefines faith to include works, so that one must believe and work in order to be saved

LXX - an abbreviation for the Septuagint, a Koine Greek translation of the Old Testament, so called because of the committee of 72 scribes who translated it

Messiah - an Anglicized spelling of the Hebrew word, meshiach (מָשִׁיחַ), which means "anointed one."

Metaphor - a figure of speech that describes something by comparing it to an unrelated object

Middle voice - a grammatical structure in which the subject performs the action for its own result (not found in English grammar)

Missional - being in relation to a mission

Parable - a simple story using familiar topics told to illustrate spiritual or moral truths

Parallelism - a literary device which compares or contrasts two or more lines in order to express a single idea

Paraphrase - a translation philosophy that expresses the translators' understanding of the text with little regard to maintaining the structure of the text itself

Partial rapture - the theory that faithful believers will be raptured, but unfaithful believers will not

Passive voice - a grammatical structure in which the subject receives the action

Personification - a literary device that ascribes characteristics or actions of a person to inanimate objects

Premillennialism - the teaching that Christ's second advent will precede a literal millennium

Primary application - the way the originally intended audience of a command or moral teaching should respond

Promised Land - the land which God promised to Abraham in Gen 15:7-20

Regenerate - those who possess eternal life

Regeneration - the reception of eternal life

Secondary application - the way someone who is not part of the originally intended audience should respond to a command or moral teaching

Simile - a comparison using like or as

Soteriological - in relation to soteriology (the doctrine of salvation)

Soteriology - the doctrine of salvation

Synecdoche - a literary device in which reference to something is made by naming one of its parts

Synonymous parallelism - a literary structure in which corresponding lines express the same idea

Synthetic parallelism - a literary structure in which the second of two corresponding lines completes the thought of the first

Translation - converting a text from one language/culture to another

Tribulation - 1. generally, a difficulty 2. specifically, a seven year period that precedes a literal millennial reign of Christ

Type - real persons, events, or things in the Old Testament that have a substantial relationship with corresponding New Testament persons, events, or things

Unregenerate - one who has yet to receive the free gift of eternal life

YHWH - the Anglicized version of the tetragrammaton the four Hebrew letters of God's name (יהוה), often pronounced Yahweh or in English, Jehovah

Zoomorphism - ascribing animal characteristics to God, to angels, or to people

Scripture Index

Acts

About Bold Grace Ministries

PURPOSE STATEMENT

Bold Grace Ministries exists to *unite* believers under the banner of God's grace (Eph 4:3-6), *share* the gospel and aid those who will proclaim it faithfully (Rom 10:14-15), *increase* believers' confidence in the power of the indwelling Christ (Gal 2:20), *love* without hypocrisy (Rom 12:9a), *proclaim* the hope of Christ's glorious kingdom (Rom 8:18-21), and *equip* the saints to share Christ's matchless grace and love with others (2 Tim 2:2).

OUR VISION

Grace is relevant. By grace God makes Himself available to us, and by grace He meets our deepest needs. Grace unites us, when we are naturally so prone to division. It frees us from pride and the tyranny of sin and effects holiness and humility.

Yet too often grace is missing or downplayed in our message about Christ, our interactions with one another, and our views on the Christian life. By God's grace, and with the help of like-minded brothers and sisters, we hope to reach out to the world with a message of God's free grace, to unite and encourage our brothers and sisters in Christ, and to teach all the ways that His grace is sufficient for us in our pursuit of Christlikeness.

MINISTRIES

E-NEWSLETTER

Our e-newsletter, *Things Above*, brings practical, grace-for-living truth to people's inbox. "Set your mind on things above, not on things on the earth" (Col 3:2). To sign up for *Things Above*, go to www.boldgrace.org.

WEB PRESENCE

Through boldgrace.org, Bold Grace Ministries seeks to help people find fellowship and answers, to see how Christ's grace is sufficient for them in every circumstance, and to equip believers for the edification of the Universal Church.

PUBLISHING

Bold Grace Ministries publishes books like this one (both electronic and traditional), gospel tracts, and other helpful materials. Visit www. boldgrace.org for an updated list of works available and in progress.

GET INVOLVED

If you have enjoyed this book and want to get involved with Bold Grace Ministries, either through financial partnership or serving with us, visit our website, www.boldgrace.org, and click on the "Get Involved" tab. There are many needs and opportunities listed there and it's growing all the time. Also, don't forget to "like" us on Facebook and "follow" us on Twitter.